We live in others. We live in words.
      Maggie Gee, *Virigina Woolf in Manhattan*

Gentle breath of yours my sail
Must fill, or else my project fails,
Which was to please.
      William Shakespeare, *The Tempest*

Gylphi Contemporary Writers: Critical Essays

Series Editor: Sarah Dillon

Gylphi Contemporary Writers: Critical Essays presents a new approach to the academic study of living authors. The titles in this series are devoted to contemporary British, Irish and American authors whose work is popularly and critically valued but on whom a significant body of academic work has yet to be established. Each of the titles in this series is developed out of the best contributions to an international conference on its author; represents the most intelligent and provocative material in current thinking about that author's work; and, suggests future avenues of thought, comparison and analysis. With each title prefaced by an author foreword, this series embraces the challenges of writing on living authors and provides the foundation stones for future critical work on significant contemporary writers.

Series Titles

David Mitchell: Critical Essays (2011)
Edited by Sarah Dillon. Foreword by David Mitchell.

Maggie Gee: Critical Essays (2015)
Edited by Sarah Dillon and Caroline Edwards. Foreword by Maggie Gee.

Maggie Gee
Critical Essays

A *Gylphi Limited* Book

First published in Great Britain in 2015
by Gylphi Limited

Copyright © Gylphi Limited, 2015

All rights reserved.

No part of this publication may be reproduced, stored in a retrieval system, or transmitted, in any form or by any means, without the prior permission in writing of the publisher, nor be otherwise circulated in any form or binding or cover other than that in which it is published and without a similar condition including this condition being imposed on the subsequent purchaser.

A CIP catalogue record for this book is available from the British Library.

ISBN 978-1-78024-033-6 (pbk)
ISBN 978-1-78024-034-3 (Kindle)
ISBN 978-1-78024-035-0 (EPUB)

Design and typesetting by Gylphi Limited. Printed by Amazon.

Gylphi Limited
Canterbury, UK

For my Charlotte
(SJD)

For the wonderful Iain
(CE)

Maggie Gee
Critical Essays

edited by
Sarah Dillon and Caroline Edwards

Gylphi

Contents

Acknowledgements	xi
List of Abbreviations	xii
Foreword *Maggie Gee*	xiii
1. Beyond the Blue: The Sorrowful Joy of Gee *Sarah Dillon and Caroline Edwards*	1
2. Burning to Tell the Tale: Negotiating Aesthetics and Politics in *The Burning Book* *Monika Szuba*	31
3. Reproductive Politics and the Public Sphere: Natalism, Natality and Apocalypse *Alex Beaumont*	51
4. 'Fall[ing] Out of the Past': Time, Ageing and Generations in *Where Are the Snows* *Sarah Falcus*	79
5. Literary Equivocation: Reproductive Futurism and *The Ice People* *Sarah Dillon*	101
6. 'One and Indivisible, A Seamless Web': Climate Change as Historical Process in *The Flood* *Chris Maughan*	133

7. 'The End Times and After': Utopia, Dystopia
and Being-Together in *The Flood* 159
Adam Welstead

8. From the 'Native Outside' to the 'Foreign Within':
Re/negotiating Urban Space in *The White Family* 181
Irene Pérez Fernández

9. Faith and Grace: Maggie Gee's Spritual Politics 209
Susan Alice Fischer

10. The Resurrection of the Author: On *Virginia
Woolf in Manhattan* 229
E. H. Wright

11. How May I Speak in My Own Voice? Language
and the Forbidden 261
Maggie Gee

Notes on Contributors 281

Index 285

Acknowledgements

This book has been a long time in the making. We first conceived the idea of a Maggie Gee conference and collection when we met at the David Mitchell Conference in 2009. Two babies later, the Maggie Gee Conference took place at the University of St Andrews in August 2012. We owe our thanks to Anthony Levings at Gylphi and the School of English at the University of St Andrews for their support of the conference. We would also like to thank Maggie's husband, Nicholas Rankin, for his presence and contributions, and Iain Robert Smith for filming the proceedings. All the paper-givers and delegates helped make the event a success, and papers delivered there but not included here, as well as the discussion they prompted, have informed this book.

We are grateful to Birkbeck College, University of London, for their support in allowing us to print Maggie Gee's 1996 William Matthews lecture – 'How May I Speak in My Own Voice? Language and the Forbidden' – included, with contemporary amendments and comments by the author, at the end of this collection. Further details on the lecture series can be found at the website: http://www.bbk.ac.uk/english/about-us/william-matthews-memorial-lectures. Thank you to Suzanne Williams for her efficient and prompt transcription of the lecture.

Two years after the Gee conference, through job moves for both editors, the collection has finally come to fruition. We thank our family and friends for their support throughout these busy years of upheaval. Above all, we owe a debt of gratitude to Maggie Gee, not just for the rich body of work she has given to the world, but for her generosity of spirit and time, and her enduring faith in us and this book. We hope we have done her proud.

Sarah and Caroline
September 2014

List of Abbreviations

Abbreviations of works cited by Maggie Gee.

Date of first publication is in parenthesis, followed by details of edition cited throughout (if different from original edition).

D   Gee, Maggie (1981) *Dying, in Other Words*. London: Flamingo, 1994.

BB   Gee, Maggie (1983) *The Burning Book*. London: Flamingo, 1994.

LY   Gee, Maggie (1985) *Light Years*. London and Boston: Faber and Faber.

G   Gee, Maggie (1988) *Grace*. London: Heinemann.

WS   Gee, Maggie (1991) *Where Are the Snows*. London: Telegram, 2006.

LC   Gee, Maggie (1994) *Lost Children*. London: Flamingo.

IP   Gee, Maggie (1998) *The Ice People*. London: Telegram, 2008.

WF   Gee, Maggie (2002) *The White Family*. London: Telegram, 2008.

TF   Gee, Maggie (2004) *The Flood*. London: Saqi Books, 2005.

MC   Gee, Maggie (2005) *My Cleaner*. London: Saqi Books.

TB   Gee, Maggie (2006) *The Blue*. London: Telegram.

MD   Gee, Maggie (2009) *My Driver*. London: Telegram, 2010.

MAL   Gee, Maggie (2010) *My Animal Life*. London: Telegram.

VW   Gee, Maggie (2014) *Virginia Woolf in Manhattan*. London: Telegram.

Foreword

Maggie Gee

The relationship between writer and reader, an unnerving intimacy with a total stranger, remains mysterious. Writing, my body is the locus of illusions that for me, in that moment, are real: scenes, faces, landscapes, flash before my eyes as I record them. My web of words, by now drained of sound and colour, is transmitted to a publisher. Then any reader empathic enough to slip into his or her cinema of dreams will convert my mute notation back into moving scenes and images, cries and gestures that mimic, but are never quite the same as, the ones I first lived through as I wrote. The ideal reader will also feel the emotions in my characters, and, at another level, the emotion encoded in the body of the text, which is in some respects an avatar of my own feeling body, though the medium, painstakingly drafted and redrafted, is specific words in a particular order. And what about the ideas in the book? They are like shifts in topography, light and weather you do or don't notice on a train trip, even though they might indicate where you are really going.

On the last page, the enigmatic transference of meaning from writer to reader is complete, as is the transference of meaning from the empathic reader to the book. Beth Wright, in her clever and insightful essay on my 2014 novel *Virginia Woolf in Manhattan*, cites Ina Schabert's translation of *Einfühlen*, usually rendered 'empathy', as 'feeling aspects of myself into the other'.

What my reader has actually heard and seen and felt, what he or she thinks I meant, I will only very rarely discover. It is just part of the cloud of unknowing that surrounds the fate of a book – the writer sends it into the world, with hopes and fears, her child, not knowing who it will meet or where it will go.

So Chaucer at the end of *Troilus and Criseyde* liberates his book like a bird from an open window:

> Go, litel bok, go, litel myn tragedye,
> ...
> ... no makyng thow n'envie,
> But subgit be to alle poesye;
> And kis the steppes, whereas thou seest pace
> Virgile, Ovide, Omer, Lucan, and Stace.
>
> ... So prey I God that noon myswrite the,
> Ne the mysmetre for defaute of tonge.
> And red wherso thow be, or elles songe,
> That thow be understonde, God I beseche!
> (*Troilus and Criseyde*, Book V, Lines 1786–98)

Here's my reworked *envoi*. 'Go, little book, go, my tragedy... don't envy other people's writing, but bow to all the other poets who went before you. Kiss the earth where Virgil, Chaucer, Shakespeare, Thackeray, Virginia Woolf, Doris Lessing, Maureen Duffy walk. I pray that no one misquotes you or mangles your rhythms. And wherever you are read, please God may you be understood!'

A book must leave home or it never becomes a book. An aesthetic unity only comes alive when, like the Grecian urn, it is held in another mind, complete, a three-dimensional virtual object.

Most human beings, and not just writers, have a deep longing to be understood. For writers, the reader is the essential Other in the fulfillment of that desire. But what does it mean, to be understood? How rarely readers talk back to the novelists who buttonhole them for hours at a time.

Reviewers offer the first response, but they write to a deadline, for money (albeit a pittance) and with space constraints. The performance element too often makes book pages or blogs an arena where reviewers turn tricks for their own readers, rather than a record of how the book has become embodied in another mind. Reviews want a verdict, good or bad, black or white, and bypass the reading experience, that slow-flowering, mutable and mutual thing which flickers into life through suspended disbelief.

Occasionally, not so many times in a lifetime, a postcard or a letter might arrive from the other side of the world saying a reader's life has in some way been changed. Personal letters come via the publisher, the more valued for being written despite the number of difficulties that stood in the way of the communication ever reaching the writer. Such readers mostly just want to give the writer a present of their enjoyment or their sense that the book expressed one of what Virginia Woolf called their 'unacted parts'. Out of the blue, five or six years ago, a Turkish scholar, Mine Özyurt Kiliç, contacted me to say she wanted to write a book about my work. The resulting study, *Maggie Gee: Writing the Condition-of-England Novel*, published in 2013 by Bloomsbury Academic, is a perceptive, resourceful and intelligent socio-political reading of all my work. To read it was like a drink of cool sweet water in a desert.

Even among your friends and family, you never know who has read you – a curious shyness infects the writer's immediate circle. Maybe they realize how much writers love their 'litel books', how much of writers' secret, deepest selves goes into them; maybe they don't want to get it wrong. Or maybe they avoid reading us because they prefer to know the easier self we show them – as is their right; the social world would shudder to a halt if everyone we met had a backlist to be read.

And so this current collection of essays is that rare excitement for a writer, a set of messages that have come back from the outposts of reading. I read them with fascination, hunger, occasional bemusement and sometimes an absolute sense of 'Yes, they heard me' – and I thank all the essay writers for their concentration, and for their courage in hazarding a response, knowing I am alive to read it.

Like Chaucer, I long to be 'understonde'. But Chaucer was lucky enough to live hundreds of years before Roland Barthes talked about the Death of the Author; before grateful theorists agreed that an author's conscious intention deserved little house-room. Of course part of every author feels the less for this. A small fierce internal voice might say 'I did know what I was doing, and only I know what I was doing – and your (but not *your*) interpretation is wrong!'

There, I did say it. A few of these essays seem to me at certain points to mis-read the text, as Chaucer said to 'mys-metre' it – but that is their right. Others speak powerfully to my longings. To cite just one example of the many who do the latter, Susan Alice Fischer's essay on faith and grace in *Grace* puts its finger on something important I instinctively know to be true but could not have formulated myself.

Because my own account of my writing can never be complete. My mind sometimes plays tricks on me, and although I am a deliberate maker of connections and internal references, much of what I do is unconscious. For the writer to write without inhibition, she often has to screen off parts of her awareness. Throughout the writing of *The Burning Book* I had to fool myself that the fictional family in it had nothing to do with my own birth family – of course, untrue.

To take a more immediately relevant example, the link between the academic conference on my work at St Andrews (organized by Caroline Edwards and Sarah Dillon) from which many of the essays in this volume derive, and the fictional conference that plays a central role in the resolution of my new novel *Virginia Woolf in Manhattan*, had not occurred to me until Sarah Dillon put the possibility to me. Yes: I sat at the back of the audience for the Maggie Gee Conference in Scotland in August 2012, and it was a surreal, moving and occasionally comic experience that surely fed into the pages of the novel where my fictional Virginia Woolf sits in the audience of an international conference about her own work.

Thank you, Sarah Dillon, and thank you, Caroline Edwards. The St Andrews conference was the first organized academic event dedicated to my writing; I am sure it took boundless courage and determination to get it off the ground, and the garnering and editing of the papers from it must have been a similar challenge. The introduction to my work that you have written together made me laugh with pleasure and recognition, albeit sometimes wry recognition – I loved it. So much of it seems true. I can't resist satirizing academic literary theory in my work, but I also know how often the academy saves serious writing from neglect. I have been delighted and energized by what these brilliant, generous younger women have done for my books. And both at the conference and here in this collection, they have given me, the living, inconvenient Author, house-room.

A suite of academic essays will not take us directly to the intimate frontiers of reading: the secret borders where the writer's conscious intent, unconscious desires and unique freight of memories touches each particular reader's unknown hinterland: where we stretch out our hands towards each other in the glimmering darkness, sensing a friend or a fellow-sufferer. But somewhere, hidden behind every essay, lies the mystery of the private experience, the quantum collisions that initially stirred an essayist to write this particular essay and no other: the tiny unpredictable transfers of energy that give me happiness and make my work complete. It is up to me, and to you, readers, to make out the private voice within the public. These essayists have searched for clues in me, and now we can search for clues in this collection. 'Go litel book...'

So it becomes part of the infinitely absorbing web of writing, the glistening thing that some of us continue feverishly weaving even as the world underneath it grows ever bigger and less containable by novelists or critics, bursting our threads on its way into an unimaginable future.

Works Cited

Chaucer, Geoffrey (1957) *The Works of Geoffrey Chaucer*, ed. F. N. Robinson. Oxford: Oxford University Press.

1

BEYOND THE BLUE
THE SORROWFUL JOY OF GEE

Sarah Dillon and Caroline Edwards

It is a risky business holding an academic conference, and publishing a collection of academic essays, on Maggie Gee. For Gee is a satirist of the most unflinching kind, and literary scholars and their conferences are mocked throughout her work. Take, for example, Gee's most recent novel, *Virginia Woolf in Manhattan* (2014). Woolf – accidentally resurrected from the dead by contemporary writer Angela Lamb – learns that Angela is to attend a Woolf conference in Istanbul and is eager to go along with her. Angela has her doubts: 'I can hardly take her to her own conference' (*VW*, 145), she writes to her daughter, Gerda; 'why not?,' thinks Gerda, in reply: 'Wouldn't it be helpful to have the actual writer telling all the academics and people like my mother where they are gong wrong? Surely it would be good for them' (*VW*, 145). Gee has a longstanding interest in the role of the author, since her doctoral thesis on self-conscious authors in Nabokov, Beckett and Woolf. Her first published novel *Dying, in Other Words* (1981), plays out that interest through fiction, in a postmodern self-conscious experimental reflection on the role of the author; her most recent novel addresses the same ideas through two author characters: the contemporary writer Angela Lamb, and the resurrected dead Woolf.[1] This miraculous resurrection provides playful opportunity for further reflection on Roland Barthes's idea of 'the death of the author', a theoretical concept on which Gee wrote in her doctoral thesis:

> "I know this will sound strange to you, but they won't believe what you say about your work."
> "Because – because I'm dead?" It was obvious. "Because they won't believe it's me?"
> "No, nothing as simple as that, Virginia ... It's because – some modern scholars think authors don't know anything about their work," she panted, over her shoulder.
> "That doesn't make sense. We are the ones who wrote it." (*VW*, 317)

Through our conversations with Gee – both at the conference and in correspondence throughout the years in which this collection has been brought together – we the editors, and our contributors, have no doubt that whilst an author may indeed not know everything about their work, the idea of intentionality is not entirely fallacious.[2] Gee is a clever, careful writer, as well as a skilled scholar (even though she did not choose that path); she knows what she is doing when she is writing and she knows what she intends. At the same time, of course, she is under no illusion that when her fictional work ventures into the world, it will be interpreted in various and different ways. We are reminded of David Mitchell's comment recently at the Guardian Reader Event for the launch of *The Bone Clocks* (2014), that: 'I know I can't have the last word on how my work is interpreted, but I will have the last word on what I meant'.[3] There is an elegant duality at play here in both Gee and Mitchell, a harmonious coexistence in one space of two ostensibly opposite concepts: first, that the author's intentions count *and*, second, that the reader's interpretations count. These need not be polar opposites, as they are so often represented in literary theory, where *either* the intention of the author is the only guide to a text and the blueprint of its meaning, *or* the author is dead and the meaning of the text lies only in the reader's response to it. Rather, neither the author nor the reader knows everything or nothing – both know something, and therein lies the wonderful productivity of literary scholars working with, and alongside, the author in producing interpretations of the text.

The power and importance of this kind of duality, of the paradoxical unity of two, is a dominant concern in Gee's fiction; in the sections that follow, we will look at the way in which it shapes a view of her writing. First, from the outside, in terms of her uneasy place on the contemporary literary scene, the importance she places in literature (its truth-telling through lies), the deep connection she finds in the personal and political, and her combination of formal experimentation and social commentary. Second, from the inside, in terms of her themes – which can always be found in dual pairs, such as that of life and death, the joy and vulnerability of our animal bodies, the potentialities and limitations of children, and the relationship between the sexes – and the formal and stylistic techniques she uses to explore them. This second section focuses on the content of each of the chapters in the collection, providing the customary guide to the details of their readings and arguments, as well as identifying threads that weave across them. As an interlude between these two sections, we have placed a short piece of close reading. 'Feeling Blue' explores the way in which Gee's characteristic concern with duality manifests itself in her careful stylistic play with the connotations and semantic reverberations across her texts of just one small word: 'blue'. The introduction ends with the playful desire that in the essays that follow Gee might glimpse trace evidence for the existence of the ideal readers she so hopes for in her memoir, *My Animal Life* (2010).

The central metaphor of Gee's fourth novel, *Grace* (1988) – a response to nuclear weapons and the Hilda Murrell murder case – is the splitting of the atom and the chaos that ensues. The novel opens with the joyful unity of father and daughter playing. Their play physically unites them – 'she fights him off as he tickles her but her strong short calves cling on for dear life' – but 'then they split apart' and 'the following night, the world grew dirtier' (*G*, 1).[4] Writing this introduction on the day of the Scottish referendum on independence, it is hard not to affected, as Gee's fiction always is, by the politics that surrounds us – succumbing to that temptation, we might assert that in Gee's fiction there is no doubt that we are 'better together', even if, and often especially if, that 'we' is composed of awkward opposites continually jostling for space and supremacy.

I. The View From Outside[5]

In Gee's second novel, *The Burning Book* (1983), Prunella – grandmother of the aforementioned character Angela Lamb, whom we first meet as a baby in this novel – decides to break free from the expectations of what a mother should be: 'There wasn't any way you could get it right by doing what everyone else did' (*BB*, 35). Such, indeed, might be Gee's own motto. Her body of work is characterized by its diversity, from early postmodern experimentation through science fiction to sceptical realism.[6] As reviewer Kathryn Hughes (2010) describes Gee's oeuvre: 'each book when it arrived seemed to emerge out of a fierce desire to write a particular book at that particular moment, rather than from any ambition to build a brand'. Gee delights in this generic freedom – 'all my books are different because they are from different genres and that's what I like doing really' (Gee cited in McKay, 1997: 220) – but she recognizes that in today's literary landscape, in which brand is just as important as in any capitalist market, it comes with its downsides: 'I never want to do anything I've done before … which is a great mistake! Publishers really like it [if you do]' (Gee cited in Williams, 2014). The contemporary publishing world has not escaped Gee's lampooning. Its fictional representation in *The Flood* (2004) is perhaps the most condemnatory: the publishing company in this novel is an institution that marks literature's resting place and demise – its name is 'Headstone'. As Sarah Dillon has discussed elsewhere, Headstone's editors have become ossified into a pattern of marketing and publication determined by their cultural environment, rather than being imaginative enough to publish material that might challenge or critique the culture and market forces upon which the company depends for its distribution and readership.[7] This company resurfaces from the waters of *The Flood* in *Virginia Woolf in Manhattan*, as Angela's publishers. Headstone Press has now been subsumed into an even larger capitalist company, the Haslet group, who in addition to publishing, 'also make large profits from chopped, reconstituted meat' (*VW*, 10). In *Virginia Woolf in Manhattan*, Angela is popularly successful but desires literary respectability: 'She's popular, yes, she's won prizes including the Iceland Prize, but she craves more: respect. To be counted as literature, which she loves – though she also likes money' (*VW*, 10). In her non-fiction writing and interviews, Gee represents herself as the opposite of her character Angela Lamb – her work is indeed considered to be 'literature', but she craves more popular success. In the new interview Kiliç includes in Part Three of her monograph on Gee, *Maggie Gee: Writing the Condition-of-England Novel* (2013), Gee states 'I would (honestly) love my writing to be more successful' (Gee cited in Kiliç, 2013: 153). This is not an evaluation of the literary quality of her work, but an estimation of its popular success, in terms of its reach and, thereby, its influence. Gee considers this kind of success to be determined by the dominance of literary prizes in the UK. In the section of her memoir subtitled '*the literary jungle*', she associates the winning of prizes not with originality but with the power of the repetition of success: 'it becomes taken for granted that certain names are landmarks, and the more they are repeated, the more it seems true, for they start to come easily to everybody's lips' (*MAL*, 193). Gee is certain, however, that this does not prove that such writers are good but, rather, that 'they are merely successful' (*MAL*, 193). Explaining this UK publishing and literary awards scene for a US audience, Gee (2009) comments in conversation with Elaine Showalter that: 'I've been short-listed but never won, and although some writers would see me as very privileged and successful, I still feel short of serious attention from the mainstream'. Literary excellence and popular success, then, are jostling for supremacy in Gee's own understanding of her oeuvre and her own aspirations for her work. She believes in doing her own thing, but she is also absolutely committed to writing 'stories that matter, for people to read' (Gee cited in McKay, 1997: 213). While she would also like the big prizes – and, like Angela and the rest of us, no doubt 'likes money' – she is also deeply conscious of the creative freedom she retains in not being subsumed by the belly of the contemporary publishing beast: 'If you don't win big prizes, it keeps you going in all sorts of different directions. There is something that isn't necessarily wholly positive about acclaim – it can be deafening' (Gee cited in O'Keefe, 2014).

Non-conformity is not just a creatively liberating practice for Gee; she believes that it also lies at the heart of the moral responsibility of the writer. In 'Why Writers Can't Be Told They Have Responsibilities', Gee's 2004 Dawson-Scott Memorial Lecture at English PEN's International Writers' Day, she observes that while Shelley believed poets were 'the unacknowledged legislators of the world', for her, the opposite is true: 'I think in many countries it is more important that they are the unacknowledged and unpaid opposition to the world; writing in isolation they go against that conformist grain' (Gee, 2004a). This may sound like such a small thing – merely 'to be oneself' – but, she argues:

> authoritarian regimes prove just how dangerous this apparently small thing is when they lock up and murder their writers. When writers are themselves, when they won't be told, when they're off-beat, satirical, lyrical, cynical, auto-biographical, fantastical, defiantly irresponsible, they are fulfilling the deepest responsibilities of writers to the world. (Gee, 2004a)

Literature – the telling of truth through lies – is of such social importance precisely because we are constantly surrounded by discourses, primarily political ones, which are telling lies while insisting they are true: 'we need fictional worlds precisely because we are surrounded by literal accounts of our world that make strident claims to accuracy, and most of them are lies' (Gee, 2004a). Ironically, as Gee (2004a) observes, 'people look to novels and poems for truthfulness' because it is easier to trust someone who acknowledges that whatever truths they are proffering are subjective, uncertain, equivocal; that they have been discovered in and through writing, through the asking of questions and the tentative discovery of some, but not all, answers.[8] The truthful lies of literature do not 'inform, convince, persuade, warn, improve' (Gee, 2004a). Rather, Gee (2004a) insists, when novels work, 'they seduce, they amuse, they astonish and shock and grieve people into attention'. Novels promise nothing other than to move you emotionally but, in another duality, only by promising you so little can they in fact offer you so much.

Another key element of the lecture 'Why Writers Can't Be Told' is the intimacy Gee sketches between the personal and the political. One of the many failings of Saul, the narrator of Gee's 1998 novel *The Ice People*, is that he does not realize the significance of this inextricable duality. When he challenges his partner Sarah about her reluctance to get married, she insists, 'It's *political* [...] You never see the political angle' (*IP*, 49, emphasis in original) – Saul's mistake is to think that 'marriage was personal, actually', that it could somehow be only 'about you and me, and – love and children...' (*IP*, 49). While Gee is often seen as a political writer, she is keen to clarify the origin of the political aspects of her work: they emerge from a deep and personal response to the present moment.[9] The satire of the international 'politics' of Tony Blair and George Bush in *The Flood*, for instance, was written 'from a deep sense of imaginative and intellectual outrage at the lies we were being told' (Gee, 2004a). Such writing is driven by emotional responses to the present, by feelings of fear and of disgust. Her political satire does not arise as obligation, but as inevitability: 'I didn't write about the war because I ought but because I must, because I could do no other, living in that society at that moment' (Gee, 2004a). Gee is a writer acutely attuned to and interested in 'the present' – she is a quintessentially *contemporary* writer in that her subject matter changes along with the shifting concerns and events of that present.[10] She writes *The Burning Book* when American Cruise missiles are sent to Britain in the early 1980s; *Grace* is inspired by the murder of the eighty-four-year-old anti-nuclear campaigner Hilda Murrell in 1984; the growing awareness of human-induced climate change and its potentially catastrophic planetary consequences drives *The Ice People* and *The Flood*; *The White Family* (2002) is Gee's bold confrontation of Britain's ingrained institutional and cultural racism which was brought to light by the murder of Black British teenager Stephen Lawrence in 1993. One could continue to draw such connections across her work, for each of Gee's novels is a deeply personal, emotionally-driven, literary political act of protest.[11]

II. Feeling Blue: An Intimate Interlude

Before we go on to trace some of the key themes in Gee's work, we want to pause for a moment. We want to do so for two reasons. The first is as a result of Gee's comment in a 1997 interview with Margaret McKay:

> ...what I hate, and I think it's a general thing in criticism, is that almost no attention is given to structure or style. My novels are reviewed as very content-based books, and given that I do have literary training and I work fantastically hard on the structure and on the style and language I always find that very distressing. (Gee in McKay, 1997: 219)[12]

We do not want to add to this distress. Each of the chapters in this collection addresses both the content of Gee's novels, *and* their style and structure. In fact, in formal literary criticism – as opposed, perhaps, to journalistic reviewing – it is impossible to fully explore the former without close attention to the latter. The overview of themes and techniques in the following section has of necessity to move swiftly and, as an introduction, dispense with some of the close analysis. But we did not want the introduction to be lacking in it entirely. The second motivation behind this interlude is provided by the publication in 2006 of Gee's first, and still only, collection of short stories, *The Blue*. The chapters in this collection focus exclusively on the novels – here, then, we wish to create space for a momentary engagement with Gee's short fiction.

The Blue's play with the word 'blue' begins not in the body of the work itself, but in the paratexts. Its cover is the most simple of all Gee's books: dark blue at the top shades down to light blue at the bottom; the title, subtitle, writer's name and suitably brief reviewer quotation float in white like gentle clouds in this otherwise clear sky. The paratexts continue the theme. The book's dedication is to Gee's friend and editor who passed away the year before the collection's publication: 'Christine Casley, 1933–2005'. But the terminal date of her death – 2005 – is not the end of this dedication. It is followed thus '1933–2005: into the blue'. Gee's work is characterized by a stark acceptance of, and an open confrontation with, our mortality, at the same time as a defiant hope that we might never end. This is another of her dualities, one which can be seen at a structural level in many of her novels, which are, as the last chapter of *The Burning Book* names it, '… *Against Ending*'. In *The Blue*, the simultaneous defiance and acceptance of endings is placed at the very beginning of the book and takes place not at the macroscopic level of novelistic structure but at the microscopic level of the paratextual dedication – even more specifically, in a single syntactical mark, a colon. The colon after '2005' both allows and defies the finality that date signifies. '2005' is not the end; the colon implies movement, transition, continuation, forward motion consolidated by the directional preposition immediately following it: 'into'. Christine has left Gee and the present she so loves, but she has not expired. Like the characters at the end of *The Flood*, she has merely relocated, 'into the blue'. The dedication ends there, but the questions it raises do not. Is the blue positive or negative for Gee? Is it an Edenic haven of restfulness free from the chains and cares of the present? Or is it the cold emptiness after death? The answer, of course, is 'both': the word 'blue' carries in its single syllable the duality that is a recurring feature of Gee's oeuvre, manifesting both across individual texts, and across levels and scales of structure and meaning.

Like a pair of matching extra-dimensional bookends, the phrase 'into the blue' brackets and encloses Gee's volume, recurring as it does as the title of the final story collected therein. Giving voice to the dead, as *Virginia Woolf in Manhattan* does in a very different way, the last story, 'Into the Blue', features a necronarrator. He is a long-forgotten, long-dead artist – contemporary to the Spanish Renaissance painter and sculptor El Greco and fiercely competitive with him in love and art alike – whom we meet as he visits a twenty-first century El Greco exhibition at a London gallery. Unlike Christine, the narrator has not dissolved into the blue, rather he is a 'restless soul' (*TB*, 132) who refuses to release his hold on the world of the living: 'I must wander forever, never dissolve into blue air' (*TB*, 132). Blue is positive here, it represents escape, freedom, rest. It is a realm that one can be taken to by death, but also by exceptional art, as the narrator begrudgingly admits when looking at El Greco's best work:

> I need not pause long to look at it, though some strange voice inside me whispers 'stay', for just once or twice, a window has opened, I have looked at his paintings and seen miracles. I have seen through into the blue blue air, the electric skies where he perhaps has – yes. The skies where he has genius. (*TB*, 135)

But Gee layers this one word with contrary semantic reverberations. For only a few moments later the narrator uses it again as an adjective, but now in a very different sense. Rather than the 'blue blue air' to which art can lift us, here the envy the two artists have of each other burns them up, 'a blue flame' (*TB*, 137).

This double attribution of contrary meaning to 'blue' recurs throughout the collection *The Blue* and, in fact, Gee's work as a whole. In the first story, 'The Blue', 'blue' is wholly positive – it represents the freedom and escape desired by the story's protagonist, an overburdened mother. Her first sensing of this freedom is described as an internal expansion: 'something like a distant pool of blue water' (*TB*, 10). From then on 'a cloud of blue butterflies' (*TB*, 10) dances alongside her, protecting her from anything that might harm her or prevent her from reaching her goal. Even the calls of her children, though they tug and pull at her heart, cannot hold her back: 'the core of her was deep blue certainty, an ocean of water' (*TB*, 12) into which, in a surfeit of blue, she finally immerses herself:

> She took off her clothes. In the distance, people shouted. But the butterflies covered every inch of her body, floating up like blue steam as she slipped into the water. Cool, edgeless, it became her skin. A blue cloud hung on the blue sea wind. She was invisible. She was her soul. Mysterious, liquid, endless, whole. (*TB*, 13)

In the story 'Thank You Tracey Emin', as a tired and disillusioned computer support technician, Joe, decides to change his life, 'he smiled at the bright blue wind from the river...' (*TB*, 30). When we meet Joe again in 'The Good Hope' he is pleased that someone has named a blue boat 'Hope' and the blue butterflies from the first story flutter in to preserve his enjoyment of the nature reserve, hiding anything that would sully his joy: 'blue butterflies hovered over the nettles' (*TB*, 50). But here 'blue' begins to be associated not just with pure freedom, since the blue butterflies disguise reality, giving false hope and skewing perception. In 'The Good People' the aeroplane may be rising 'steeply into blue heaven' (*TB*, 59), but it does so only to fall out of the air. The blue may be a place of solace, but it also a vast, potentially threatening, unknown – 'the great blue unsteadiness outside their thin shell' (*TB*, 62) – as well as a form of false consolation, such as in Joe's nostalgia about a happiness with his wife Amber that is long gone, '*her cool white flesh in the bright blue waves*' (*TB*, 79, emphasis in original). In the third Joe and Amber story, 'Starting at Last', 'the promise of the blue above him' (*TB*, 83) represents both Joe's intense pleasure in the beauty of the natural world, his acute joy in life, and the death that is soon to befall him. In 'The Money', the small tragedy of that story announces itself with 'the blueing and darkening of the clouds ahead' (*TB*, 67); in 'Ring-barking', 'the cold blue yew' (*TB*, 85) stands in for the absence of widow Una's lost husband. Moving outside of *The Blue*, the duality of blue continues to shade Gee's writing. In *My Driver* (2009) it represents the 'ghastly blue light on their faces' (*MD*, 83), the faces of today's travellers who are chained to their technology rather than open to each other. In *Dying, in Other Words* it is the 'savagely blue' joy that Felicity feels now that her husband's lover is dead as well as the depths of her grief when she in turn loses him: 'And now blue, blue, nothing but blue' (*D*, 111).

In the last room of the exhibition in 'Into the Blue', the narrator arrives at a portrait, attributed to El Greco but of which he is in fact the painter. It is of the mistress they shared who suddenly speaks to him, reminding him of their son – his son, not El Greco's – whose paternity has been as misattributed as that of the painting whose featured mistress is now talking to him. And 'as she reminds me, I am released' (*TB*, 139): all the envy fades away, the blue flame finally sputtering out. Gone is the burning hunger for fame and success, for acknowledgement and recognition. It is replaced by a sense of the real worth of his life: 'my son and my picture' (*TB*, 140). Given how the title 'Into the Blue' recalls the personal dedication to *The Blue*, it is difficult not to read this final story as self-reflexive. Just as Prospero in *The Tempest* is read as a figure for Shakespeare and his thoughts about his own art, here our necronarrator is ghosting Gee. Does this collection release her too, from her own freely acknowledged burning desire for success and recognition? Does she too come to the realization in the final story that the meaning of her life lies in her art, whether it receives attention or not, and in 'her only child, our only child' (*TB*, 140)? Despite the alluring 'patch of true azure in the gallery window' (*TB*, 140), the narrator does not disappear into the blue. He goes even further than this:

> I've had enough. It is time to go home. Those wild white clouds, their flanks of silver, clear air showing through the oil-black *disegno*...
>
> A blessed blankness beyond the blue. (*TB*, 140)

Home is not the blue, but the 'blessed blankness' beyond it, represented by the 'wild white clouds' which recall the floating titles on the cover of the volume. True escape, true release, for Gee it seems, lies not in the blue – whether it be a heaven or a hell – but in what those titular clouds name: literature. Gee's Eden is writing itself – the pure bliss both showing through but achieved by the black ink of the words (the *disengo* which represent the intellectual craft necessary to the creation of seemingly effortless beauty). Here Gee finds her strength to confront the sorrowful joy, the overwhelming intensity, of the intimate partners that are life and death, love and loss: 'words for the world I loved: the end that I fear is silence... Let it not come today. May the sheets of memory hold us' (*D*, 249).

III. The View From Inside

In 1996, Gee gave the William Matthews Lecture at Birkbeck College, London. The lecture – entitled, 'How May I Speak in My Own Voice?: Language and the Forbidden' – is an insightful piece of critical writing by Gee on Gee and we are delighted to be able to print it in full as the concluding chapter of this collection. In the lecture, Gee describes her attraction to fiction since in it, 'the unsayable can be said' (Gee, 1996a). She explains that the main concerns of her writing are precisely those things that cause 'the English to fall silent': 'sex, the emotions, class, race, money, success, failure, excretion of course, illness, age and death' (Gee, 1996a, emphasis in original). She identifies in her work 'a consistent desire to go against the grain of English repression, to reach out for the ruby glowing in the darkness of denial, to find the forbidden truth, to transgress' (Gee, 1996a). In doing so, she is in good company since this is, she believes, 'what writers have always done' (Gee, 1996a). In an interview conducted the following year, Gee reiterates this drive to say the unsayable, to address in her writing issues that are so often repressed by English society. 'I like to write,' she tells, Margaret McKay, 'about things that are in some way forbidden' (Gee cited in McKay, 1997: 214). All of these themes as played out in Gee's writing are characterized by the dualism we have been tracing. We wish to give just a few specific examples here – working primarily through another text that does not have a chapter devoted to it in the body of the collection, Gee's 2010 memoir, *My Animal Life*. We will then present the chapter summaries that detail the ways in which the contributors to this collection have engaged with these and other themes in Gee's fiction through close attention to the formal characteristics of her work.

Gee's work is characterized by what Joe in 'The Good Hope' describes as 'a piercing gladness to be alive' (*TB*, 51). We find this in the opening of her memoir, *My Animal Life* in which she wonders at our momentary and incredible vitality:

> I am alive at the time of writing this. And so are you. For nearly four billion years on earth, neither of us existed: we were a blank. For the next billion years before the sun burns up the earth, our bodies will be bones under the ground, or ash, asleep.
>
> But now, in this astonishing living moment, we are between two states of non-being, two endless nights [...] Suddenly, this is our chance; our luck, our animal luck. (*MAL*, 7)

Inextricably coexisting with this joy is deep sadness at the brevity of the one chance we have at life. Her emotional side wishes we might come back, after death, resurrected in order to have another shot; her rational side tells her that 'we have to make room' (*MAL*, 39) for others, 'for the not-yet-born' (*MAL*, 39). 'Our "once-ness"' (*MAL*, 39) is the source of both the joyful preciousness of life, and the sorrow of it: 'It will just be hard to say goodbye, one day' (*MAL*, 39). Gee addresses this acute awareness of mortality in 'How May I Speak in My Own Voice?', where she states that the title of her first novel is actually a subtitle: '*Dying, in Other Words* really means Living: *Dying, in Other Words*' (Gee, 1996a, emphasis in original). Each second that we live our bodies are dying in a continuous process of senescence and gradual decay. 'I was saying in that title,' she explains, 'that living implies dying, that they are implicitly connected. Of course this is obvious enough, but not in my family. Not in my country, either' (Gee, 1996a). The predominance in Western societies of what has been called a 'death denial thesis' animates a collective disavowal of the natural processes of ageing and dying – as well as arousing a shocking resistance to the visual signs of ageing in multi-billion dollar industries, such as cosmetics and plastic surgery.[13] This disavowal offers Gee a forbidden subject that reverberates across her fiction.

Gee entitles her memoir *My Animal Life*, as she says, 'not to degrade my life, but to celebrate it' (*MAL*, 13). Her physicality – her joy in her own embodiment – joins her, 'tiny though it is, to all the life in the universe' (*MAL*, 13). This physicality enables Gee to do all the things she loves in addition to writing – run, have sex, bear a child. But that very embodiment also renders her vulnerable, to the physical violence of her father, to sexual violation, to her body's betrayal in multiple miscarriages. In *Virginia Woolf in Manhattan*, Gee gifts this physical joy to Woolf who, after a breathless run, thinks 'briefly, clearly, "I love my body"' (*VW*, 305). Woolf 'had not felt that since I was a girl' (*VW*, 305). Gee does indeed identify this joy with youth – with the children in perpetual motion who cartwheel through her work – and the concomitant threat to such youthful joyfulness is ageing, a 'class and a place of its own' (*MAL*, 76). It comes as no surprise, then, that Gee's fiction is populated by characters 'just at the end of being young' (*VW*, 323).

Gee's memoir opens with an account of illness (her own), and ends with the moving memories of the loss of her mother, which she depicts as a personal apocalypse. The more, it seems, that one perceives the joy in life, the more one is haunted by its inevitable end. Gee's work is repeatedly, even compulsively, obsessed with death, at all levels from the individual to the planetary. She traces this back to her father's refusal to confront death – 'my father refused to consider himself mortal until he actually began to die' (Gee, 1996a: 9) – and to the dire warnings of a childhood teacher on the eve of the Suez crisis in 1956 when Gee was just eight-years old: 'I sometimes think one reason for the apocalyptic streak that runs through so many of my novels might be the burden of terror Mr Norris gave me, which lingered long after the crisis went away' (*MAL*, 91). But these two levels are not discrete; the threats of each repeatedly manifest together. Consider, for example, Joe's intimately bound personal and planetary apocalyptic fears in the short story 'Thank You Tracey Emin': '"Do *you* still like me?" he suddenly asked. "We could all be killed tomorrow, with the world as it is. Do you love me, Amber? Tell me you do"' (*TB*, 32–33, emphasis in original). Gee's work repeatedly confronts the reality of the end, but always encodes it with a determined faith in continuance, a repeated insistence – in both the content and structure of her works, and in the consistent resurrection of characters across her oeuvre –that 'Nobody would ever die…' (*TB*, 52). Apocalypse is always both the end and a new beginning for Gee: 'The world left them, they began again – ' (*TB*, 61).[14] Nowhere is the duality of Gee's acceptance and denial of endings presented more succinctly than in the double meaning enclosed in the final line of *Dying, in Other Words* – 'No-one. No-one. Gone' (*D*, 253) – which means both that there is no one left, that everyone has gone, *and also* that no-one has gone.[15]

This preoccupation with the apocalyptic – at the personal, as well as the political, or even global planetary, level – is addressed in Monika Szuba's chapter – 'Burning to Tell the Tale: Negotiating Aesthetics and Politics in *The Burning Book*'. Focusing on Gee's second novel, Szuba considers the thematic and formal implications of this text, which combines the social conscience of nineteenth-century Realist writers as well as the experimental narrative forms pioneered by early twentieth-century Modernists. Szuba argues that Gee presents her readers with a novel that is both political and experimental, although experimental within the restrictions of her own type of realism. Structurally, *The Burning Book* proleptically unveils its apocalyptic ending at the beginning, enacting a circularity of structure that plays with readers' expectations while also conveying the fractured temporality through which we all live as individuals. Interweaving the catastrophic events of Nagasaki and Hiroshima with the private lives of two families, the Lambs and the Ships, Szuba traces Gee's investigation of the formal and ethical possibilities of storytelling in the novel, in which 'small stories' are revealed to be the most apposite to bear witness to unrepresentable horrors like the allied atomic bombings of Japan. Szuba considers Gee's typographic experimentation with the layout of words and images on the page, connecting the charred bodies of Japan's *hibakusha* (or 'explosion-affected people') with the burned pages of books during the novel's concluding nuclear apocalypse. Such experimentation, Szuba concludes, depicts the multiple local historical narratives and subjective experiences that make up global historical time. It cracks asunder the façade of realism in order to make Gee's readers complicit in the meaning-making of narrative via authorial intrusion, non-linear narrative structure, and typographic creativity.

Bringing this discussion of the apocalyptic to bear on gender relations, Alexander Beaumont's chapter – 'Reproductive Politics and the Public Sphere: Natalism, Natality and Apocalypse' – considers the relationship between biological reproduction and global cataclysm in Gee's work, examining novels such as *The Burning Book*, *The Ice People*, *The White Family* and *The Flood*. Beaumont develops the concept of natalism, as theorized by Lauren Berlant, in dialogue with Hannah Arendt's concept of natality. Both concepts illustrate the way in which the public sphere is ideologically constructed around ideas of hope for the future, as embodied in the figure of the unborn, or the very young, child. Beaumont traces the way in which Gee's fiction brings together the genres of family saga and apocalyptic or dystopian fiction to reflect upon the role that hope for the future (embodied in children) plays in our contemporary political discourses, shaping our imagined collective journey into the future. In Gee's fiction, the world must be protected and preserved *for* our children (as in *The Burning Book*, *Where Are the Snows* and *The Flood*), as well as *from* newly savage children (as in *The Ice People*). Beaumont concludes that Gee's interest in the political implications of reproduction and child-rearing across many of her novels thus encourages us to make the world anew.

Continuing this discussion of the significance of reproduction and child-rearing in Gee's fiction, Sarah Falcus focuses on the gendered politics underpinning social and familial roles in her chapter – '"Fall[ing] Out of the Past": Time, Ageing and Generations in *Where Are the Snows*'. Falcus explores how in *Where Are the Snows* the protagonists Alexandra and Christopher refuse to accept their own ageing bodies in a futile attempt to prolong their middle-aged (but also youthful) energy, and live outside of time. Falcus argues that in exhibiting a Thatcherite concern for the individual and disregard for the social, as well as a selfish form of globe-trotting consumerism, Alexandra and Christopher express a particular kind of affluent 1980s consciousness that leaves them both outside of, or free from, family, society, nation and the meaning-conferring powers of all of those things. As Falcus demonstrates, this story of escapism from the responsibilities of family life serves to reflect upon contemporary discourses of ageing, in particular, the limitations they place upon women, whose value is socially determined by their youthful appearance and the fecundity it suggests. Falcus notes that in depicting the sexual lives of older men and women (indeed, showing sex being enjoyed into old age), *Where Are the Snows* critiques our contemporary silencing of older voices (and bodies) from discourses of physicality and sexuality. However, Falcus concludes that the novel's protagonists are ultimately shown to be pursuing an impossible attempt to escape time, ageing and death – and, as in Gee's other fiction, must come to accept their own decaying bodies and inescapable mortality.

Sarah Dillon takes this discussion of familial responsibility one step further in her chapter – 'Literary Equivocation: Reproductive Futurism and *The Ice People*'. Dillon enters into the debates that have arisen around the concept of 'reproductive futurism' – a term coined by queer theorist Lee Edelman to name all politics which, he believes, is determined by the future, and invested in the figure of the child. Formulating a literary critical response to Edelman's theory, Dillon positions Maggie Gee's novel *The Ice People* within a number of twentieth and twenty-first century texts that deal with dystopian futures and population crises. Such dystopias of demography (or 'demodystopias') as Zoe Fairbairns's *Benefits* (1979), Margaret Atwood's *The Handmaid's Tale* (1985), P. D. James's *The Children of Men* (1992) and Jane Rogers's *The Testament of Jessie Lamb* (2011), Dillon argues, confront the generalizing, universal theory of reproductive futurism with a resounding sense of literary *equivocation*: we cannot equate reproduction as being synonymous with reproductive futurism; nor can we assign the child the privileged role of securing that future. Crucial to Dillon's close reading of *The Ice People* is her exploration of the disruptive force of irony. For instance, Dillon argues that in the novel the messianic child Luke is depicted as a queer child, disrupting the heteronormativity of a future guaranteed by reproduction and complicating Edelman's structural political model of futurity. Edelman cites queer adults as the only actors excluded from a future shaped by concerns over species survival, and fails to consider the important role that the queer child can play in complicating societal expectations of the figure of the Child-as-future. Dillon also pays attention to the dramatic irony – a common technique in Gee's fiction – whereby the narrator of the novel, Saul, repeatedly exposes the problems with his own investment in reproductive futurism through his self-representation to the reader. Drawing a connection between the compulsive nature of both Saul and Edelman's investment in the idea of reproductive futurism, Dillon argues that against their tenacious universal fantasies stands literature and its power to equivocate; a power that defines the literary as opposed to other forms of discourse, and which Gee's novel embraces in its critique of any totalizing approach to thinking about futurity.

This discussion concerning the political significance of futurity in our contemporary thinking is extended by Chris Maughan into an analysis of the relevance of Gee's fiction for rethinking our approaches to climate change. In his chapter – '"One and Indivisible, a Seamless Web": Climate Change as Historical Process in *The Flood*' – Maughan argues that Gee's novel underscores the way in which the natural environment, and its rapidly encroaching ecocatastrophe, needs to be understood not as external to human labour, but as integrally bound up with human activity. He argues that *The Flood* engages with environmental problems as dynamic, historical processes, and schools us into refining a new hermeneutic of reading that can engage on three levels: the individual utterance, the broader social context, and the totalizing historical perspective. Maughan considers the engagement in Marxist theory with studies of ecocriticism in his reading of *The Flood*, drawing in particular on the work of Marxist literary and social critic Fredric Jameson, whose three horizons of interpretation in his 1981 text *The Political Unconscious* shape Maughan's close reading of the novel. Since ecological change, Maughan argues, is so slow and accretive, its effects are hard to grasp. Similarly, history – which as a set of real-life processes is fundamentally non-narrative – can only be grasped in its representative (textualized) effects. *The Flood* thus allows us to consider the implications of climate change in a way that non-fictional, political and empirical discourses struggle to do. Gee's web of interconnected characters within the novel, as well as across her oeuvre – where individuals and families appear in different contexts – thus opens up a reflection upon the human causes of ecological change: specifically, social antagonisms clustered around race, gender and class that destructive globalized capitalism propagates. Maughan concludes that Gee's non-naturalistic framing of the novel thus presents us with a formal narrative resolution that is too neat, too paradisiacal, and too totalizing to be read at face value. Rather, it should be read as an aesthetic attempt to deny the complexity of historical and anthropogenic climate change, a formal repression that in fact reveals the 'political unconscious' latent within texts: a textual 'unconscious' that the discerning literary critic must uncover as an indispensable critical instrument in understanding climate change.

Climate change and its utopian–dystopian critique of contemporary society is also the subject of Adam Welstead's analysis in his chapter – '"The End Times and After": Utopia, Dystopia and

Being-Together in *The Flood*'. Welstead similarly focuses on *The Flood* but offers a very different account, interrogating the mode of communal and social 'being-together' that Gee constructs in her 2004 novel of rising sea levels and an apocalyptic tsunami. Welstead situates Gee's text as the literary inheritor of a twentieth century tradition of seminal dystopian novels dealing with totalitarian regimes that illustrate a brutal attitude towards their own citizens: figured, variously, as crowds, homogeneous masses, frenzied and violent mobs, or de-individualized, indoctrinated party members. Welstead notes that this twentieth century desubjectification was considered synonymous with the utopian imagination, and texts such as H. G. Wells's *The Sleeper Awakes* (1910), Aldous Huxley's *Brave New World* (1932), George Orwell's *Nineteen Eighty Four* (1949) have been read as articulations of a narrow and static implementation of utopian engineering. In company with other twenty-first century British dystopian texts by J. G. Ballard, Sarah Hall, Rupert Thompson and Sam Taylor, however, *The Flood* reveals that despite the decline of such problematic utopian thought in the twenty-first century, the dystopian imagination has continued to flourish. Applying Hannah Arendt's notion of 'being together' and 'acting together', Welstead uncovers in Gee's novel a more contemporary utopian formulation of heterogeneous collectivities that do not erase the individuality of each participating subject. Many of the gatherings in *The Flood* depict what Guy Debord called 'the lonely crowd' – riven by divisions of class and social opportunity, undercut by poverty or political protest, and expressing 'dystopian being-together'. However, Welstead argues that Gee's narrative prologue and epilogue functions as a quasi-utopian scene at Kew Gardens that refutes traditional, homogenizing utopias to present an image of interconnectedness among the novel's diverse cast of characters; what Michel Foucault would call a 'heterotopia'. This redeeming post-apocalyptic space thus hints at a new beginning and new modes of being-together; but in its heavenly contours it is a place that remains self-reflexively impossible and external to the world of *The Flood*.

The significance of heterotopian spaces in Gee's work is given further consideration in Irene Pérez-Fernández's chapter – 'From the "Native Outside" to the "Foreigner Within": Re/negotiating Urban Space in *The White Family*'. Pérez-Fernández reflects upon the difficult publication of *The White Family* within the context of attitudes towards im/migration and cross-culturalism in Britain in the 1990s and early 2000s. Written in the shadow of Stephen Lawrence's murder and subsequent investigations into the institutional racism of the British Metropolitan Police, Pérez-Fernández argues that Gee's novel presents its central family – the White family – as a trope for contemporary Britain, a society still engaged in redefining Britishness. Pérez-Fernández develops the terms 'the native outside' and 'the foreign within' to describe the two ends of a multicultural spectrum in which space – particularly the diasporic spaces that make up contemporary London – is shared by two groups of characters: indigenous characters like Alfred, Dirk and May who have failed to adapt to their city's changing population and become positioned 'outside' of society, clinging to older, imperial visions of Britain; as well as characters (both indigenous as well as immigrant) like Elroy, Shirley and Winston who have constructed a sense of belonging in contemporary multiethnic Britain. The lived spaces of the novel's key locations – particularly Hillesden's Albion Park – thus structure the novel's heterotopian sites, which present Gee's reader with 'slices of time' as they become embodied within sites and counter-sites where social reality is represented and contested. Pérez-Fernández concludes that Gee's novel thus reveals the abiding importance of negotiating 'lived space' in a changing society whose fluid and adaptive sense of identity shapes its shared community.

Gee's concern with developing an empathic vision in her fiction in order to confront racism, misogyny and intolerance informs a different kind of study in Susan Alice Fischer's chapter – 'Faith and Grace: Maggie Gee's Spiritual Politics'. Fischer is concerned with uncovering Gee's 'spiritual politics' – an intertwining of the spiritual with the political that she finds most profoundly suggested in Gee's preoccupation with the natural world. Fischer argues that the two characters, Faith and Grace, who appear in Gee's 1988 novel, *Grace*, demonstrate Gee's recourse to religious imagery. This informs her reflection upon the central importance of compassion, hope and luck that recurs in other texts throughout Gee's oeuvre, including *Light Years* (1985), *My Cleaner* (2005), *My Driver* (2009) and her recent memoir, *My Animal Life*. Whilst Gee refers frequently to 'miracles' or 'luck', Fischer contends that it is the concept of grace that best describes Gee's compassion for the planet and her adherence to the concept of Gaia. The spiritual figure of the *anawim* (meaning 'poor ones'), who appear in the Old Testament, offers Fischer a useful critical approach for reading Gee's two, interconnected novels, *My Cleaner* and *My Driver*. Fischer reads these two novels as a literary diptych: each text offers an inverted reflection of the other; taken together, they construct a kind of altarpiece, asking us to contemplate the spirituality that connects us to a life force greater than ourselves, one which is deserving of reverence in all its form, human and otherwise. The interconnected lives of the middle-class white author Vanessa Henman and her former domestic worker Mary Tendo thus refract one another until the spiritually-invested roles of cleaner and driver become so intertwined that they attain a transcendent state of grace.

Bringing this empathic concern for the other to bear on Gee's earlier-discussed interest in beginnings and endings, and the possibilities of necronarrators or characters raised from the dead, E. H. Wright's chapter – 'The Resurrection of the Author: On *Virginia Woolf in Manhattan*' – examines Gee's most recently published novel. In many ways, *Virginia Woolf in Manhattan* brings Gee's literary career full circle: returning to her doctoral study of modernist innovators Woolf, Nabokov and Beckett with the deliciously satisfying literary conceit of bringing Woolf back to life as a character in the twenty-first century. As Wright attests, such 'biofiction' or 'author fiction' (which features well-known authors as characters in novels that fill in unknown historical blanks with fictional speculation) has become increasingly prevalent over the past thirty years. Woolf herself has become a particularly popular writer to recreate in fiction, featuring as a character in a number of novels by writers such as Michael Cunningham, Sigrid Nunez, Gillian Freeman, Susan Sellers, Clare Morgan and Stephanie Barron. Wright considers the way in which such texts suggest the 'ownership' of a historical figure like Woolf, who reappears in Gee's novel to assert her own authorial voice and autonomy – most amusingly, at a conference in Istanbul dedicated to her work. Wright interrogates the relationship between Woolf as influential precursor and Gee as literary inheritor. She explores the way in which revivifying Woolf allows Gee to: play with Woolfian idiom, archaism and synaesthetic language; experiment with narrative structure (what Gee calls 'pattern') and stream of consciousness soliloquies; make thematic links with Woolf's oeuvre – most notably Woolf's notorious contempt for contemporary critics of her work; and, to recall Woolf's own fictionalized biographies, *Orlando* (1928) and *Flush* (1933). Wright suggests that this authorial playfulness has a serious purpose in highlighting a feminist counter-canon on which Gee is drawing, in order to open up sufficient historical distance to confront modern attitudes towards race, religion, class and money. These are issues that, like many of the forbidden topics Gee's fiction explores, impact upon women's lives asymmetrically, in comparison with their male counterparts. Gee's so-called 'author fiction', Wright concludes, enables her to hurl Woolf into the twenty-first century precisely to challenge our contemporary world.

IV. The Reader

We opened this introduction with the observation that Gee is a satirist. This is something readers sometimes fail to grasp in her work, thereby missing its humour, but also its careful non-representation of real life. She observes to McKay that sometimes readers 'don't know what I'm doing and I think that makes them feel unsafe because they can't work out what my attitude is to my characters' (Gee cited in McKay, 1997: 219). In a characteristic dualism, Gee both loves and mocks her characters, she satirizes 'where there's a grain of truth' (Gee in Williams, 2014), but she also understands them all. Gee explains that the closer she feels to the opinions or traits of a character, the more she satirizes them:

> whenever in a novel I come to a character who more or less reflects my own opinions in real life, especially if they are around my own age

and gender, a squirm of embarrassment and distaste sees me heading very fast to the opposite pole of authorial sympathy. [...] the nearer they come to my own views, these characters, the more I feel I have to separate myself from them through irony. (Gee, 2004a)

Herein we find a guarantee against the risk we have taken with this collection – according to this logic, academics are most fiercely satirized in Gee's work because she senses her own affinity to them most acutely; she may mock us powerfully, but she loves us with equal strength.

In the story 'Thank You Tracey Emin', Joe seeks out artwork to populate his new gallery space. He visits a young artist called Faith, who is ridiculed for the empty pseudo-intellectualism she spouts about her art works: '"I think they're, I don't know, you know, there's a dialectic of self I haven't quite....like, it's a socially constructed thing...and it's gendered..."' (*TB*, 35). Joe's response is far more simple:

> He loved them at once. They were small polished suitcases made out of shiny paper she had worked to look like leather, with miniature labels, miniature chalk marks from Customs, miniature leather tags, tiny bright locks no bigger than the purple fragment of nail on her little finger. He touched one with wonder.
> 'Do they open up?'
> 'You see that's not the ... Obviously it's more about the tension between the inner and the outer, which questions – '
> 'I think they're beautiful.' (*TB*, 36)

Here intellectual engagement with art is presented as polar opposite to pure aesthetic appreciation. We hope the chapters that follow demonstrate the combination of these into a further dualism; we believe they show that an academic response to a work of art need not preclude a love of it, but rather in fact that the two are mutually productive. The editors and contributors alike have worked hard to avoid Gee's most acute objects of academic satire which can be found in the conference that takes place in *My Driver*: 'long or repellent' (*MD*, 24) titles; 'longwindedness' (*MD*, 24); 'contorted style' (*MD*, 141). There are, we admit, some 'French deconstructionist words' (*MD*, 191) but we believe that where theory is employed, it brings insight and clarity of argument and perception, rather than mystification.

To return at the end to Gee's first novel: *Dying, in Other Words* might most clearly and predominantly be about the author, but hidden at the heart of it is a recognition of the importance of the reader:

> But the papers stayed real and full-size on a desk, it no longer mattered on whose desk as long as they lay to be read on someone's … someone with brains and a heart, someone living (dying, in other words) [...] the world which supported the papers had (randomly) opened and closed: and a face with its pleased self-invention, a name with its bright self-invention is no longer needed to hold the fiction together … all that is needed is somebody else's hands: for the hands which have sculpted a world must be first and last self-destroying.
>
> Reach out and touch me, reader. Flying, flying and falling. Other chance hands will support me. (*D*, 196)

In the contemporary literary jungle there may well be no 'literary angels' (*MAL*, 193), but we hope that the chapters that follow prove at least the existence of Gee's imagined 'skilled taxonomists, Nabokovian naturalists, protected like jurors from prevailing opinions, ideal readers who sift slowly and carefully and add to knowledge with what they tell us' (*MAL*, 193). Taxonomy, though, seems such an earthbound enterprise; buoyed up by the power of Gee's writing, we hope that we might soar a little higher than that, maybe not to the angelic heavens, but at least into the blue.

Notes

1 In the first academic monograph on Gee's work, Mine Özyurt Kiliç (2013: 29) summarizes her account of *Dying, in Other Words* thus: 'The novel poses the question of what it means to be an author in this world, what it means for the characters and what it means for the reader. Gee starts her writing career by probing the question of the death of the author and, in a sense, asks what has become of fiction, and what the function of fiction is. These questions about the nature of authorship and fiction were the very

questions that literary critics and theorists of the 1980s were discussing. In making her debut with a novel exploring this vital literary discussion both thematically and stylistically, Gee was placing herself at a significant juncture in contemporary fiction.' Elisabeth Bronfen (1992: 425–32) includes an engaging discussion of *Dying, in Other Words* in the context of her analysis of the relationship between authorship and feminine death in the final chapter of her now classic work *Over Her Dead Body*.

2 Woolf is right to see 'the influence of Dr Freud' (*VW*, 317–8) in this suspicion of conscious intentions. From a psychoanalytic perspective, it is not just authors who do not consciously know what they are doing; none of us does.

3 The Guardian Reader Event took place on Wednesday 3 September 2014 at the Royal Geographical Society in London. Mitchell was in conversation with the *Guardian*'s Books Editor, Claire Armistead. He was driven to this statement after Armistead insisted that one of his satirical characters was clearly a well-known contemporary author; Mitchell avowed that it was not intended to be so.

4 Discussing the novel in interview with Margaret McKay, Gee traces the character Bruno's disturbing nature and behaviour back to a splitting, this time of masculine from feminine: 'I thought because Bruno has to be so masculine and has to split off his feminine self this is what makes him so dangerous' (Gee cited in McKay, 1997: 217).

5 This subtitle is lifted from Gee's (2004b) excellent review of the Tate Modern's 2004 'Edward Hopper' exhibition, which demonstrates Gee's sensitivity as a lover and critic of the visual arts, and discusses themes and techniques in Hopper's work which reflect back on similar concerns and practices in her own.

6 When editing the prose selection for the Fiction Supplement of the 1996 edition of Virago's *Writing Women*, an annual anthology of poetry and prose, Gee (1996b: 26) responded to submissions that evidenced the same adventurousness and originality that drives her own work: 'I found myself excited by pieces that took risks and tried something different'. In interview with Elaine Showalter, despite her innate resistance to categorization, Gee (2009) responds positively to the description of her work as sceptical realism: 'I have been called a skeptical realist, and the name instantly made sense to me. I am socially and culturally skeptical, but I also habitually look at the "reality" of the book skeptically. In other words, I belong, in part, to what Robert Alter called "the other great

tradition," meaning self-conscious novelists from Sterne onwards who are holding fictionality to the light every now and then'.

7 For a fuller discussion of the representation of the publishing industry in *The Flood* see Dillon (2007: 387–8).

8 Gee expresses a similar sentiment in 'How May I Speak?' (1996a): 'Writing fiction,' she says, 'offers an additional kind of freedom because it comes, in effect, with a disclaimer. The novelist is usually very aware that his or her novel is, in a deep sense, true. And yet there is an escape clause, because everyone knows (though they sometimes forget) that fiction is not literally copied from life'.

9 Gee considers herself in good company here. In 'Writers Can't be Told' (Gee, 2004a), Gee responds to an audience question in which previous writers of social conscience are mentioned – such as 'Dickens, San Jenettson, Steinbeck, Andre Brink' – that 'in order for those writers to write well it has to have affected their imagination in the deepest sense. It was not that Dickens thought "I really ought to write a novel on social criticism." It was that his imagination, his visual sense, his sense of humour, his sense of pity were all deeply involved in what he saw around him. And from that comes good writing. I just think that first of all it has to have sunk in in a personal way and that's what makes it work'.

10 As she explains in interview with Kiliç, 'the present is what fascinates me. It's so exciting'; Gee wants to understand 'what is really happening that isn't in journalists' reports or politicians' claims' (Gee cited in Kiliç, 2013: 161).

11 In *My Animal Life*, Gee articulates her reaction to the Stephen Lawrence murder: 'I wanted to protest; as Dickens did against the evils of his day, and Thackeray and George Eliot – so many great nineteenth-century novelists' (*MAL*, 175). Such protest is not, she insists, inimical to literariness; rather, she draws attention to the way in which social commentary and stylistic experimentation form another dualism in her writing: 'Many of my literary models are modernist – Virginia Woolf, Vladimir Nabokov – but for me the modernist aesthetic breaks down when it isolates the writer from the world. Like the modernists, I love pattern, and try to give each book an overall controlling form, but I also have one eye on reality. I want my books to express the whole of me, politics and jokes as well as love of beauty' (*MAL*, 175). This dualism is not addressed at length in this introduction since it is the sustained focus of Mine Özyurt Kiliç's monograph.

12 In her comments on gender and genre in the contemporary publishing industry, recorded in *A Woman's Business* (1998), Gee (1998: 173) argues that this inattention to technique is to some extent specific to criticism of women writers by male reviewers: 'In general, I have to say that I think women writers suffer from a lack of attention to style and even more particularly to form. Form is something that critics apparently only expect to find in the work of male literary writers...'. In the male-dominated critical domain, it would appear that 'women "write *about*" – by which I mean that reviewers look first at our subject matter. Men simply "write" – a primary, literary activity' (Gee, 1998: 174, emphasis in the original).

13 For an authoritative account of the pervasive 'death denial thesis' in Western literature and culture, see Ernst Becker (1973/1997).

14 For extended discussions of Gee and apocalypse see Steven Connor (1996: 238–45) and Andrew Hammond (2013), in relation to *The Burning Book*, and Dillon (2007) in relation to *The Flood*.

15 So many other dualisms – thematic and technical – that we do not have space to explore at length here, can also be found in Gee's writing, such as ambition and the restrictions of working motherhood – Virginia, for instance, notices a fellow passenger on a plane trying to juggle care of her baby with her work, 'her drive to write [...] chained to duty' (*VW*, 227) – or the continual dance between the sexes. In her later work, this dualism manifests at a character level, as she uses a pair of characters to explore issues of class and race, for example Vanessa and Mary in the two novels *My Cleaner* (2005) and *My Driver* (2009).

Works Cited

Becker, Ernest (1973/1977) *The Denial of Death*. New York: Simon and Schuster.

Bronfen, Elisabeth (1992) *Over Her Dead Body: Death, Femininity and the Aesthetic*. Manchester: Manchester University Press.

Connor, Steven (1996) *The English Novel in History: 1950–95*. London: Routledge.

Dillon, Sarah (2007) 'Imagining Apocalypse: Maggie Gee's *The Flood*', *Contemporary Literature* 48(3): 374–97.

Gee, Maggie (1996a) 'How May I Speak in My Own Voice?: Language and the Forbidden', The William Matthews Lecture 1996 delivered at Birkbeck College, London, 23 May. (Printed at the end of this collection.)

Gee, Maggie (1996b), 'Editorial', *Writing Women* 12(3): 26.

Gee, Maggie (1998) 'The Contemporary Writer: Gender and Genre', in Judy Simons and Kate Fullbrook (eds), *Writing, A Woman's Business: Women, Writing and the Marketplace*, pp. 172–82. Manchester: Manchester University Press.

Gee, Maggie (2004a) 'Why Writers Can't Be Told They Have Responsibilities', The Dawson-Scott Memorial Lecture, English PEN's International Writers's Day, 29 May, URL (consulted 21 September 2014): http://www.englishpen.org/legacy/downloads/Events/maggiegee_why_writers_cant_be_told.pdf

Gee, Maggie (2004b) 'View From Outside', *New Statesman*, 24 May, URL (consulted 22 September 2014): http://www.newstatesman.com/node/148027

Gee, Maggie (2009), 'Five Questions For…', Maggie Gee in Interview with Elaine Showalter, SHEWRITES.com, URL (consulted 21 September 2014): http://www.shewrites.com/profiles/blogs/five-questions-for-5

Hammond, Andrew (2013) *British Fiction and the Cold War*. Basingstoke: Palgrave Macmillan.

Hughes, Kathryn (2010) '*My Animal Life* by Maggie Gee', Review, *The Guardian*, Saturday 15 May, URL (consulted 22 September 2014): http://www.theguardian.com/books/2010/may/15/my-animal-life-maggie-gee

Kiliç, Mine Özyurt (2013) *Maggie Gee: Writing the Condition-of-England Novel*. London: Bloomsbury.

McKay, Margaret (1997) 'An Interview with Maggie Gee', *Studia Neophilologica* 69(2): 213–21.

O'Keefe, Alice (2014) 'Maggie Gee interview: "Writing novels is a ghastly profession"', *The Observer*, Sunday 15 June, URL (consulted 22 September 2014): http://www.theguardian.com/books/2014/jun/15/maggie-gee-interview-writing-novels-ghastly-profession-virginia-woolf

Williams, Holly (2014) 'Maggie Gee: "My Manhattan Transfer with Woolf"', *The Independent*, Sunday 15 June, URL (consulted 22 September 2014): http://www.independent.co.uk/arts-entertainment/books/features/maggie-gee-my-manhattan-transfer-with-virginia-woolf-9536272.html

2

Burning To Tell The Tale
Negotiating Aesthetics and Politics in *The Burning Book*

Monika Szuba

The Burning Book, Maggie Gee's second novel, opens with an epigraph, a Buddhist *kōan* – 'If all is reduced to the One, to what is the One reduced?' – which introduces a paradox to arouse doubt and incite progress on the way to enlightenment, thus turning the reader into a Zen practitioner. Since the kōan cannot be understood by logical thinking but only through intuition or lateral thinking, its function is to open one's eyes. Arousing great inquiry or 'Great Doubt' is an essential element of kōan practice. As the author of *Three Pillars of Zen*, Philip Kapleau, explains:

> Kōans take as their subjects tangible, down-to-earth objects such as a dog, a tree, a face, a finger, to make us see, on the one hand that every object has absolute value and, on the other, to arrest the tendency of the intellect to anchor itself in abstract concepts. But the import of every kōan is the same: the world is one interdependent Whole and that each separate one of us is that Whole ... In the process they pry us loose from our tightly held dogmas and prejudices, and empty us of the false notion of self-and-other, to the end that we may one day

perceive that the world of Perfection is in fact no different from that in which we eat and excrete, laugh and weep. (Kapleau, 1980: 64)

The puzzle at the beginning of the novel is not a typical kōan as it does not refer to a 'tangible, down-to-earth object' exemplified by Kapleau. However, it still serves its purpose, namely to 'pry us loose from our tightly held dogmas and prejudices'. Thus, not only does the opening kōan initiate the process of inquiry, but it also foreshadows Buddhist echoes, which resound throughout the whole text, including the idea of the cyclical nature of things and the suffering of all beings. Thanks to its Zen context, the kōan announces the meditative aspect of narrative and urges the reader to start a process of questioning. The kōan offers an invitation to Gee's reader to consider the paradoxes of reality, the nagging questions that cannot be ignored; it announces that logic cannot be used on the way to enlightenment. Thus, the narrative of *The Burning Book* is introduced as a kōan, which will represent the world as an interdependent whole, with the Ship and Lamb families inextricably part of that narrative world. What is more, by signaling at its opening that the novel intends to initiate a great enquiry, the text operates within what Roland Barthes (2002: 18–9) calls 'the hermeneutic code': a way of creating suspense in narrative by the anticipation of the action's resolution. That is, it foregrounds that some elements of the story are not going to be explained, that part of the reading process will be the solving of a puzzle. However, the narrative in *The Burning Book* disrupts this hermeneutic code, unveiling the end before it arrives and summarizing the events in the characters's lives in its very first chapter. By doing so, and by introducing and repeating the motif of the final violence, the text thwarts readers's expectations of the suspense and resolution usually promised in narrative.

Despite being first published, as Gee (*MAL*, 175) admits, in 1983 as a direct response to the American Cruise missile crisis, the novel's finely wrought exploration of the personal consequences of political decisions remains as urgent as ever. The novel has lost none of its relevance: it remains topical in the times of impending doom repeated every day in the media. By offering a critique of an anthropocentric vision of the world, *The Burning Book* explores those concepts closely related to the etymology of the term 'ecopoetics', where *oikos* refers to dwelling, home, and *poesis* means creation. That is, the novel is concerned with how literature nurtures and cultivates the sense of our being in the world. The narrative hinges on the tension between fictional events and historical ones – the nuclear disasters of Hiroshima and Nagasaki are interwoven into the story of the Lambs and the Ships. Moreover, the text presents a mode of living that persists in Western countries into the twenty-first century; one that is short-sighted, consumerist, greedy, and based on the irresponsible use of natural resources. It voices concerns over nuclear or environmental, human-induced disaster, shared by many people: it depicts a world where final violence looms, warning readers that such an eventuality is not as fictitious as it may seem. Uncannily prescient as Gee's fiction has often proved to be, *The Burning Book* captures the anxiety of the contemporary moment and what Ursula Heise (1997: 4) calls 'the temporal disintegration of the individual'.[1] Heise's analysis of Beckett's and Robbe-Grillet's late modernist texts may be useful in our discussion of Gee's novel: time disintegrates and becomes fractured, the narrative is broken by numerous insertions and interruptions. As a result, both the characters and the readers find themselves without a hold on past or present (Heise, 1997: 4). Gee's novel is a rare and powerful combination – experimental fiction that engages with fundamental political and ethical concerns and explicitly aims to raise public consciousness of them.[2]

In *My Animal Life* (2010), Gee observes that:

> Many of my literary models are modernist – Virginia Woolf, Vladimir Nabokov – but for me the modernist aesthetic breaks down when it isolates the writer from the world. Like the modernists, I love pattern, and try to give each book an overall controlling form, but I also have one eye on reality. I want my books to express the whole of me, politics and jokes as well as love of beauty. (*MAL*, 175)

Gee uses fiction as a political response, and writing as a way to protest against inequities: she says, 'I wanted to protest; as Dickens did against the evils of his day, and Thackeray, and George Eliot – so many great nineteenth-century novelists. It didn't make them less literary' (*MAL*, 175). Modelled on the innovation of twentieth-century modernists and the social conscience of nineteenth-century realists, Gee's fiction is both experimental *and* political. In *My Animal Life*, for instance, she talks about the killing of Stephen Lawrence and her feeling, as a white person, of complicity: 'But I still felt accountable. What had I actually done to dissociate myself from the murderers?' (*MAL*, 175). Gee's response to such feelings of accountability is to write: 'In 1982, when American Cruise missiles were about to be sent to Britain, I had written my anti-war novel *The Burning Book*; in 1988, the murder of eighty-four-year-old anti-nuclear campaigner Hilda Murrell had inspired my fourth novel, *Grace*. What was I going to do this time?' (*MAL*, 175). What she did was to write *The White Family* (2002), a book so bold in its confrontation of racism in a Britain still in denial of that racism that it took years to secure a publisher.

Gee thus clearly articulates the stakes at play in her work – for her the novel is not a purely formal or aesthetic enterprise, even though she remains committed to formalism and aesthetics. Rather, in addition, it is a political mode of discourse, one that is obliged to reconfigure experimental techniques within the context of realism. A prime example of this political aesthetic, *The Burning Book* contains avant-garde elements – offering formal experimentation with narrative and time, but also engaging with important problems of memory, silence and suffering. As Gee says, '[i]n fiction, lost selves can be found, and new selves constantly created. In fiction the unsayable can be said' (Gee, 1996: 1). Gee insists that it is necessary to write 'on what is repressed and what the novelist is impelled most urgently to say' (Gee, 1996: 15). This chapter will examine the tension between the formally experimental, self-referential nature of Gee's novel and its underlying social message; in so doing, it will investigate the important relationship between aesthetics and politics in Gee's work.

1. Telling Small Stories

Employing an experimental form, Gee challenges readers to reflect upon the message of *The Burning Book*, which, as we have seen, takes the form of a kōan – offering a non-standard vision of reality. Despite its formal inventiveness, the novel remains a compelling read, proving that Gee is an excellent *raconteuse*. The text stresses the power of telling stories: as the title of this chapter implies, the narrator burns to tell the tale as she arouses curiosity and the desire to know in readers who, as a result, are compelled into an awareness of social, ecological and pacifist issues relevant both in the 1908s and in the twenty-first century.[3] Storytelling is skilfully employed in the novel as a powerful instrument aimed at forcing its readers to confront the repressed, and the purposefully forgotten. As I have already mentioned, despite the narrative strategy of Gee's novel – which involves self-conscious, self-reflective devices – *The Burning Book* is aware of the social meaning implied by formal experiment. The author herself confirms this when she observes that:

> Books sometimes help by keeping memories alive and getting things out there where they can be discussed. They are a slightly less pressured place where people can sometimes see things more clearly. People are not on the line so much in imaginary spaces – the writers are on the line but their readers are not – so books lift things out of the everyday world where people's ideas are quite fixed into a space where they are free to think again. (Gee cited in Jaggi, 2004: 309)

Published one year before the English edition of Jean-François Lyotard's *The Postmodern Condition: A Report on Knowledge* (1984), which suggests that metanarratives and their reliance on some form of transcendent and universal truth are exhausted, *The Burning Book* equally stresses incredulity toward metanarratives; advocating *petits récits*, small, local narratives instead (Lyotard, 1984: xxiv–xxv). Gee's novel offers an apology for small stories, set against a background of history, and individual lives are contrasted (but also intertwined) with a bigger entity. Lyotard's (1984: 82) closing words in *The Postmodern Condition* read: 'Let us wage a war on totality; let us be witnesses to the unpresentable; let us activate the differences and save the honor of the name'. As Gee (1996: 1) similarly agues, bearing witness to the 'unpresentable' presents writers with a particular dilemma: 'for all writers, each silence is a challenge. The small internal voice asks, what is the silence saying? Enforced silence is an affront writers are almost honour-bound to redress'. The importance of this bearing witness, or telling (and the power of storytelling), is highlighted by another storyteller of our times, John Berger. In *And Our Faces, My Heart, Brief as Photos*, John Berger (1984: 31) writes: 'If we storytellers are Death's Secretaries, we are so because, in our brief mortal lives, we are grinders of these lenses', where the lenses are 'the secret of narration, ground anew in every story'. Telling stories thus requires sharp optics, and Gee trains her own narrative lens on the contemporary world, focusing on the way in which the circularity of stories can be identified as akin to the cycles of nature. Published in the same year as Graham Swift's *Waterland* (1983), *The Burning Book* equally insists on the need for storytelling and the circularity of history, rejecting totalizing grand narratives in order to focus on *petits récits*.[4]

The Burning Book confronts the fractured temporality experienced more and more acutely in the contemporary world: a world of short attention spans, flickering screens feeding people glimpses of images, ever faster means of transport, rapid scientific development, and an overall obsession with speed. In *Chronoschisms: Time, Narrative and Postmodernism*, Ursula K. Heise (1997: 6) calls this 'fragmentation into multiple temporal itineraries'. She argues that 'the accelerated temporal rhythms of late-capitalist technologies of production and consumption, [...] tend to make long-term developments more difficult to envision and construct' (Heise, 1997: 6). The fragmented temporalities of contemporary life have therefore consolidated the loss of faith Lyotard first articulated in postmodernism's rejection of the Enlightenment idea of grand historical narratives stretching seamlessly from the past, through the present, into the future. This 'rapidly decreasing belief in narratives of progress, enlightenment, emancipation, liberation or revolution, especially since the 1960s, has become', Heise (1997: 16) argues, 'one of the hallmarks of postmodernist culture, that, in the view of many theorists, mostly clearly marks its difference from modernist thinking'. By returning to, and highlighting, the importance of small narratives in the face of this postmodernist disbelief in narrative altogether, *The Burning Book* participates in a late twentieth century 'interest in histories understood as more local and concrete narratives' (Heise, 1997: 16). In doing so, the novel gives a renewed coherence to the experiences of the characters whose lives could otherwise seem fragmentary, or even irrelevant, if viewed within the context of a globalized technological time.

2. Self-awareness and Self-extinction

From the very first sentence of *The Burning Book* we are made aware that we are reading fiction – no illusion, no suspended disbelief is possible. With the opening words: 'This is the story of ...' (BB, 15), the narrator announces her presence and makes visible the individual threads that combine to make the fabric of telling. To extend our metaphor of narrative yarn, we might argue that the stitches of Gee's text can be viewed as conspicuous: on the outside for all to see. The oral aspect of this telling is repeatedly highlighted: there are numerous ellipses, which imitate pauses occurring when the teller loses the plot, drifts away, or becomes distracted. Frequent authorial intrusions comment on the processes involved in storytelling, thereby violating any illusion of omniscient narration and disturbing the impression of realism. Through statements such as 'Henry Ship will be one of our heroes' (BB, 15) the façade of realism is fractured and readers are rendered complicit in the making of the fiction: with the possessive pronoun 'our' we are invited to participate actively in creating the story. Thus the book also alludes to the novel tradition, in which early British novels such as Laurence Sterne's *Tristram Shandy* (1759–1767) engaged readers in the story, using the narrator to draw them in, inviting them to participate by employing conversational devices. Yet these authorial intrusions and the metanarrative frame they create sometimes disappear in a text, and when they do so suspended disbelief resumes in order for the fiction to work. Confronted with this challenging experience, the reader is denied any oblivious immersion in the story, which, like a kōan, resists simple explanation.

Disrupted temporality, narrative intrusions and self-consciousness are examples of the formally experimental nature of Gee's *The Burning Book*. Furthermore, numerous other self-reflexive devices heighten the effect of the novel's fictionality, creating what Linda Hutcheon (1984: 1) calls 'narcissistic narrative' aimed at enhancing 'textual self-awareness'. There are sentences that introduce metafictional elements, for instance: 'She had told some terrible stories, to neaten the narrative ends' (*BB*, 19); or, 'They never saw the *hibakusha*, creeping back into this chapter' (*BB*, 158, emphasis in original); or, 'She did discover real love in a world which was mostly fiction. But she lived, like most of her neighbours, in a novel too late to be bought. There wouldn't be time for this novel, there wouldn't be space for this novel' (*BB*, 52). The narrative also offers self-reflective comments about synopses: 'There is comfort about a synopsis. Except that it doesn't quite fit' (*BB*, 18); or, 'the running fauna of dreams whose names don't fit in the synopses' (*BB*, 18). Authorial interjections throughout the text, delivered in italics, provide a metanarrative: a voice narrating from outside of the main story, which disrupts the immersion of the reader in the story. For instance: '*with such a hubbub outside, great cracks appear in my novel*' (*BB*, 52, emphasis in original); or, '*this chapter is no longer sealed*' (*BB*, 114, emphasis in original); or else, 'I know I am writing a novel, and novels are not for them. I know that novels need detail, the vivid detail of life...' (*BB*, 116). The employment of self-referential devices even includes the appearance in Angela's attic flat of '*Dying, in Other Words*, by Maggie Gee, open at the last few pages' (*BB*, 155). This double temporality, or narrative 'metalepsis' as the French narratologist Gérard Genette calls it, involves transgressions in telling: 'introducing into one situation, by means of a discourse, the knowledge of another situation' (Genette, 1980: 234). All the above devices result in an extremely self-conscious narrative: the machinery of fiction is thus laid bare on many occasions and the reader is constantly jolted into the realization that they are reading a novel.

However, the political aspect of the narrative is equally highlighted. The reader follows the story, witnessing how the protagonists's worst fears come true. The novel tells a story of a British family whose lives are torn apart by world wars, juxtaposed with sections about Nagasaki and Hiroshima. The tension between fictional events, such as the problems of the Ship family, and historical ones, when the nuclear disasters of Hiroshima and Nagasaki are evoked, serves to enhance Gee's devastating account of the real perpetuated atrocities, which seem more horrifying than any fictional account. The fiction provides an opportunity to record the lives of those who died in camps, wars, famines or prisons, supplanting them, standing in for them. As we read: 'Because their names and details are lost their voices can never stop calling. They add their terrible volume to the cries of those who survive' (*BB*, 116). The word *hibakusha*, meaning 'explosion-affected people' (which is used by the narrator to describe the surviving victims of the atomic bombings of Hiroshima and Nagasaki), is repeated throughout the novel, illustrating the cyclical ruthlessness of history. The first reference to the *hibakusha* appears in the first chapter of the novel. Their plight as the disenfranchised and the rejected is demonstrated by the narrator's objectifying phrase, 'something broken pleading for life' (*BB*, 21). A fuller description is subsequently given: 'There are people not spoken about, people not written about, people whose name is a way of saying they are not there. Hibakusha, atomic victims – the scarred who carry our scars. They reminded the Japanese of the horrors that come with defeat' (*BB*, 21). The narrator depicts them as 'the scarcely human' (*BB*, 21), people pushed to the margin of society because they remind us of historical events that are too painful and have been repressed. In Gee's narrative, however, they are invited in: '*Hibakusha, hibakusha.* Let us in, let us darken this space' (*BB*, 21, emphasis in original). The verb 'darken' has a double meaning here: they will fill the pages of the novel as ink darkens the blank page, but the *hibakusha* also render the story ominous and sombre.

At the same time, we follow a set of fictional characters' more ordinary lives: Lorna's choice of husband, her menial job at the supermarket, her affair, Henry's obsession with clocks and watches, Angela's reading habits, George's goodwill, and Guy's death. Despite the experimental fiction in which they appear, these are characters whose dreams, fears and aspirations are often close to our own. This impression is further enhanced by the sweeping statements of universality which abound in the novel, for instance: 'as most people do' (*BB*, 15); 'They married, like everyone else' (*BB*, 16); 'People do love their children' (*BB*, 36); or else, 'Lorna just liked to feel loved and safe, exactly like everyone else does' (*BB*, 73); to quote just a few. These characters can seem schematic at times, whilst 'they all start different, [...] they mostly end up the same' (*BB*, 15), but this renders them less as caricatures than universal archetypes; representatives of us, our petty concerns and our naïveté in the face of impending disaster. Like them, we share a blind faith that '[t]hings will come right in the end' (*BB*, 243). As the narration zooms out to show characters' lives in perspective, it heightens the atmosphere of sadness and sorrow at the inevitable fate of the little people; cogs in the machinery of an irrational and inevitable historical fate or 'final violence'.

The 'big people' are no better. *The Burning Book* is outspokenly critical of our supposed leaders, described as 'people so famous that they are more real than life' (*BB*, 21), who 'wear contact lenses of sapphire which glitter with cold blue fire' through which 'they see nothing [...], and no one outside can see in' (*BB*, 21). Such people may seem more real than Lorna, Henry, Angela, and the others, but this is only because 'they are proved by oceans of print and mountains of newsreel footage' (*BB*, 21). In fact, 'their size is a trick of the light. Their outsides are frail lacquered cases. Their sound effects come from machines. Their scripts are written by hacks...' (*BB*, 21–2). More terrifying for Gee than the disempowerment of the ordinary man or woman is the empty or irresponsible power of those who appear to be in charge: 'Our children, should any survive, will try to make sense of those speeches. But they will find nothing there. There never was anything there. We give real power and glory to dying, neon-dipped actors' (*BB*, 22). The bleak irony is that while the Lambs and families like them will be burnt away without trace by a nuclear apocalypse they seem powerless to prevent, the leaders whose actions could or should have done so, will be the ones who survive: they are 'booked for embalming, the finest bunkers reserved' (*BB*, 21). All that will survive of humanity is their 'greed and glitter and lying' (*BB*, 22).[5]

The novel's constant impression of impending doom is intensified by the device of prolepsis: that is, 'any narrative maneuver that consists of narrating or evoking an event that will take place later' (Genette, 1980: 40). In *The Burning Book* this provokes fear and anxiety in the reader, since its prophecies concerning our future are very grim: the nuclear disaster it foresees casts a shadow over the lives of ordinary people, both then and now. Between 'lived time' and 'universal time', to use Paul Ricœur's expression (1988: 104), Gee's characters experience the pitiless pressure of grand, or totalizing, history. The employment of prolepsis gives the impression of impending doom and further staves off the illusion of realism by offering the reader the uncanny sensation of having impossibly glimpsed the future. This enhances the artificiality of Gee's created world, but at the same time it points to the novel's major political concern, providing powerful criticism of the present situation. The tensions between aesthetics and politics are clearly visible here. It can be argued that the oracular nature of the text exposes its fictionality but, at the same time, that it is also part of the novel's political power – in this sense, like much of Gee's work, *The Burning Book* is aligned with speculative fiction and that genre's important political function as a literature of 'cognitive estrangement' (to use the influential concept coined by Darko Suvin [1979: 4], one of the leading critics of speculative and science fiction), which imagines the future in order to reflect critically upon, and incite change within, the present.

3. Authorial Intrusion

In addition to the omniscient and omnipresent narrator, authorial narration operates in *The Burning Book* within the convention of 'telling rather than showing', offering intrusive comments which are most striking in the opening chapter but which continue throughout the whole novel. In the first chapter mimesis is denied, as the narrator refuses to dramatize the story. The illusion that we are seeing and hearing things for ourselves (Genette, 1980: 162) is only introduced in the next chapter. At the beginning, therefore, the story is not presented in a dramatic or a scenic way: there is no description of setting; there are no dialogues. Diegesis – the concept described in detail by Genette (who borrows it from Plato) to describe telling or relating – is rapid, panoramic, and functions as a way of summarizing narration. This prevails in some parts of the novel, especially in 'Chapter of Beginning', helping the author to link information as efficiently as possible, without trying to create the illusion that the events are taking place before our eyes (Genette, 1980: 162). This mode of narration, the amount of information it provides, and the manner in which it presents characters and events, is a way of creating distance. As Genette writes: 'the narrative can furnish the reader with more or fewer details and in a more or less direct way, and can thus seem ... to keep at a greater or lesser distance from what it tells' (Genette, 1982: 162). By employing diegesis in the opening section of the novel Gee's author maintains her distance, providing the readers with a distant perspective of the Ships's lives. Due to this narratorial device essential information is foregrounded, but it also adds to the overwhelming impression of the futility and ephemerality of individual lives by compressing many years of hopes and fears into a few sentences. The first chapter diegetically summarizes the events of the story, and relates them in a shortened manner, thus functioning (to borrow a film metaphor) as a trailer to the whole plot. The act of narration throughout the novel resembles fast-forwarding, with the author in full control of the remote. Furthermore, the intrusive narrator is burning to tell the reader what is awaiting the characters around the corner, which highlights the puppet-like nature of her protagonists and endows Gee's narrator with God-like qualities: turning her into a puppeteer who decides about the fate of her creations, which constitutes another example of the novel's preoccupation with self-referentiality.

Authorial intrusions such as 'I am sorry', 'I fear' (*BB*, 18) abound in the novel. Here we find a heterodiegetic narrator – a narrator who self-consciously presents her/himself as the author of a narrative – describing the book as 'my pages' (*BB*, 132). She is not involved in the story (that is, she does not appear within narrative events as one of the novel's characters) and has a tendency to explain her choices. For instance, she says: 'That was how Guy came to be left out of the final chapter of burning' (*BB*, 18). As a result, the reader has a chance to learn about the process of writing as well as to step back from, or proleptically ahead of, the story in order to consider its significant themes. For the intrusive authorial voice has seen the future and her tale is shadowed by it: 'But there's something more fundamental, fogging my diagrams. There are shadows stretching on down from the darkness before it began. There is something more frightening as well. There is laughter, but also screams. The screams seem unwritable' (*BB*, 20). The family stories presented in *The Burning Book* are interspersed with statements based on what narratologists, borrowing from Jacques Derrida, call the 'future anterior': which Mark Currie (2006: 50n) defines as 'a future which comes before as well as a past which will exist in the future'. For instance: 'But none of this was to happen. The candles would never burn. The cake would never be baked' (*BB*, 38). At times the narrator's style is merely informative, with laconic statements and short sentences which react against over-sentimentalization of the narrative theme. At other times, when the narrative style becomes highly metaphorical, the authorial voice brings the reader back down to earth: '*But this is the language of novels, the architecture of novels. There are other and brisker languages, other lessons to learn*' (*BB*, 52, emphasis in original). The authorial voice articulates Gee's struggle with the relationship between aesthetics and politics, literature and life, and the different languages used to express each. Which speaks loudest? Which has more power? Which bears more truth? These are urgent questions for an author whose political response is to write. While the language of politics is often brisk and informed by references to specific policies or research findings, when it enters the realm of the political fiction has a unique power of its own that, through language, can take us beyond signification or representation. This enables fiction to approach Lyotard's 'unpresentable': 'sometimes the lie is true [...] Sometimes the world flashes love like a miracle, leaving words dim as stone' (*BB*, 84).

Towards the end of the novel, the fear is not that the language of politics overpowers that of literature, but that history prevails over fiction which as a result seems erased, or rather crushed under its weight: '*A bigger and better fiction, closing down on my story...*' (*BB*, 287, emphasis in original). Literature survives only as long as its material inscription upon the page: 'Nothing was lost which was written down [...] *until the Chapter of Burning*' (*BB*, 223, emphasis in original).[6] Gee's use of italics and parentheses to indicate these authorial intrusions creates an impression of a double whisper, a voice that is trying to pierce the surface in order to be heard. However, the author seems to know, or at least hope, that sometimes a whisper is more powerful than a scream. And if not a whisper, then possibly a laugh? The language in *The Burning Book* is at times imbued with a lightness that blends with the seriousness of its theme. For instance, consider the following passage – a darkly comic mixture of sadness, melancholy and flippancy: 'It's hard to find a new man when your skin has those mulberry stains, when your scalp is a ruined city of stubble and blind pink shine' (*BB*, 40). This flippant remark derives its pathos from the notion that the worst consequences of nuclear catastrophe are its effect on one's dating prospects. Offering irony in the face of tragedy, the novel is thus able to confront themes of nuclear disaster and death, without avoiding or downplaying them.

4. Inventive Typography

Gee's inventive use of typography is one of the many devices in the novel aimed at flaunting the text's fictionality and advertising its literariness, but it also clearly reflects the disintegration of the social and political world depicted in *The Burning Book*; here aesthetics and politics merge, as the language used to describe the world breaks down as that world itself shatters. The non-standard typography (italics, capital letters, spacing) reflects the events that cause chaos and dissolution, and eventually a complete breakdown of narrative. Usually it takes form of interjections, breaking the narrative flow and adding blank spaces on the pages. For instance:

... the pool of light from the central light-bulb cascaded down Lorna's red rivers of hair, light like a whole sinful city glowing and burning
—*never for her*—
and then in a frenzy of maddened puppet-like motion Prunella was up on her flat slippered feet and had seized the thin arm and pushed her towards the door. (*BB*, 32, emphasis in original)

There are phrases torn out of context, for example '(*all the water this chapter weeps won't put out the fires of the future*)' (*BB*, 135, emphasis in original), '*all the worst things are secret*' (*BB*, 42, emphasis in original), preceded and followed by white space on the page. There are also ellipses intensified towards the end of the novel, creating the impression of precariousness and disintegration, such as: 'Silly childish questions ... *why is it dark this morning*?)' (*BB*, 240, emphasis in original). The latter is also an example of a bracket closing without being opened, a device which highlights the breakdown of grammatical rules. Gee's recurrent references to war and bombings, in italics or in the form of scattered words, heighten the impression of the chaos caused by the dramatic events depicted in *The Burning Book*. The whole novel abounds in such intrusions, which create undercurrents below the main story.

In the final part of the novel the words bleed across the pages: scattered, flakes of utterances, incoherent sentences, torn out of their place, embodying the final violence, incorporating burnt and blackened beings. After the bombs have exploded, blackening people and paper alike, three black pages follow – they represent the total absence of life, and of literature. When nuclear apocalypse comes, real lives are affected, as literature is. Although 'books in their charred skins feel less pain ... ' (*BB*, 298), they also symbolize those fragile lives, their pages, spines and covers reflecting human bodies, as delicate and vulnerable as paper: they symbolize fragile bodies turned into blackened carcasses or lifeless objects. Even though books are analogous to bodies, they endure more, they resist, and this makes them more suitable to engage in a fight. The novel's political engagement is thus stressed, confirming its status as *littérature*

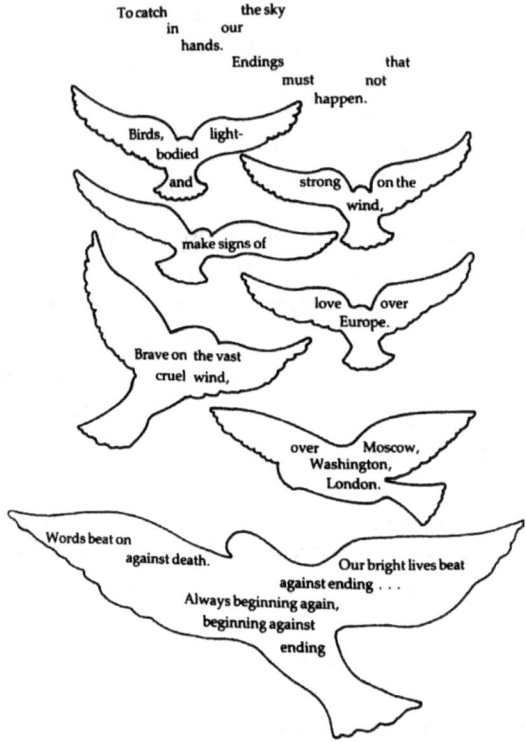

Figure 1. This image reproduces the final page of Maggie Gee's *The Burning Book* (BB, 304).

engagée, that is, literature of commitment, which takes responsibility for engaging in serious social and political discussions.[7]

As such, Gee's novel should also be considered as contributing to a literature of hope. For the novel does not end with blacked out lives and charred literary fragments. It ends, as Gee's work so often does, with hope in the face of despair – with faith in human and nonhuman agents (primarily animals), in the persistence of life and words. The birds of peace literally figured on the final page (Figure 1) carry that message of hope; they are a literary and political plea to our leaders, and to ourselves, to prevent 'endings that must not happen' (*BB*, 304). The employment of graphic elements here reinforces the disappointment with, or perhaps even the betrayal of, language: the birds flock the last page, transcending the limits of coherent language, enveloping the messages, embracing the words and carrying them outside the page which cannot contain them. But at the same time, the message they contain is that '[w]ords beat on against death' (*BB*, 302).

Like a kōan, *The Burning Book* arouses doubt in Gee's readers and makes us think whether the kind of world where the final violence is a real possibility is a world we want to inhabit. Language, this fiery tool, merges with the liquid matter of history and at this seething junction stories are forged. The narrator's final appeal – 'against ending' – is an appreciation of the cyclical nature of things and the circularity of all narratives. The story always beginning again, beginning against ending. As Gee reminds us, nuclear weapons endanger all stories but storytelling continues in the face of such threatened obliteration. This power of storytelling is stressed by Paul Ricœur, who claims that identity and self-understanding is acquired through the mediation of narrative and is thus a function of fiction (Ricœur, 1990: 27–35). The French philosopher points out that all human experience is 'mediated by all sorts of stories that we have heard' (Ricœur, 1991: 29). As Walter Benjamin (1999: 83) similarly notes in his essay 'The Storyteller: Reflections on the Works of Nikolai Leskov', experience 'has fallen in value', concluding that 'the storyteller joins the ranks of the teachers and sages' (Benjamin, 1999: 107). Gee can thus be considered a sage who draws upon shared experience; her powerful, memorable statements – both political and literary – resound in our times.

Acknowledgements

Attempts were made by the editors on several occasions to obtain formal permission from HarperCollins to reproduce the image in Figure 1 but no response was received.

Notes

1 See Sarah Dillon's (2007: 390) observation that 'with its tsunami and Islamic suicide bomber, *The Flood*'s eerily prescient narrative evidences the uncannily prophetic nature of literature'. *The Flood* was published in 2004, just prior to that year's Boxing Day tsunami and the 7/7 London bombings in 2005.

2 Consider as a comparative example John Berger's *G.* (1972), which is *both* highly experimental in its form (often referred to as a cubist novel), involving experimental typography, narratorial intrusions, and radical time shifts, *and* which raises the issue of an individual's detachment from history.

3 In 1982, a year before the publication of *The Burning Book*, Gee edited *Anthology of Writing Against War: For Life on Earth*, which raises similar issues as the novel.

4 Although different in many respects from *The Burning Book*, Graham Swift's novel demonstrates the same preoccupations, such as the entanglement of human lives with history, its circular nature, the impact of historical events on the individual, and the power of storytelling.

5 In David Mitchell's *Cloud Atlas* (2004), the revolutionary clone Somni~451 is adopted as a god in the post-apocalyptic story that follows hers, 'Sloosha's Crossin' an' Ev'rythin' After'. In *The Burning Book*, it is not the revolutionary who becomes the god after the apocalypse, but the vacuous leaders who survive on film, if not in the flesh: 'Our children may not understand how to read these pictures of God. They will use primitive logic to try to make sense of our end. They will think these are love's own deities, call on their names as they mate, softly for fear of the dark and the rats and the wild men in the old sewers' (*BB*, 22). These 'glittering tinpot gods' (*BB*, 222) recur at the end of *The Burning Book* where we learn that all along they have been '(*Staring down over our story, watching how far we are going*)' (*BB*, 223, emphasis in original).

6 See Sarah Dillon (2007) for an extended discussion of the relationship between literature and apocalypse in the context of Jacques Derrida's thought and Maggie Gee's *The Flood* (2004): 'Literature therefore belongs to the nuclear epoch, because its "existence, possibility, and significance are the most radically threatened, for the first and last time, by the nuclear catastrophe" (27). This is because the movement of literature's inscription, the constitution of itself in the archivizing act, is at the

same time the "very possibility of its effacement"' (Dillon, 2007: 383). Dillon is citing Derrida's essay 'No Apocalypse, Not Now (Full Speed Ahead, Seven Missiles, Seven Missives)' (1984), which was published the year after *The Burning Book* and is therefore responding to the same historical moment, in particular, to the pre-eminent concern with nuclear apocalypse in the early 1980s.

7 It is interesting to note the similarity between Gee's novel and Ray Bradbury's classic, *Fahrenheit 451* (1953), published exactly thirty years before, where the motif of burning books is used by the author to voice criticism against political decisions, in this case the oppressive nature of the state.

Works Cited

Barthes, Roland (1975) *S/Z*, trans. Richard Miller. London: Cape.
Benjamin, Walter (1999) *Illuminations*, trans. Harry Zohn. London: Pimlico.
Berger, John (1972) *G*. London: Bloomsbury.
Berger, John (1984) *And Our Faces, My Heart, Brief as Photos*. London: Bloomsbury.
Bradbury, Ray (1953) *Fahrenheit 451*. New York: Ballantine Books.
Currie, Mark (2006) *About Time: Narrative, Fiction and the Philosophy of Time*. Oxford: Oxford University Press.
Derrida, Jacques (1984) 'No Apocalypse, Not Now (Full Speed Ahead, Seven Missiles, Seven Missives)', trans. Catherine Porter and Philip Lewis. *Diacritics* 14 (2): 20–31.
Dillon, Sarah (2007) 'Imagining Apocalypse: Maggie Gee's *The Flood*', *Contemporary Literature* 48(3): 374–97.
Gee, Maggie (ed.) (1982) *Anthology of Writing Against War: For Life on Earth*. Norwich: University of East Anglia.
Gee, Maggie (1996) *How May I Speak in My Own Voice?: Language and the Forbidden*. London: Birkbeck College.
Genette, Gérard (1980) *Narrative Discourse: An Essay in Method*, trans. Jane E. Lewin. New York: Cornell University Press.
Heise, Ursula K. (1997) *Chronoschisms: Time, Narrative and Postmodernism*. Cambridge: Cambridge University Press.
Hutcheon, Linda (1984) *Narcissistic Narrative: The Metafictional Paradox*. New York and London: Methuen.
Jaggi, Maya (2004) 'Maggie Gee in Conversation with Maya Jaggi' in Shusheila Nasta (ed.) *Writing Across Words Contemporary Writers Talk*, pp. 301–14. Abingdon: Routledge.

Kapleau, Roshi Philip (1980) *The Three Pillars of Zen*. London: Rider.
Mitchell, David (2004) *Cloud Atlas*. London: Sceptre.
Ricœur, Paul (1988) *Time and Narrative, Vol. 3*, trans. Kathleen McLaughlin and David Pellauer. Chicago and London: University of Chicago Press.
Ricœur, Paul (1990) *Soi-même comme un autre*. Paris: Éditions du Seuil.
Ricœur, Paul (1991) 'Life in Quest of Narrative' in David Wood (ed.) *On Paul Ricœur: Narrative and Interpretation*, pp. 20–33. London and New York: Routledge.
Suvin, Darko (1979) *Metamorphoses of Science Fiction: On the Poetics and History of a Literary Genre*. New Haven: Yale University Press.
Swift, Graham (1983) *Waterland*. London: Picador.

3

REPRODUCTIVE POLITICS AND THE PUBLIC SPHERE
NATALISM, NATALITY AND APOCALYPSE

Alexander Beaumont

Over the course of a career that recently entered its fourth decade, Maggie Gee has persistently revisited two key themes: the existential imperative to bear and raise children, and the possibility of world-destruction through various forms of apocalypse. These themes deserve close examination in any discussion of Gee's work. The relationship between biological reproduction and global cataclysm is central to understanding the politics of her fictions, which are heavily invested in the maintenance of the material and phenomenal world as a common public sphere. In the most aesthetically successful and politically compelling of Gee's novels, reproduction and apocalypse are brought into a dialectical relationship with one another; instead of representing a foreclosure of the public sphere, the apocalyptic mode functions as an aesthetic means of vouchsafing its continued reproduction. It is thus, paradoxically, when her novels are at their most apocalyptic – as in *The Burning Book* (1983), *The Ice People* (1998) and *The Flood* (2004) – that Gee's politics are most radically promissory. By contrast, when Gee retreats from the apocalyptic mode – as in *Where Are the Snows* (1991) and *The White Family*

(2002) – her portrayal of human reproduction results in a limited conceptualization of the public sphere marked by the ideological effects of natalism.

The term natalism is rich in historical, philosophical and theological applications, but it is used here in a narrow sense to describe the ideological position critiqued by Lauren Berlant in her work on public intimacy.[1] In the essays on sexual politics and American culture collected in *The Queen of America Goes to Washington City*, Berlant (1997: 1) identifies a natalist ideology that 'collaps[es] the political and the personal' and transforms a public sphere 'made for adult citizens' into 'one imagined for fetuses and children'. In this new version of the public, she argues, the purpose of political action is to engender and protect an 'Edenic conjunction of [sex] act and [national] identity', which places the heteronormative account of human sexuality at the centre of public life (Berlant, 1997: 59). And she suggests that, while such acts necessarily take place in the private sphere, they are nonetheless laid bare to public scrutiny and sentimental ownership in the service of national recuperation (Berlant, 1997: 59). The public sphere is thus constructed in such a fashion that the most private acts – heteronormative sex acts – 'take place in the abstract idealized time and space of citizenship', and the most private citizens – children – become 'custodian[s] of the promise of zones of privacy that national culture relies on' for its social reproduction (Berlant, 1997: 60). The foetus, child and pregnant woman *become* the common world through an affective logic of public intimacy that promises to reconstitute the nation in the private sphere. Female bodily autonomy is subjugated to the needs of national recuperation, the foetus become an ideal citizen and the life process is rendered public in a way that makes policing the womb a justifiable political act. Most importantly of all, rather than describing the performative maelstrom of public life, politics itself is reoriented towards the preservation of '[i]dentities not live, or in play, but dead, frozen, fixed or at rest' (Berlant, 1997: 60).

It is this compromised understanding of the public sphere that begins to encroach on Gee's representation of human reproduction whenever her novels eschew the apocalyptic mode. By contrast, those texts that bring reproduction and apocalypse into a dialectical relationship with one another demonstrate a more radical politics, which can productively be read using Hannah Arendt's concept of natality. Simply put, this term describes 'the birth of new men' and women, and 'the new beginning, the action they are capable of by virtue of being born' (Arendt, 1958a: 247). Arguably, it forms the basis for all of Arendt's thought, since it is a prerequisite for the life of free, public action – the *'vita activa'* (Arendt, 1958a: 7) – around which she organizes her critique of political modernity, from *The Origins of Totalitarianism* (1951) through to *On Violence* (1970). For Arendt (1958a: 7), the *vita activa* is the highest form of life to which a human being can aspire, because through it we are able to introduce newness into the public realm in the form of what she terms 'action'. However, the *vita activa* can only be realized through the possession of 'a place in the world which makes opinions significant and actions effective' (Arendt, 1967: 296), and this requires us both to tend to the world as well as to ensure the continuation of human life within it.[2] For Arendt (1958a: 7), the world is a fabricated thing that human beings are obligated to produce and reproduce through the activity of 'work' in our capacity as *homo faber*. '[W]here God creates *ex nihilio*', she writes, 'man creates out of given substance', and the result of this act of creation is the world (Arendt, 1958a: 139). By contrast, life is a natural thing that 'corresponds to the biological process of the human body' (Arendt, 1958a: 7). However, we are nonetheless required to maintain it and ensure its perpetuation from one generation to the next, and we do this through 'labor' in our capacity as *animal laborans* (Arendt, 1958a: 7). The imperatives undergirding our obligation to engage in all these activities can be described as *amor mundi* ('for love of the world') and *volo ut sis* ('I will that you be'). If it is by fabricating and tending to our world that we express love for it, it is by bringing other human beings into existence – and valuing their existence – that we express our hope for it. And this is what lies at the heart of natality: a feeling of hope which anticipates the renewal of the life process, the world and – most importantly – the *vita activa*, along with all the new action the latter makes possible in the future.

Such a feeling of hope, Arendt (1958a: 247) writes, receives 'perhaps its most glorious and most succinct expression in the few words with which the Gospels announced their "glad tidings": "A child has been born to us". We see from this that symbolic investment in the figure of the child is important to the concept of natality, just as it is to natalism. However, it is crucial to note that, unlike natalism, natality never substitutes the perpetuation of the life process itself for the public sphere. Natality's children *inherit* the world; they do not *become* it. While it is certainly a logic of biological and social reproduction, natality describes the binding together of the various forms of human activity – labour, work and action – into political imperatives whose ultimate purpose is to make possible new, free, public action both now and in the future. Where this distinction between natalism and natality is useful in discussing Gee's work is in relation to the way in which her engagement with apocalypse results in representations of human reproduction that produce superficially similar but actually profoundly different understandings of the public sphere. Where Gee indulges her apocalyptic imagination most vividly, the representation of reproductive politics in her works remains oriented towards a vital public sphere whose maintenance rests at the heart of natality. By contrast, when she limits this part of her imagination, the novels tend to result in conservative publics that are equated with the preservation of the life process itself. At the heart of all of the novels discussed in this chapter lies a fear of our contempt for the world and a sense of our obligation to maintain it as a common public sphere. But where, in her less apocalyptic fictions, the public sphere inheres in the frozen, fixed and messianic symbolic economy of the foetus, child and pregnant woman, in her most cataclysmic fantasies the possibility of a genuinely public life is opened up through a radical reproductive politics; even as Gee's narrative worlds undergo catastrophes that appear to foreclose the possibility of human action ever taking place again.

1. Natality and Apocalypse in *The Burning Book*

It is not difficult to locate in Gee's work a feeling that the world could at any moment be completely destroyed, along with a sense that we are failing in our responsibility to ensure its perpetuation.[3] Indeed, these sentiments are nowhere more apparent than in her remarkable second novel, *The Burning Book*, which combines the narrative experimentation of her first novel, *Dying, in Other Words* (1981), with the generic make-up of the realist novel.[4] An unusual combination of family saga and apocalyptic fiction, *The Burning Book* recounts how the lives of two generations of a working-class family from Wolverhampton are shaped by alcoholism and domestic violence, immigration and racism, the legacy of World War II and – overbearingly – the perpetual threat of nuclear war between the USA and USSR. The character who most urgently expresses the terror accompanying the threat of nuclear conflict is Angela: bookish and idealistically left-wing, she is a precocious girl who seems forever to approach the threshold of public life without ever quite reaching it. Above all, Angela is intensely fearful of what she sees as the inevitability that the world will be destroyed before she has had the opportunity to take proper custodianship of it. Lying beside her boyfriend one night, she points to the bleakly rational basis for her fear, given the sheer amount of destructive potential ranged against the world: 'You talk about being reasonable', she says, 'Well being terrified *is*. What do you think he was really saying, that man on the bus last night? *Cheer up, it may never happen*. What do they mean by *it*? I feel it *is* going to happen. I feel we're all going to die' (*BB*, 228, emphasis in original). This fear is thrown into relief a few pages later when Angela recalls an argument with her mother, Lorna, after the latter walked in on her reading *The Diary of Anne Frank* as a teenager and shouted, 'You're *obsessed* with war […] I can't understand it, what's the matter with you? Why can't you be like other girls your age?' (*BB*, 237, emphasis in original).

It is significant that Anne Frank provides a link in the novel between nuclear apocalypse and the European Holocaust, because she has functioned for many decades as the most potent embodiment of a potentiality that never had the opportunity to be fulfilled. Although Angela reaches an age Frank did not, it is nonetheless notable that Gee places her in a similar position of potentiality when she writes that Angela 'couldn't stay young (though she wouldn't ever grow very old)' (*BB*, 244). The novel thus concatenates two events – Nazi totalitarianism and nuclear war – that Arendt associated with contempt for the world and identified as key threats to natality. *The Origins of Totalitarianism* and *Eichmann in Jerusalem* (1963) have now become classic texts in the study of Nazism; however, Arendt considered the threat of nuclear war to be just as sinister, and perhaps even the greater threat of the two. In *On Violence* (1970: 17–8), she suggests that, were a person to ask two simple questions of the post-war generation – 'How do you want the world to be in fifty years?' and 'What do you want your life to be like five years from now?' – the answers would likely be preceded by 'Provided there is still a world' and 'Provided I am still alive'. Nonetheless, as early as 1958 she was arguing that the 'threat of destruction to the existence of mankind, even to the existence of organic life on earth' renders 'all past political thought about war, its possible justification for the sake of freedom, its role as an *ultima ratio* in foreign affairs, perfectly obsolete' (Arendt, 1958b: 20–1). As Patricia Bowen-Moore has argued:

> Nothing stands in such contrast to Arendt's philosophy as [...] nuclearism. Under the cloud of the possibility of nuclear extinction, the worldly attitude of *amor mundi* and its concomitant imperative *volo ut sis* seems a weak, if not superfluous recommendation to a world seemingly bent on its own destruction [...T]he fact that human beings themselves, we, have made this ominous possibility our present reality says something about our failure to appropriate the meaning of natality and its bond with the common world. (Bowen-Moore, 1989: 130)

What is more, Bowen-Moore argues, to Arendt the political crisis represented by 'nuclearism' represents only the concluding passages of a narrative that stretches back past Soviet gulags, Nazi extermination camps and the colonial outposts of European empires to the revolutionary tribunals of the Great Terror. It is merely the logical end to an entire 'tradition of philosophical and political thought' that has 'failed to grasp, and thus to sustain, the true nature of political action and freedom' (Bowen-Moore, 1989: 131).

As I explore further towards the end of this chapter, Gee's fiction also seems less concerned with the particular nature of the apocalyptic event than it is with apocalypse as an aesthetic means of revealing to us our contempt for the world. This said, Bowen-Moore's comments on nuclearism certainly help us to identify Angela as the sole character in *The Burning Book* to demonstrate the 'worldly attitude' of *amor mundi*. With the possible exception of her brother George, a thoughtful and religious soldier with 'a sweet nature' (*BB*, 84), nobody else in the novel appears particularly concerned about the threat to the world posed by nuclear war. This threat is repeatedly communicated by the presence of the hibakusha, the Japanese civilians who escaped the firestorms of Hiroshima and Nagasaki but bore the irradiated legacy of these cataclysmic events on their bodies. The hibakusha's voices frequently punctuate the narrative with dire warnings about '*the wounded [who] walked in a living chain from the burning cit[ies...] searching for water in which to drown*' (*BB*, 244, emphasis in original). However, only Angela appears to have any cognisance of these warnings, and only she seems to understand the miraculous nature of the world in which she lives, set out by Gee in the 'Author's Note' that opens the book:

> Throughout this novel 'miracle' is used in senses (1), (7) and (14) of the *Oxford English Dictionary*, revised edition: '...ad L. *miraculum*, object of wonder: object of earthly wonder eg the Siberian birch-forest, the Colorado Desert, the Hanging Gardens of Babylon ... [or] ... marvellous event (or change in the course of events) brought about by human agents ... [or] ... a miraculous story, play, legend.' (*BB*, 11)

In light of this passage it is worth noting that the term 'miracle' is of some importance to the concept of natality. The child itself – as indicated in Arendt's quotation of Isaiah 9.6 – is of course miraculous but also, more importantly, so is the public action that its birth anticipates. The preciousness of natality resides in its capacity to introduce the new into the world, whether that newness is a person or an action. And, as Arendt writes in her posthumously-published *Promise of Politics* (2005: 111–2), 'whenever something new occurs, it bursts into the context of predictable processes as something unexpected, unpredictable, and ultimately causally inexplicable – just like a miracle'. By the time the bombs fall, then, Angela appears to be the only character in *The Burning Book* to understand the miraculous nature of the world in which she lives, a world into which newness might irrupt in newly miraculous ways, and the only character to fully comprehend the perilous situation it is in. Only she, in other words, really grasps the lesson of natality.

This is not to suggest that Gee intentionally meditates on Arendt's thinking in *The Burning Book*. Rather, the concept of natality can be used to make sense of the novel's treatment of the relationship between apocalypse, on the one hand, and its representation of the dilemmas of family life, on the other. It is important, therefore, that the novel focuses not just on the experiences of childhood and youth, but also on the difficulties posed by parenting too. *The Burning Book* abounds in intergenerational conflict, which takes on a potent meaning in the context of its apocalyptic ending, since it becomes clear that, while Lorna's generation certainly fails to preserve the world *for* their children, there is an equally urgent suggestion that they also fail to protect it *from* their children. This reflects another key aspect of natality, for just as actions can have unforeseen and sometimes terrible consequences, the irruption of new life – which speaks of the possibility of new acts in the future – is also dangerous precisely because of its unpredictability, and so it behoves us to contain and control it. Hence parents are charged with a double task: '[T]he child requires protection and care so that nothing destructive may happen to him from the world,' Arendt writes (1961: 185–6), '[b]ut the world, too, needs protection to keep it from being overrun and destroyed by the onslaught of the new that bursts upon it with each generation'.

The character Gee uses to dramatize Lorna and Henry's failure to protect the world from their child is Guy, whose poisonous right-wing politics are established as a threat that neither parent adequately confronts. Crucially, this responsibility is expressed in terms of their son's anger at the lack of love he finds in the adult world: 'grownups told lies all the time,' Guy thinks, '[t]hey all pretended to love one another, but [he] would never be fooled' (*BB*, 85). As Gee writes: 'Guy never *had* any love. As a child he had tried to get some from his mother, but she had run out, run dry. In the weary process of growing up he had tried every member of the family' (*BB*, 160, emphasis in original). This is why he embraces the tribal politics of racism and misogyny he considers to be 'the nearest thing to love', and finds a surrogate father figure in Big Ray, who introduces him to the New British Empire Party (*BB*, 160). Having failed in their parental duty to protect their child from the lovelessness of the world, Lorna and Henry fail all over again to protect the world from the dangerous hatred of their child. Unloved by his parents, Guy is swept up into the politics of the far right before being pointlessly crushed to death during a violent rally in London. However, while the pathos of Guy's fate is clear, Gee refuses to sentimentalize the 'lost child' of her narrative by insistently representing the worst aspects of his character and, more importantly, redirecting the reader's concern for him into a concern for the world that has destroyed him, and which he ultimately sought to destroy. As Gee tells us, 'The summer that Guy was lost it was clear that trouble was coming' (*BB*, 224); 'trouble', of course, meaning the nuclear attack which concludes the novel. Guy's death, then, functions not to consolidate a sentimental attachment to the figure of the child, however common a figure in anti-nuclear propaganda the latter might be.[5] Rather, it serves to facilitate a reinvestment of the reader's concern in a narrative world against which enormously destructive power has been ranged, and which will shortly be consumed in flame.

When it comes, this apocalypse is chillingly effective in demonstrating the sheer totality of nuclear annihilation. In the final chapter, the narrative of *The Burning Book* begins to fragment as a multitude of voices and texts intrude and interrupt the novel's exegesis: newspaper headlines describing a tense standoff between the US and USSR; the signs that Lorna and Henry read during a visit to Kew Gardens; and above all the tortured voices of the hibakusha. Finally the bombs fall and Gee's whole cast of characters – her entire narrative world, including every insignificant creature and every record of it ever having existed – is destroyed:

> Some died instantly, some took time. Bags of skinned organs, spilling, crawling. A thing called *lethality*, a thing called time. Time was a measure of terror and pain   no   I can't bear it
>   please stop time
> The last light shone with no one to see it. The final photograph made its print. Everything was on it, nothing escaped. The pattern had an unearthly clarity. Melted eyeballs, shattering bone. Miracles of form became crackling bacon, miracles of feeling flashed to hot fat. Bleeding and terrified things pushed blindly against the pain which put out the light. Some died instantly, most took time. Nothing was too little for poison to reach it. Mice and sparrows found nowhere to hide. Black burst crusts which were rainbow fishes. Balls of burnt feathers on the burnt black ground. Flakes of ash were once soft moths quivering. Books in their charred skins feel less pain .... [...]
>   All was as if it had never been.
>   Blackening paper, the last leaves burning.
>   (BB, 297–8, emphasis in original)

The increasingly strange and strained expression in this passage – the imperfect images and stertorous grammar with its confusion of tenses – gestures at a language-world that is now in the process of being torn apart, its miraculous construction incapable of withstanding the man-made power ranged against it. And, as if the totality of this end were not clear enough, Gee then forces her readers to confront the ensuing nothingness by including three blacked-out pages before finishing with an epilogue – simultaneously an expression of hope and a warning about our contempt for our own world – which she entitles '… Against Ending'.

This arresting technique – which is only one among many textual experiments whose playfulness is chillingly at odds with the novel's sobering subject matter – reflects an important characteristic of fictions of nuclear disaster written in the wake of Hiroshima and Nagasaki.[6] As David Dowling (1987: 47) writes, '[t]he memory of the Japanese holocaust acts both as a brake and a stimulus to the apocalyptic imagination' because 'the attempt to write about *that* experience commands us to be faithful to the dead and the living survivors, and also exposes the limits of our language and our imaginations'.

The memory of past destruction raises the prospect of a more total apocalypse in the future, which confronts us with the unimaginable nature of our own extinction; in turn, this failure to imagine demands that we remember earlier moments in which the possibility of world-destruction was rehearsed. In this way, the need simultaneously to remember and to imagine (or rather, fail to imagine) becomes a moral and epistemological tautology that contains within it an urgent lesson about the preciousness of the world and our obligation to protect it.

Perhaps this is why Gee includes the epilogue, a kind of revelation that impels us to recognize our human capacity for action and to guarantee that it will last into the future. She laments the stubborn inaction of her characters – their refusal, as Arendt (1958a: 5) would put it, 'to think what [they] are doing' – and draws a distinction between her love of their world, her will that they be, and their own myopia; declaring that they 'died in formation, nearsighted, their eyes on the ground. I loved them all, but they died. I had thought such things could not happen' (*BB*, 303). Crucially, however, in stepping out of her narrative world and addressing the reader directly, she also reminds us that we have not died, that our world still exists and must be cared for. She does this before presenting us with a final image [see Figure 1 in Chapter 2], at once haunting and redeeming, which comprises a pictorial representation of seven birds ascending the page, wings spread from edge to crease, bearing the message: 'Words beat on against death […] Always beginning again, beginning against ending' (*BB*, 304).

2. Encroaching Natalism in *Where Are the Snows*, *The Ice People* and *The White Family*

Although Gee retained an interest in world-destruction over the course of the 1980s and 90s, none of the novels she produced in this period reaches the apocalyptic intensity of *The Burning Book*. Indeed it was not until the attacks of 11 September 2001 that she was reminded of the fragility of the world in such a haunting way that she was prompted to revisit the terrain with similar urgency, and wrote

The Flood. Nonetheless, the novels in between continue to evidence the kind of fear for the world witnessed in *The Burning Book,* and, moreover, demonstrate an intensification of her belief in the crucial role of human reproduction in its ongoing renewal as a common public realm. However, they also demonstrate that, when Gee retreats from the apocalyptic mode, her politics begin to lose their radicalism and appear somewhat more marked by the ideological effects of natalism. Such a tendency can be recognized if we rearrange the order of three of her novels from this period – *Where Are the Snows* (1991), *The Ice People* (1998) and *The White Family* (2002) – and examine them in order of their diminishing engagement with apocalypse, from *The Ice People* to *Where Are the Snows* to *The White Family.* In doing so, we are able to trace from a political point of view the ways in which, as the texts move away from the apocalyptic form, the representation of human reproduction is increasingly marked by a sentimental politics of public intimacy.

The Ice People draws much more readily on the semantics of science fiction than *The Burning Book,* though it too recounts what Derrida (1992: 31) describes as 'the *eskhaton,* the end, or rather the extreme, the limit, the term, the last, what comes *in extremis* to close a history, a genealogy'. As the first sentence of the novel reads, 'I, Saul, Teller of Tales, Keeper of Doves, Slayer of Wolves, shall tell the story of my times. Of the best of days, and the end of days' (*IP,* 13). Moreover, it too is structured around 'an *apokalupsis,* disclosure, uncovering, unveiling' (Derrida, 1992: 27), in that it appears designed to urge in us a recognition of the vulnerability of our world and a sense of the need for us to care for it. While *The Ice People* is lighter in tone, its conclusion is arguably gloomier than that of *The Burning Book,* since the biblically-named characters at the heart of the narrative all speak of a future terminally disallowed, postponed or lost. Saul recalls both King Saul, ordained and then forsaken by God (1 Sam. 9.16, 1 Sam. 13.14), and the apostle Paul – only here he is denied his Damascene experience (Acts 9.3–9) and dies unconverted, incomplete. Sarah recalls Abraham's barren wife who miraculously conceives a son, except rather than being treated as the miracle that he is, in Gee's novel Luke is reduced to the spoils of an acrimonious separation between his parents; indeed, his name raises the possibility of 'glad tidings' that are nonetheless silenced as a consequence of his final absence from the narrative. Once more, then, we witness a concatenation of the miraculous nature of birth – the introduction of new life, which speaks of the possibility of new action in future – and an apocalyptic mode that urges us to recognize the fragility of the world.

Like *The Ice People*, *Where Are the Snows* narrates a journey from a fractious present into a perilous future while evidencing a similar concern for reproduction to *The Burning Book*. In this novel, however, Gee retreats from the apocalyptic mode somewhat, relying on the longstanding status of Venice as a city in peril in order to hint at a wider crisis in the world. As Christopher, one of the protagonists, announces: '[T]he tours are bypassing Venice again, with the water-level rising and grave men telling us our half-drowned ballroom will slide into the sea' (*WS*, 33). A feeling that these are the end times persists; however, the future is by no means ruled out, and there is an implication that the new generation might just prove responsible enough to make it happen. As the novel's other protagonist, Alexandra, says of her step-daughter: 'She's done better than me. Her generation will have to' (*WS*, 399); indeed, she asserts at one point that '[t]he world would be there even when I was gone [...] We hadn't quite destroyed it' (*WS*, 380). Yet the result of this more ambiguous relationship with apocalypse is a novel wont at times to strike the reader as conservative. This is largely due to the way it substitutes the body of its female protagonist for the world and then treats corporeal apocalypse as the localized consequence not of a failure of *amor mundi*, but a refusal to capitulate to a regressively gendered reproductive imperative. Like Angela in *The Burning Book* and Sarah in *The Ice People*, Alexandra identifies as a feminist; however, the punishment for insisting on her own sexual agency is a body that refuses to yield that which, too late, she comes to desire most of all: a child. Instead, she conceives the cancer that ultimately kills her, and the novel quickly confirms our suspicion that the tumor is intended to function as both the symbolic opposite of the child and the consequence of Alexandra's radical (and radically selfish) politics.[7] As she laments: 'Christopher [...] loved young children, I didn't see that because I didn't want to, I didn't take it in till it was too late, and even when I did I only thought about *my* hunger, *my* loss ... He wanted children. I left it too late' (*WS*, 380, emphasis in original). Unlike *The Burning Book*, then, in which the apocalyptic mode is mobilized in order to enact a transgression of diegetic boundaries that throws the reader back on reality, thereby forcing him or her to confront the ways in which he or she is neglecting the world in which he or she lives, here the reader is directed *into* the body of the novel's protagonist. In a manoeuvre that has much in common with natalism's tendency to substitute the female body for the public sphere, Alexandra's dying body is rendered public in playing host to a more mundane apocalypse (cancer), which is used as an aesthetic means of passing judgment on her refusal to subordinate herself to natalism's reproductive imperative. This represents a dramatic inversion of Berlant's logic, since in her critique public intimacy functions in a politically regressive way to open up the pregnant body to a *celebratory* form of sentimental ownership. What we are provided with in *Where Are the Snows* is the opposite (though not the negation) of this process: as a penalty for her refusal to fulfil her biological destiny, Alexandra's body is opened up – again, in a politically regressive way – to a *condemnatory* form of sentimental ownership and punished by the same logic of internality by which the pregnant body is canonized. The implication is that if those women who accede to natalism's reproductive imperative are rewarded with idealization and their bodies celebrated publicly as fecund, those like Alexandra who refuse to yield to this imperative can be punished with vilification and their bodies condemned – again, publicly – as sites of entropy and death.

The key point, however, is that in this novel some of the more problematic aspects of natalism raise their heads at exactly the moment when the text begins to retreat from the apocalyptic mode. *The White Family* sees the natalist account of human reproduction intrude even further upon its narrative, lending it a problematic politics despite the fact that it is probably Gee's most politically earnest novel, having gone through a long and difficult genesis in the wake of the murder of Stephen Lawrence in 1993. What is important to note is that here it is the complete withdrawal of the apocalyptic mode that lies at the heart of the novel's troubling rehearsal of natalist ideology. The novel certainly attempts to resolve itself by recuperating an embattled public sphere; however, this recuperation is achieved through a textual strategy that embraces the redemptive and reconciliatory possibilities of reproduction to such a degree that the latter *become* the public world the novel seeks to preserve. The novel's solution to the public problem posed by Stephen Lawrence's murder might be born of deep political feeling, but it nonetheless results in a regressive sentimentalization of the pregnant body and a characterization of the child which borders on the messianic.

The crucial figure in this respect is Shirley, a pious and self-effacing woman who is the inverse of Alexandra in *Where Are the Snows* in virtually every respect, except that she too yearns for an escape from her family. This impulse is represented as far more understandable in her case, however, since her father is a racist, misogynistic bully who raises his son, Dirk – Shirley's brother – in his own image, until the latter murders a young black man in a park toilet after an encounter that reveals to him his own homosexual desires. Though she is married to a black man named Elroy, on the night of the murder Shirley has a one-night stand with a white family friend named Thomas, who worries after they have sex that Shirley might become pregnant. 'Don't worry about the contraception angle', she tells him, 'I was trying to get pregnant for over six years' (*WF*, 317). Miraculously, however, she does conceive a child: after her infidelity Shirley returns home, falls asleep and wakes a few hours later 'with Elroy inside her, home from work, tense, exhausted, desperate to lose himself in her body [...] deep inside, his sperm joined Thomas's' (*WF*, 319). This conception – an image of reconciliation staged deep inside Shirley's body – is thus represented explicitly as a moment of redemption which answers the violent act of her brother. As a narrative resolution, it is nothing if not affirmative; however, it is difficult for the reader to escape the sense that it is, at root, a profoundly sentimental response to the Stephen Lawrence case that offers a solution to the public problem of racially aggravated murder only at the expense of female sexual autonomy. The two sex-acts of which it is a product – neither of which speaks of empowerment, since Shirley responds to Thomas's advances only after he pulls her out of the way of a speeding car, and Elroy merely uses (and arguably rapes) her – are perfect examples of Berlant's public intimacy. The solution to a national crisis precipitated by murder is located in the 'Edenic' moment at which a sex act produces an identity that then *becomes* the public sphere. In playing host to the recuperative mingling of 'black' and 'white' sperm, the intimate spaces of Shirley's body are opened up to a sentimental investment that renders them public. A political imperative is then attached to organizing the public sphere around a 'commitment to making a world that could sustain [the] idealized infant citizen' (Berlant, 1997: 28) that will result from her union with Thomas and Elroy. Shirley's autonomy is thus diminished even as the novel celebrates her body as a site of national recuperation whose mixed-race issue, it is implied, will eventually replace the cracked and divisive public sphere the novel seeks to map.

In a perversion of the apocalyptic mode mobilized in *The Burning Book*, we witness here a *messianic* mode, in which Shirley's conception bears the status of what Arthur Bradley and Paul Fletcher (2011: 1) describe as a 'messianic event'. Her child becomes 'the agent or *telos* of [a] historical process', which opens up the possibility of a 'politics to come' that might answer the intractable political problems of the present (Bradley and Fletcher, 2011: 2, 4). Bradley and Fletcher are writing in light of Derrida's concept of the 'messianic without messianism', of which they ask the reasonable question, 'can we even speak of a messianic without a messiah?' (Bradley and Fletcher, 2011: 3). At least as far as *The White Family* is concerned, the answer appears to be an emphatic 'no', since rather than a politics which directs us to the need to preserve a common public world in which future action might take place, we witness instead a kind of secular messianism in which the child-to-be becomes the sentimental object of a national culture which no longer locates the solutions to its problems in the public world. Rather, it arrogates to itself the intensely private spaces of the bedroom and the womb, and identifies in them the conditions of its own recuperation and reproduction.

In light of such an appropriation of the female body, it is not too flippant to attend to the nature of the 'coming' that accompanies this messianic natalism. Gee's representation of Shirley's pleasure with Thomas and Elroy seems, given its miraculous result, to subordinate the potentially transgressive nature of *jouissance* to reproductive destiny. A series of orgasms accompanies the conception: with Thomas 'nothing could stop it, she came, she came – she came with a great deep moan of pleasure that seemed to go on and on' (*WF*, 316); after Elroy she is '[f]lushed with contentment' (*WF*, 350) and tells him, 'You made me come [...] I loved the way you made me come' (*WF*, 350); and later, when she and Elroy return to bed, it isn't long until she is 'coming, already coming from deep deep inside' (*WF*, 354). All this pleasure convinces her that she is 'a scarlet woman, with sperm from two different men inside [her]' (*WF*, 351), but of course she is performing nothing more than her destiny as the guarantor of the public sphere's reconstitution; she is, contrary to her opinion of herself, being a good sexual citizen. By contrast, Alexandra's orgasm as she leaves her step-children behind in *Where Are the Snows* could never result in conception: 'I was due to menstruate next day' she tells us as she and Christopher have sex on the aeroplane carrying them out from London: 'but he didn't know, only I knew that; he was an idiot who wanted to make babies [...] I shook with Christopher's dying moments. We died together [...] "What if we just made a baby?" Chris asked [...] I didn't disillusion him. Let him dream' (*WS*, 24). Unlike Shirley, whose 'productive' orgasms speak of '[a]ll that life, deep, deep inside' (*WF*, 319), then, Alexandra's 'unproductive' pleasure leads only and inevitably to death.

3. Apocalyptic Natality in *The Flood*

If *Where Are the Snows* and *The White Family* retreat from the apocalyptic natality of *The Burning Book*, it returns in perhaps its most compelling and successful form in *The Flood* (2004). The novel is set in an unnamed city-state that forms 'part of the satellite lands of the Hespirican empire, in its final decades' (*TF*, 54) and which is ruled by an ingratiating but superficial president named Mr Bliss who is only too happy to collude with Hesperica's endless wars against other cities. *The Flood* sees the formal experimentalism of *The Burning Book* pushed to gleefully satirical extremes. Characters from all over Gee's oeuvre have been transplanted into a single narrative world that bears little in common with those of the novels in which they previously appeared, and yet they continue their lives without noticing the monumental authorial intervention that has deracinated them. A comic tone, almost entirely absent from *The Burning Book*, enables Gee to derive a great deal of sympathetic humour from the teenagers Lola and Gracie, for example, along with much cattier comedy from her representation of the publishing industry. There is a narrator, who remains unnamed, but no one protagonist; instead, the novel is dizzyingly polyvocal and multifaceted, featuring a huge cast of characters who range from male to female, black to white, gay to straight, old to young and even human to non-human. And while *The Flood* possesses palpable narrative impetus, there is nothing in it that could be described as a discrete and singular plot. In the simplest terms, Gee achieves little else over the course of three hundred pages except to provide her readers with an insight into the diverse lives of her ensemble while building a sense of impending disaster, and then to wipe out her entire narrative world in one final deluge. Indeed, if *The Burning Book* augments its broadly realist aesthetic with a handful of experiments designed to draw attention to its textual status, *The Flood* discards virtually every formal constraint of the realist novel except psychological verisimilitude, offering its readers a vision of contemporary Britain which, though easily recognizable, is allegorized to the point of parody.

This means that Gee is able to engage with the contemporary milieu in a robustly satirical fashion while reflecting on the satirical method itself. 'Bliss', for instance, transparently functions as a portmanteau of 'Blair' and 'Bush', and satirizes the cozy relationship between the two leaders by turning them into a gestalt. But while her characters never appear to doubt the integrity of the absurd narrative world in which they are situated, they are far from stupid. On the contrary, they are drawn with a degree of psychological realism that renders them complex and reflexive. Consequently, Gee is able to reveal, complicate and even undermine her own satirical technique, gazing through the intelligent eyes of her characters at the world she has created in order to foreground the novel's use of irony and expose it to critique. One instance of this is when she describes a group of characters going to see *Madame Butterfly*. Following the performance, one of them praises the opera's allegorical power: "'So good on imperialism," Harold enthused, afterwards' (*TF*, 140); he then goes on to praise "'the way they used the American flag [...] It was just like the way Mr Bliss and Mr Bare make use of the flag of the Hesperican empire. The director was very strong on satire'" (*TF*, 141). But not all the others agree: while sitting in the theatre, Davey leans across to Delorice to inform her that, "'America is really Hesperica, of course'" (*TF*, 140). Delorice – a respectable publisher dismayed by the parlous state of the cultural industries – hisses back, "'That's obvious'" (*TF*, 140). In this passage, Gee maps Puccini's opera onto *The Flood*'s narrative world, then has one of her characters – an academic, no less – acknowledge the capabilities of allegory. She thereby foregrounds and affirms her own rhetorical technique while simultaneously using another character to describe this technique as 'obvious', self-consciously drawing attention to the ways in which her own narrative discourse 'devolves' into caricature. The result is a text that hybridizes culturally legitimate forms (allegory, opera, narrative realism) with their 'baser' counterparts (caricature, burlesque, the fantastical) in such a way that their collective relationship with the world they represent – our world – is simultaneously earnest without being po-faced, and parodic without being reductive. This strategy has the added benefit of allowing the novel to remain formally playful without ever becoming arch or self-indulgent. Dowling (1987: 186) dismisses many of the textual experiments that Gee conducts in *The Burning Book* as 'obvious and tedious [...] postmodernist exercises in exposing the fictionality of the text in order to create a genuine sense of crisis'; *The Flood*, by contrast, could never be accused of this, because its rhetorical technique allows it to be formally innovative while maintaining a ruthless focus on the world it is satirizing. Consequently, despite the fact that the narrative world of *The Flood* is (superficially) further removed from our own world when compared to that of *The Burning Book*, it feels intensely politically engaged throughout.

The success of this engagement is also a result of Gee's decision to conclude the narrative with a degree of apocalyptic intensity unseen since her second novel. In order to understand the aesthetic and political functions of the cataclysm that ends *The Flood*, however, it is necessary to acknowledge straight away that it is of a very different nature to the one that ends *The Burning Book*. After all, the impact of ecological catastrophe is quite distinct from nuclear armageddon, as Mike Davis points out:

> [G]lobal warming is not H. G. Wells's *War of the Worlds*, where invading Martians democratically annihilate humanity without class or ethnic distinction. Climate change, instead, will produce dramatically unequal impacts across regions and social classes, inflicting the greatest damage upon poor countries with the fewest resources for meaningful adaptation. (Davis, 2010: 37)

Moreover, this kind of catastrophe takes place over far greater periods of time than the photographic flash of nuclear apocalypse in *The Burning Book*, and is thus more likely to be characterized by what Rob Nixon (2009) has termed 'slow violence'. In contrast to nuclear apocalypse, the slow violence of environmental collapse is 'deficient in the recognizable special effects that fill movie seats and flat-screen TVs with the pyrotechnics of Shock and Awe' and tends instead to be 'driven inward, [and] somatized into cellular dramas of mutation' (Nixon, 2009: 445). The spatially uneven and temporally elastic nature of ecological catastrophe is something that Gee seems to acknowledge in *The Ice People*, and yet in *The Flood* she contrives a return to the total destruction represented in *The Burning Book*. In some ways this is strange, given that her description of 'flood sickness' seems to recognize Davis and Nixon's observations. The rising floodwater, Gee writes, is considered 'dangerous [...] [t]here's talk about some virus' (*TF*, 224); soon after falling into a murky pool of the stuff one child begins to show 'the strange red buboes [...] the sharp stigmata of flood sickness' (*TF*, 281). Given their physical proximity to the floodwater and systematic neglect by the health authorities, the residents of the Towers – decrepit housing blocks in low-lying areas, separated from the city and each other by the rising tide – are the most likely to suffer the kind of spatially uneven and somatic violence Davis and Nixon describe. Indeed, this is perhaps why Gee characterizes the waterbuses that shuttle residents between their homes and their menial jobs in the city as 'floating hospitals' (*TF*, 174).

In wiping out every one of her characters in a final deluge, irrespective of social status, Gee could be argued to foreclose this critique of the intersection between catastrophe and political and spatial exclusion in favour of a narrative strategy that reasserts the primacy of the spectacular event. In an apparent nod to *The Burning Book*, we are told that the characters of *The Flood* 'do not end in fire, but water' (*TF*, 318), though the effect, as this pithy comment suggests, is much the same. If this conflation of the different natures of the cataclysms strikes the reader as a limitation, however, it does have the effect of identifying *The Flood* as a continuation of the enterprise initiated in *The Burning Book*, and allows us to read it as another episode in an ongoing engagement with the concepts of newness and renewal initiated in that text. Sarah Dillon (2007: 375–6) argues that 'apocalyptic narratives [...] both confront and diffuse the threat of total destruction, since they describe, reveal or predict cataclysmic events but only and always with the guarantee of a postcataclysmic continuance'. As we have seen, in the context of Gee's novels, 'postcataclysmic continuance' might really take the form of a return to our world and a reminder to love and protect it. Even so, to the extent that this also applies to *The Burning Book*, we might read both novels as points in a singular narrative that uses the concept of 'postcataclysmic continuance' inherent to apocalyptic discourse as a means of encouraging us to recognize our capacity to introduce newness into the world in the form of new life and new action, as well as to acknowledge and protect the essential fact of natality which makes free, public action possible both now and in the future. Indeed, this reading only becomes more persuasive when we consider the number of characters from Gee's earlier texts who reappear in the 2004 novel. Some, having already experienced one apocalypse, are resurrected solely in order to suffer another: Angela, Lorna and Henry, for instance, are all alive and well despite the nuclear fire that supposedly killed them and everything else at the end of *The Burning Book*. And they are not the only characters to have miraculously survived violent deaths: as Dillon (2007: 380) points out, '[T]he writer Moira Penny is very much alive and kicking despite presumably falling to her death in Gee's first novel *Dying, in Other Words* (1981)' and 'Isaac, the homosexual art dealer who definitely died of AIDS in *Where Are the Snows* is here resurrected' only to endure a new death by drowning.

This is certainly a remarkable strategy, but it is one that Dillon (2007: 381), drawing on the analyses of M. H. Abrams, argues to be wholly of a piece with the apocalyptic tradition, since its 'recursive procedure [...] replicates that of Revelation, which "represents the present and future by replicating or alluding to passages in earlier biblical texts"'. What is more, while the spatial and temporal aspects of ecological catastrophe might be marginalized, Gee's particular way of representing environmental catastrophe in *The Flood* ultimately serves to make the novel more urgent, since it divorces her preoccupation with apocalypse from atomic weapons and draws attention to the broader ways in which the world is being placed under threat. Our capacity for world-destruction might nowadays be measured more in terms of emissions per capita than in stockpiles and lethality. However, the lesson of *The Flood*, when read alongside *The Burning Book*, is that the menace to natality consists no more or less in the current ecological crisis than it did in the crisis that emerged when particularly invidious relations between two ideological belligerents coincided with the development of especially destructive weapons technologies during the Cold War. The particular nature of the threat is less important than the fact that the threat exists in the first place, since mutual assured destruction, peak oil and even the evolution of the anthropocene are merely different ways of talking about a much grander historical narrative of far graver political significance. Gee implies as much by resurrecting characters from her own work already associated with death and world-destruction and destroying them all over again using different means. This spectacular representational strategy enables her to import the concerns of *The Burning Book* into a new and more contemporary setting while suggesting that, though the specifics of the threat may have changed, the reasons behind it remain the same: contempt for the world, and a failure to recognize the importance of ensuring the possibility of new public action now and in the future.

It is thus worth noting that *The Flood* continues the concerns with reproduction and child-rearing initiated in *The Burning Book*. A resurrected Angela is now struggling with the demands of motherhood herself, inflicting the wounds she received from Lorna in the earlier novel upon her own daughter, Gerda. In an echo of *The Burning Book* that is so transparent it must surely have been self-conscious, she shouts during an argument with her daughter, 'Why can't you just be normal?' (*TF*, 210), despite the fact that she was hardly a normal child herself, and was rebuked in similar terms by her own mother as a teenager when Lorna spotted her reading *The Diary of Anne Frank* (*BB*, 237). The repeated complaint that the child is not 'normal' recalls the radical contingency that the latter embodies, the possibility of new public action that she brings into the world by virtue of being born. But more importantly, in light of the conversation between Gee's texts and the discourse of natalism staged in this chapter, Lorna's complaint also urges the reader to recognize that the political significance of the child does not lie in its function as the object of a sentimental attachment which forecloses the *vita activa* by collapsing the public into the private. Instead of functioning *as* the world, the child should instead be conceptualized as a fundamental component *of* a public world – whether of the present or the future – that requires cultivation and care if it is to play host to action.

What is crucial to note about *The Flood*, therefore, is that its return to the apocalyptic mode facilitates a reminder of our obligations to the public sphere, of our need to answer the worldly imperative *volo ut sis*, if our capacity to introduce newness into the world is to be maintained. At the end of the novel 'the white line of water [...] mov[es] in' (*TF*, 308) and crashes over Gee's characters, who 'suddenly see how puny they are' (*TF*, 318) as the maelstrom pulls them in and under. Afterwards, however, as the water subsides, 'three thousand generations of humans / stiff and damp from their spell underground / push [...] up alive from the flood-washed catacombs / pulling themselves to their feet like apes' (*TF*, 320). In another epilogue that uses the representation of 'post-cataclysmic continuance' to remind us of the preciousness of the world while warning that the threat of its destruction remains, Gee describes her characters emerging into a new city, a heavenly city: after they have 'burst up' out of the water the victims of the apocalypse find themselves 'in a round house full of water-lilies' (*TF*, 321) before running into the sunlight through 'cast-iron doors with their Victorian name-plate, "Kew Gardens, London"' (*TF*, 322). For those readers who remember, this is exactly where Lorna and Henry were when the bombs fell in *The Burning Book*, and the implication seems to be that, rather than the destruction of a language-world (as happened in the earlier novel), we are witnessing a new engagement with that world. The narrator, previously inconspicuous but now an emphatic presence, describes how, 'stunned by the arc of the sun through the sky' (*TF*, 324):

> they come now, arm in arm, flowing like water into their future. They pass without seeing us, homing, home, here in the city whose name is time, glimpsed long ago, across the river, the ideal city which was always waiting [...]
>
> Above the waters that have covered the earth, stained waters, bloody waters, water heaving with wreck and horror, pulling down papers, pictures, people [...]
>
> See, here they come, where all are welcome.
>
> Here we come, to lie down at last. (*TF*, 324–5)

The voice here is presumably the same one that narrates the entirety of the novel, but at no other point is it foregrounded more explicitly, begging the question: who is speaking? Given the importance of apocalyptic natality to Gee's politics, I would be prepared to wager that it belongs to a child. But if a miracle has occurred, if a child has indeed been born to us, we must recognize that what she or he is describing in this passage is a world – our world – and that this world is the most miraculous thing of all.

This radical understanding of a common public sphere is what Gee's dialectic of apocalypse and reproduction can achieve when it is developed to its greatest potential. Her most radical novels are successful because they guide us away from the stultifying politics of natalism, with its sentimental attachments to hypostatized ontologies that devalue public life by locating it in the private sphere. Instead, they imagine a promissory politics of natality to which the child remains central, but only because it anticipates the perpetuation of the public sphere and the possibility of new public action in the future. As Arendt (1958a: 9) argues in *The Human Condition*, 'the new beginning inherent to birth can make itself felt in the world only because the newcomer possesses the capacity of beginning something anew, that is, of acting'. In Gee's best fiction the apocalyptic mode forces us to confront the complete destruction of any possibility of beginning anew while simultaneously allowing us to recognize the truth in Arendt's words. It is, in other words, the great virtue of Maggie Gee's apocalyptic natality to find new beginnings in the most apparently final of endings.

Notes

1 For other usages, consider for example its use in political demography to explain the Francophone *'ravanche du burceau'* in Quebec, or its (not unconnected) centrality to the Roman Catholic Church's position on contraception. There are numerous forms of antinatalism, too, which is put to significant but different uses in the work of Arthur Schopenhauer and Thomas Malthus, and remains an important component of some contemporary queer theory, such as Lee Edelman's concept of 'reproductive futurism' in *No Future: Queer Theory and the Death Drive* (2004). For an extended discussion of Edelman's theory in relation to Gee's novel *The Ice People* see Sarah Dillon's essay in this collection.

2 The phenomenological and existential dimensions of Arendt's use of the term 'world' are, of course, inherited from Martin Heidegger's *Being and Time* (1927). It is clear from *The Human Condition* (Arendt, 1958a: 52) that Arendt sees a direct equivalence between the world and the public: 'the term "public",' she writes, 'signifies the world itself, in so far as it is

common to all of us and distinguished from our privately owned place in it'.

3 In her memoir, *My Animal Life* (2010), Gee traces her lifelong interest in apocalypse back to her primary school teacher, Mr Norris, who in 1956, when she was eight years old, addressed her and her classmates at their village school at the height of the Suez crisis: '"The next few days," he told us, slowly, "will decide if the world will go to war. Planes are already in the air…" That is all I remember of the speech that followed, and all it needed to infect me with terror' (*MAL*, 89–90). 'I sometimes think,' Gee continues, 'one reason for the apocalyptic streak that runs through so many of my novels might be the burden of terror Mr Norris gave me, which lingered long after the crisis went away' (*MAL*, 91).

4 Such experimentation includes: multiple planes of narration; autoreferentiality; a structure which foregrounds the status of the text rather than obscuring it; and a preoccupation with the relationship between language and the phenomenological presentation of reality. For an extended discussion of *The Burning Book* that addresses the tension between realism and the experimental, as well as the relationship between Gee's aesthetics and politics, see Monika Szuba's essay in this collection.

5 Images of youth have frequently been deployed in such material to symbolize the death of the future that would be the consequence of global nuclear war. Most notorious among these is Lyndon B. Johnson's 'Daisy Girl' advertisement during the 1964 US presidential election, available to view here: https://www.youtube.com/watch?v=dDTBnsqxZ3k.

6 Other examples include the bathetic relationship between the fairy tale tone of the chapter titles ('The Chapter of Beginning', 'of Rules and Red Hair', 'of Humming' and so on) and their frequently troubling content, and the fact that among the many books to burn in *The Burning Book* is Gee's own debut novel *Dying, in Other Words*, which we learn Angela may be reading when the bombs eventually fall.

7 For an extended discussion of *Where Are the Snows* in relation to these feminist politics and to time, ageing and generational supercession in the novel, see Sarah Falcus's essay in this collection.

Works Cited

Arendt, Hannah (1958a) *The Human Condition*. Chicago, IL: University of Chicago Press.

Arendt, Hannah (1958b) 'Totalitarian Imperialism: Reflections on the Hungarian Revolution', *The Journal of Politics* 20(1): 5–43.
Arendt, Hannah (1961) *Between Past and Future*. London: Faber and Faber.
Arendt, Hannah (1967) *The Origins of Totalitarianism*. London: George Allen and Unwin.
Arendt, Hannah (1970) *On Violence*. London: Allen Lane.
Arendt, Hannah (2005) *The Promise of Politics*. New York: Schoken.
Berlant, Lauren (1997) *The Queen of America Goes to Washington City: Essays on Sex and Citizenship*. Durham: Duke University Press.
Bowen-Moore, Patricia (1989) *Hannah Arendt's Philosophy of Natality*. London: Macmillan.
Bradley, Arthur and Fletcher, Paul (2011) 'The Politics to Come: A History of Futurity' in Arthur Bradley and Paul Fletcher (eds) *The Politics to Come: Power, Modernity and the Messianic*, pp. 1–11. London: Routledge.
Davis, Mike (2010) 'Who Will Build the Ark?', *New Left Review* 61: 29–46.
Derrida, Jacques (1992) 'Of an Apocalyptic Tone Newly Adopted in Philosophy' in H. Coward and T. Foshay (eds) *Derrida and Negative Theology*, pp. 25–71. Albany: State University Press of New York.
Dillon, Sarah (2007) 'Imagining Apocalypse: Maggie Gee's *The Flood*', *Contemporary Literature* 48(3): 374–97.
Dowling, David (1987) *Fictions of Nuclear Disaster*. London: Macmillan.
Edelman, Lee (2004) *No Future: Queer Theory and the Death Drive*. Durham: Duke University Press.
Nixon, Rob (2009) 'Neoliberalism, Slow Violence, and the Environmental Picaresque', *Modern Fiction Studies* 55(3): 443–67.
The Bible: Authorized King James Version (2005) Robert Carroll and Stephen Prickett (eds). Oxford: Oxford University Press.

4

'FALL[ING] OUT OF THE PAST'
TIME, AGEING AND GENERATIONS IN *WHERE ARE THE SNOWS*

Sarah Falcus

In Maggie Gee's *Where Are the Snows* (1991), Alexandra and Christopher – the perfect couple – run away from family, friends and social networks in order to escape the quotidian aspects of family and work life. They crave an excitement and romance that they assume – in this 1980s world – can be bought. The world becomes their playground and their shopping mall. A novel of consumption and excess, of irresponsibility and exploitation, this is nevertheless also a novel driven by the need to escape time. Alex and Chris use the lure of the spatial (afforded by travel between different spaces), in order to escape the temporal: the time of generations and responsibility, the time of ageing (and death), the time of work and the clock. In doing so, they become out of time and anachronistic, symbolized by the myriad of broken and dismembered items in the market they visit in Portugal: 'miles and miles of solidified time, for all of them had fallen out of the past, beached as the tide moved on without them' (*WS*, 123). The novel, therefore, suggests that the consequence of trying to live out of time is a form of homelessness. *Where Are the Snows* does not deny the restrictions that age and generational identity may bring. As this chapter will argue, the novel is explicit about the way ageism and age-appropriateness may limit and constrict the lives of men and women, the latter especially. Nevertheless, this novel makes clear the irresponsibility of an atemporality that refuses ageing, death, familial and environmental concerns, in favour of what is depicted as selfish global consumerism. In this, the novel echoes many of the concerns found in Gee's other novels, notably social responsibility and environmental degradation; and, as in her other work, in *Where Are the Snows* Gee deftly links the fate of the individual with these wider issues, bearing out Mine Özyurt Kiliç's (2013: 4) observation that Gee's work sees 'the whole and the link between the individual and the whole, rather than simply looking at the particular'.

1. Time

Time is significant in many ways in this text, not least in its publishing history. The novel was first published in 1991 by Heinemann and then updated and published again in 2005 by Saqi Books and 2006 by Telegram Books. The original publication therefore coincides with the end of Thatcherism and the consumer-driven culture of the 1980s, echoing the treatment of this period in *Light Years* (1985), an earlier Gee novel in which time is also a significant formal and thematic issue. In *Where Are the Snows*, the culture of the 1980s is critiqued particularly in the text's representation of consumption and individualism. The protagonists Christopher and Alexandra, a couple seeking to escape their commitments, take to its furthest extent Thatcher's pronouncement that there is no such thing as society, instead valuing above all else the individual (and the couple). In doing so, they also reject the nuclear family – something Thatcher prized. So this novel explores the very contradictions and paradoxes that are at the heart of Thatcherism: individual versus the family, freedom versus constraint, innovation versus tradition.[1] Alex actually dismisses Thatcher, however, despite engaging with aspects of what could be seen as Thatcherism: 'Margaret Thatcher! – I have never had the slightest interest in politics, but everything about her offended me – her joylessness, her sexlessness. She was the Britain we had left behind' (*WS*, 233). Thatcher represents the grey London that even consumer-driven and individualistic Alex rejects, but Alex is also blind to aspects of herself and her decisions, so she does not recognize the links between her own behaviour and Thatcherite ideals. Even Alex's career – writing sensational fiction – accords to some extent with a Thatcherite approach to the arts and culture, in the sense that her writing is preoccupied with individual success and wealth creation, something she achieves thanks to becoming a celebrity. As Kiliç (2013: 81) notes, Alex also uses her family to fuel her writing in her second book, with the consequence that 'her wealth is produced by bestselling novels based on her own poverty, a form of alienation'. Alex thus embodies a self-made woman of the capitalist and consumerist 1980s.

The significance of time in the novel is also highlighted by its structure and the number of temporal planes that Gee places within it: the period 2005–7 (loosely representing the present), episodes in 1986 and 1995 (narrated from that time), and then the sweep of memory, which mainly encompasses 1986–2007, but also stretches further back into childhood. The novel is told from a variety of first-person perspectives, mainly those of Chris and Alex, but also Mary Brown (a family friend) and Susy (Chris's daughter). This makes it a truly polyphonic novel where interior life promotes a form of psychological realism. The narratives, particularly those of Chris and Alex, are largely retrospective, with Chris now in his seventies and Alex in her fifties. Therefore, both main characters are engaging in a process of life review, described by Robert Butler (1963: 66) as a way of evaluating and giving experience some sort of coherence as one reaches the end of life. This is certainly the case with Chris, as he feels the loss of friends and the sense that he is approaching death: 'People fall from my life like snow, these days. So many white-haired tiny bodies sinking beneath their obituaries or dying as quiet as snow in letters' (*WS*, 35). This leads Chris to review his life and want to tell his story before his death: 'Now at the age of seventy I want to say things for myself' (*WS*, 35). However, as Kathleen Woodward (1997: 3) acknowledges, drawing on the work of psychologists and psychiatrists, life review – in the form of reminiscence – actually begins in middle age. And this is the case with Alex, who is only in her fifties as she undertakes her own life review. For both Alex and Chris, reviewing and narrating the past are ways not only of evaluating it, but also of justifying the decisions they have made. Alex, in particular, is an erratic and in some ways unreliable narrator. She is aware of, and makes the reader aware of, the ways in which she is moulding her story to justify her actions and turn her past into an acceptable narrative, despite the flashes of guilt that emerge at points.[2] The life reviews here are also, crucially, a battle of stories and offer competing versions of the past. This is something that Chris worries about; for example, as he imagines Alex shaping the past to suit her own purposes:

> If she tries to change our story – *my story, mine, it is I who stayed faithful* – I hope they'll have burned and scattered my body so thoroughly that I shan't have to know. I don't want to haunt the margins of her fiction, bitterly disputing times and places, bodiless, impotent, a hissing ghost. (*WS*, 35, emphasis in original)

Alex and Chris thus self-consciously write for the other, needing an addressee in order to make sense of their shared past. Their competing narratives engage in a battle for the time now gone.

The foregrounding of time in the novel – reference to which is included in every chapter title except the last – is a structural reminder of its inescapability, acting as a constant ironic echo throughout the novel as Chris and Alex fight to deny its passing. Looking back, Chris reflects: 'I thought, we don't *have* to grow old' (*WS*, 47, emphasis in original). This denial of ageing and of time itself, however, leaves Chris and Alex anachronistic, out of time. As Mary Russo explains (1992: 21):

> Anachronism means literally 'against time.' More, generally, however, it refers to an historical misplacement [...] Nowadays, anachronism is a kind of historical faux pas, involving the projecting of attitudes or ideologies that are contemporary onto a former time. Thus as I understand it, anachronism is a mistake in a normative systemization of time. As such, one *risks* anachronism. (emphasis in original)

The definitions of anachronism as both 'against time' and 'a mistake in the normative systemization of time' offer ways of conceptualizing the aims and results of Chris's and Alex's attempt to escape time. This sense of Alex and Chris moving out of time in their travels is clear in the way that the novel's other narrators, Susy and Mary Brown, think about the couple. Alex and Chris are memories to their families and friends, memories that depend upon younger selves and blurred pictures; they are part of the past and not the present. We also see this challenge to linear time and the ordered generational model of temporality in the way Alex and Chris are constantly referred to, and refer to themselves, as looking and seeming younger than they are. Mary, for example, argues that Alex and Chris 'seemed to grow younger as their kids grew up' (*WS*, 26). This 'untimeliness' puts Chris and Alex, but particularly Alex, at risk of 'anachronism' and 'scandal'. 'In my view,' as Mary Russo writes, 'anachronism is a risk which is both necessary and inevitable as *a sign of life*. Given the common placement of women's lives within the symbolic confines of birth, reproduction, and death, the risk of anachronism is scandal' (Russo, 1999: 21, emphasis in original). Alex and Chris can therefore be read as grasping the opportunity of anachronism as 'a sign of life', a way of challenging models of temporality, ageing and generations that may be restricting to them. And the novel makes clear that familial and social responsibility, as well as the discourses of ageing, are indeed limiting, particularly for women. However, Chris and Alex end up trying to deny ageing and temporality altogether, constructing a mode of anachronism far less positive than this, and offering merely a fruitless quest for a way to live forever in youth; a way to age without ageing. And this leaves them in a position of homelessness: without family, society, nation or meaning.

At the beginning of *Where Are the Snows*, Alex looks back to the moment where she and Chris walked out on their children – Susy (aged 16) and Isaac (aged 19) – for a life of travel and enjoyment:

> For a moment there we were a normal family, standing on the edge of another world, where we would simply have fitted together and gone on together into the future, the children growing bigger and brighter,

us getting smaller and fading away; it was not too late, we could have changed our minds…

And then we turned, my eyes searched for Chris's, a hibiscus bloom was reflected in his lens, then Susy and Isaac, smaller, distorted; the red silk bloomed on the back of his lens, a giant hibiscus, a tiny family; our fingers met, our fingers twined, we were leaving together for paradise. (*WS*, 20–1)

In the image of the children growing while the adults fade is the narrative of linear temporality – of ageing and generations – that Alex and Chris are escaping in favour of romance and the preservation of youthfulness. As the reflection of Susy and Isaac in Chris's lens makes clear, what Chris and Alex are attempting is a reversal, or at least a cessation, of this narrative, where they remain prominent and their children fade into the background of their lives. Therefore, time in the form of ageing and the passing of generations is significant right from the beginning of this novel, as it is in other works by Gee, such as the stories 'What Was Important' and 'Starting at Last' in her collection *The Blue* (2006). *Where Are the Snows* may be read as a novel of escapism and individualism, indeed selfishness, but it is also a novel in which age and the fear of the passing of time drive the narrative.

2. Consuming Youth

Alex and Chris are driven by individualistic desires centred around consumption, glamour and freedom. And all of these things are linked to youth. Chris remembers Alex's view of their position: 'She always said how lucky we were. She said we had everything – looks, love, money' (*WS*, 33). These three things are what motivate the couple and lead them to make the decision to leave the family home and Chris's teenage children. Alex has clawed her way up from poverty (flirting with prostitution and exploitation) into marriage, money and a middle-class life with a 'daily' and the 'best china' (*WS*, 13). But the materiality of this middle-class home weighs heavily on her and she craves the excitement that her money can buy beyond the home, something symbolized by the red hibiscus she plants amongst the 'browned rhododendrons and the monkey-puzzle tree' (*WS*, 16) in the garden in Islington. Alex presents home as boring, mundane and confining, linking this to time and ageing:

> Houses and families are deadly I think. They're what everyone wants, but they eat you up, they waste your time, they weigh you down. It's why the very young are so delicious; they're not dragging all that dull baggage around. (*WS*, 62)

The children, the house itself, and home owning, all constrict Alex and she wants to escape to be young and to be free. To some extent, this functions in the novel as a critique of the traditional family and domestic life for women, where they are buried under the detritus and responsibilities of the familial home. This is certainly what Alex wants to leave, even if, by her own admission, she refuses to take on many of the tasks expected of her as wife and stepmother. Susy's reluctance to accept the traditional familial home when she becomes pregnant, and her insistence on her independence, suggests that there are dangers in the nuclear family, which must be approached warily. Nevertheless, the solution for Alex, and Chris, is one that simply rejects the 'problem' of the family in favour of selfish individualism – Alex's myopia even leads her to read the children's sadness at their departure in terms of her own feelings: 'They are just being sad to upset me' (*WS*, 12) – a judgement that the novel makes clear is ultimately wrong, as Isaac and Susy do find the parting difficult and their lives are clearly blighted by this abandonment by their parents.

Ironically, part of what stifles Alex is the endless clutter in the house, which is the result of the family's materialism and consumption: 'Every corner of the house had its ghosts, my "Speak Russian" cassettes, my trampoline, Isaac's skating boots, Susy's oil-paints, things I had half put away, half-used, and paper and dust and old-fashioned dirt' (*WS*, 64). But consumption is something that Alex fails to evade through travel and as she is travelling with Chris, she continually shops – Gee present this as an exercise of power as Alex exploits her wealth (something she did not have when she was a child), but it is also a demonstration of the web of consumption within which Alex is trapped. This excessive expenditure is closely bound up both with Alex's sense of identity and with temporality. As Chris describes the habit:

> Of all the anxiously narrow rituals that hotel life imposed on us, shopping was one of the oddest, though it never seemed so at the time. Alexandra had what's called 'an eye for beauty'; in other words, she collected things. (*WS*, 122)

The ritualistic and constraining aspect of this endless shopping indicates its importance to Alex's sense of who she is: someone with taste, and the money to exercise this. As Margaret Morganroth Gullette argues, in the cycle of purchasing '[w]e sidle up close to any "choice" we make and think of it, naively, as an "expression" of self. There's flattery in this marketeers' view: the buyer is made to seem creative and expressive, individual, intentional, potent' (Gullette, 1999: 43). But the other side of shopping, as Gullette points out (1999: 35–6), is loss, as we are socialized into a cycle of desire, possession and rejection. For Alex and Chris, rejection and loss are dealt with simply by the movement afforded by travelling: 'We left a stream of things behind us, gifts for the maids, who would have preferred money. Every new purchase displaced an old one. She had to have what she wanted, you see' (*WS*, 122). Shopping itself is presented here as a way of living in the present and escaping time and ageing: consumption bestows a sense of newness upon the couple. As Gullette argues in relation to consumption and the fashion cycle: 'It's not that the past is shameful, it is we who incur shame if we ally ourselves with the past, the unwanted, the "old"' (Gullette, 1999: 49). Alex's investment in consumer culture is part of her rejection of the passing of time and of 'the old'. She is tied to a cycle of consumption that 'implicitly devalues our sense of prior selfhood' (Gullette, 1999: 49), which leaves her endlessly chasing novelty and newness in an increasingly vain attempt to escape time itself, and her past in particular.

3. Eternal Youth

This love of newness is a love of youth. And key to the youthful identities that Chris and Alex wish to maintain throughout *Where Are the Snows* is appearance, part of the 'looks, love, money' that Alex prizes; but keeping one's 'looks' is, of course, problematic with the passing of time. In a Western consumer culture that values youth above age (Gullette, 2004, 2011; Wearing, 2007), staying young is also about continuing to look young. This can be read in terms of 'new ageing', where societal pressures impress upon the individual that the body must maintain its youthfulness, something linked to both consumerism and individualism: 'No longer viewed as a process through which the subject becomes an object to be managed by others, bodily ageing has emerged as (another) arena for self-care, for lifestyle fashioning' (Gilleard and Higgs, 2013: xi). New ageing is thus imbricated within a commodified network of lifestyle, leisure and consumption that creates 'the dilemmas of how to age by not becoming old' (Gilleard and Higgs, 2013: xii). Chris and Alex battle with precisely this dilemma as the years pass and the body itself comes to intrude more and more upon their romantic and sexual idyll. Chris is happy that he looks 60 rather than 70 whilst in Venice (*WS*, 33), and Alex revels in the idea that she is still aesthetically pleasing at 50: 'Fifty years old, but still fit to be painted' (*WS*, 238). But Chris comes to realize, in large part through his bodily infirmities, that he is old: 'I'm just an old man with too much money and too much time to dislike myself, waiting for death in a dying city' (*WS*, 247). He is very conscious of his ageing body when dressing in Venice, and during sex with his new, younger girlfriend Madonna. Chris's dream of living outside of time, of not ageing, is thus shattered at the end of the novel. Nevertheless, Chris is able to negotiate his ageing body more easily than Alex, which we might read as a result of the societal intersection of ageing and gender as well as the fact that ageing has a cultural impact upon women at a younger age, and to a harsher extent, than men. This gender inequality concerning attitudes towards the ageing bodies of men and women can be discerned when Chris's lover, Madonna, makes him change the hair colour of his avatar to grey when he plays in an online virtual world, a sign of the way in which ageing in men is appreciated, even valued, for the wisdom and maturity it suggests. Alex, on the other hand, hides her greying hair and her efforts to dye it from her lover, Benjy, keeping up the appearance of youthfulness at all costs.

Gee thus presents Alex as acutely aware of the loss of her cultural currency: her appearance and desirability are signalled by her red hair, something of which she has always been proud.[3] Attracting the gaze of men has always been important to Alex and provides her with evidence of her own desirability and her identity as a youthful woman. Chris offers Alex with much of this affirmation when they are together, but after they separate Alex finds this in other, usually younger, men. However, Alex comes to recognize that 'now I am old I'm invisible' (*WS*, 323). In the West, ageing women find themselves increasingly undervalued as they move beyond childbearing years and youth, in a culture that still associates female value very much with the nubile body and its desirability. As Kathleen Woodward (1999: xiii) argues, women experience ageism more harshly and earlier in their lives than men. Our postfeminist, popular culture is imbued with new ageing ideals, trapping women within often contradictory ageist discourses. As Sadie Wearing (2007: 278) argues, escaping time through 'rejuvenation' (a return to or prolongation of youthfulness) is endemic in popular culture, but is both 'necessary and impossible':

> Necessary because in complex ways the aging body is pathologized and disavowed; impossible because [...] deference to quite rigid demarcations of the appropriate, the decorous, and the "natural" still exerts a profound influence over representations of age and aging. (Wearing, 2007: 278)

Where Are the Snows thus makes clear the way that the discourse of ageing operates to confine women within definitions of age-appropriateness. Alex is visible and admired as long as she is able to keep up her appearance of youthfulness, something she strives to achieve throughout most of the novel. However, when she stops dying her hair and keeping up other regimes of bodily maintenance, she becomes largely invisible, as is clear in the scene at the Louvre, when Mary Brown sees Alex lying prostrate at the foot of a Munch mural, ignored by other visitors. Mary describes a hysterical or itinerant figure: 'an old woman; long wavy grey hair, the lightless yellowish-grey of the poor who can never afford to get their hair done; a tired face, very thin; perhaps a faint remnant of crazy beauty' (*WS*, 365). Despite being largely overlooked by those around her, the ageing Alex finds that any behaviour deemed inappropriate continues to be policed, as is the case in the Jardin de Luxembourg in Paris. As Alex crouches, crying, on the grass, she is helped up by a gendarme 'more indignant than solicitous'. As she narrates: 'I said I had tripped; he didn't seem surprised; old women fell down all the time, but (his expression seemed to say) they shouldn't do it in a public place' (*WS*, 381). The enforcement of proper behaviour is demonstrated very differently in the case of Mary Brown, who is an example of an age-appropriate woman whose beauty is seen to increase with age. She represents the perfect wife and mother, even nursing her dying husband. Though her dress is 'scruffy' (*WS*, 342), she does not look anachronistic and her manners and habits are calm, soothing and domestic, making her adherence to 'the appropriate' and 'the decorous' clear. Mary Brown and Alex therefore function as diametrically opposed examples of ageing women, but the behaviour of both women is nevertheless circumscribed by social and cultural determinations of age-appropriateness.

Alex does revisit regimes of bodily maintenance, however, when looking for Chris in Paris. Here, she returns to her old habits of glamorous dress, make-up and hair in order to become the younger self that Chris remembers and resurrect the cultural value that accompanies such a performance of desirability. This is a form of age denial, as described by Julia Twigg (2004), and it is made clear in the novel in the discomfort Alex now feels in her high-heeled shoes. Although they were once in vogue, these shoes have now become unfashionable suggesting that in denying her aged contemporary self, Alex is trying to live anachronistically, out of time. In this moment, Alex becomes a victim of the double standards applied to ageing women in Western cultural formations of age-appropriate appearance, no longer valued for her youth and beauty in a culture which prizes these things in women above age and its accompanying maturity, knowledge and greater experience.

Linked to the maintenance of the youthful body in *Where Are the Snows* is the connection it makes between sex and youth. Gee offers her reader an explicit novel that is not afraid to deal with sexuality in older age, both in Alex's midlife and Chris's 'third age'. This is significant at a very basic level because sexuality in older age is rarely fully explored in fiction.[4] As Zoe Brennan (2005: 93) argues, to some extent 'the sexuality of older people can be seen as parallel to that of children: officially it does not exist; nonetheless it is anticipated and prevented by those with discursive social influence'. Brennan is focusing on those 'older people' in the third and fourth ages, so her observations can be applied to the novel in the reading of Chris, rather than Alex. However, in light of the fact that Woodward suggests the shadow of old age also falls upon women in midlife (Woodward, 1999: xiii), this negation of sexuality is pertinent to an earlier stage of life for women than for men, and is therefore applicable to Alex too. There are undeniably contemporary novels which foreground the exploration of romance and sexuality in later life – the works of Fay Weldon, Alison Lurie and Philip Roth are varied and not always necessarily unproblematic examples of this – but *Where Are the Snows* is still relatively unusual in its explicit celebration of male and female sexuality across the life course: from the middle-aged Chris and Alex in the early years of their travels and their very active sex life together, to the later years, where sexual desire is still very much part of their relationship but clouded by increasing friction between them. In this sense, the novel presents midlife romance as both necessary and satisfying. It also includes the loving, if less passionate, relationship between Mary and Chris, where Chris is surprised by the openness of Mary's expression of desire and her need for sexual satisfaction. Mary, for her part, is slightly disappointed with the undeniably older body she encounters in their intimacy.

Where Are The Snows certainly goes some way towards countering the prevailing tendency in both literary fiction as well as Western popular culture to efface or make opaque the sexual lives of older women and men. However, the novel also explores the way that sexuality becomes anachronistic for Chris and Alex as both attempt to maintain youthfulness into mid and old age. Sexuality remains intimately connected to youth by both Chris and Alex (Chris even counts the number of erections he is still able to have in order to assert his continuing virility) in terms that can be associated with new or positive ageing:

> As positive aging has loosened sexual decline from the aging body in order to redress ageist stereotypes about sexual activity and pleasure, sexual health has become reassigned to a broad range of factors considered vital to identity in midlife and successful aging thereafter. By realigning sexuality, gender, age, the body, lifecourse, and identity and in seeking 'new sex for old', our culture exposes its impossible ideal that people live outside of time. (Katz and Marshall, 2003: 13)

Connected closely to consumer culture and the vast range of technological products and services that enable continuing sexual activity, this 'new sex for old' promotes an ideal of anachronism that is dependent upon the posthuman:

> posthuman bodies are today exemplified by sexual functionality and the idealization of its lifelong possibilities. It is through sexual functionality and the anxieties provoked around its maintenance that the aging subject is connected to the wondrous, interlocking, and illimitable worlds of cosmetic, prosthetic, virtual, informational, and consumerist technology and, in turn, is rewarded with the promise of a direct channel to the secrets of posthuman longevity. (Katz and Marshall, 2003: 6)

This connection to the posthuman can be seen very clearly in Gee's portrayal of Chris, an old man driven by his desire for sex, with frequent erections and a seeming inability to adequately control his appetites. This lack of control finds its apotheosis in his use of the virtual world, where Chris utilizes the posthuman as a way to ward off ageing, a melding of the technological and human with a long tradition in fiction and film.[5] Here, Chris is not limited by his ageing body and is able to indulge his sexual whims as he pleases, making his own avatar much younger than himself and inventing an avatar that looks like

Alex, from whom he is now separated. Sexual expression becomes linked with anachronistic desire: a way of living out of time and out of the ageing body to achieve the satisfaction and the experience of youth. While playing in the virtual world, Chris is literally out of time: lost to the clock time of his real world, and living in the past of his youth. The fact that these virtual games are provided by his daughter's friend – the youthful and sexually adventurous Madonna, who is presented as a version of the young Alex – emphasizes the anachronistic aspect of this pastime. The relationship between Chris and Madonna is an echo of that between Chris and Alex: Madonna is the younger woman who wants to take him away, '[s]o we can escape. We can be really free' (*WS*, 393). Significantly, Madonna wants to have Chris's child, though she recognizes that using his frozen sperm (which he had frozen when he was younger) will be sensible. This offers Gee's readers another link between sexual desire (or, in this case, reproduction) and the posthuman, where the human body and technology come together to test 'the limits of human life' (Katz and Marshall, 2003: 6). Buoyed by drugs and sex with Madonna, Chris considers this and almost leaves London again, this time for New York, repeating his youthful decision and in the process making clear the way in which little has changed in the decades since his first departure.

The exploration of the posthuman through the extension of fertility as a way to prolong youth is also central to Alex's narrative. She, too, ends up entwining sexuality and youth, using her relationship with the much younger Benjy as a way of reclaiming lost youthfulness. Gee takes this narrative to its logical extreme as Alex tries to extend her fertility and become a mother in her later middle age. This desire for a child is presented as desperate and clearly as a way in which she can extend her own youthfulness by proving her fecundity: if not through biological motherhood, then through her ability to be a carer and thus useful to a dependent. It is also an extension of Alex's habits of consumption as she desires a child that will be hers, offering another example of her need for possession. Later life fertility is a challenge to the linear model of the life course and risks anachronism. It is, as Russo (1999: 24–5) argues, one of those things 'which disrupt[s] the developmental model of a woman's life and emphasize[s] an untimeliness in relations between women'. While Russo is not necessarily critical of this untimeliness in her analysis of later life fertility, in the novel Alex is punished for her anachronistic desire. The sense of untimeliness is emphasized by Susy's successful pregnancy in her late thirties. Susy embraces motherhood and becomes satisfied, perhaps for the first time in her life, whilst Alex is left without either a biological or an adoptive child, a figure to be both pitied and mocked (as she and Benjy are in Bolivia, where they try to buy a child, by the locals who see them as naive, cash-cow 'gringos' [WS, 87]). Having or not having children – an ability determined by social and economic factors as well as biology – is a matter of concern in other Gee novels, too, most obviously *Lost Children* (1994), where children are a source of hope, but also of grief. The comparison of generations in *Where Are the Snows* sees Alex reduced in the face of Susy's successful motherhood, in almost exactly the way Alex imagined at the start of the novel as she saw the children taking over from the parents. Alex's diagnosis of breast cancer then seems to be almost too symbolic on top of this. Her woman's body, and the breasts that might have fed her baby, instead of being desirable and youthful, come to represent decline and death. This does not, nevertheless, suggest a conservative message that women must live only within family time, their lives circumscribed by the cultural mores of generational succession. As this analysis demonstrates, the novel is very aware of the limitations such potentially ageist structures may impose. In this novel, trying to live out of time through the utilization of the posthuman functions as a specific critique of individualism, selfishness and exploitation, where untimeliness is presented not as a challenge to ageism, but as a way of satisfying self-centred desire.

4. The End

Gee does not, however, leave the temporal at the level of the individual in this novel. Instead, temporality takes on a monumental, environmental aspect, as dystopic elements are scattered lightly through the narrative, with mention of floods in London (*WS*, 162-3), global warming (*WS*, 213, 305), Venice's imminent submergence (*WS*, 33), and shrinking ice (*WS*, 38–9, connected to the snows of the title). This echoes the environmental awareness found in much of Gee's fiction, from the dystopic *The Ice People* (1998) and *The Flood* (2004), to *Light Years* (1985) and *Grace* (1988). The sense that the 'world is dying' (*WS*, 212) is linked closely to the selfishness of Alex and Chris, as they become superficial world tourists, jetting across the globe on carbon-emitting aeroplanes. Alex rejects this for quite some time (*WS*, 213), even when harangued by a Marxist one-night-stand who makes the connection between her travel – which Alex and Chris refuse to acknowledge as tourism – and environmental degradation.

The sense of exploiting the world's resources is, of course, clearest in the episode with Anna Maria. Alex tries to buy a child when it becomes clear that, despite the latest medical advances, she is too old to bear one herself. She travels around South America with her young boyfriend in order to find a family willing to give up a baby to rich 'gringos'. But the final purchase is a disaster as the couple is unable to take care of the grief-stricken three-year-old and in the end they return her to the poverty and emotional richness of her life with her biological family. A comment on global adoption of this sort, this episode is also at one with Alex's (and Chris's) entitled sense of their right to the world's resources and experiences. Reading Alex's difficulty in learning about the cultures she encounters abroad in similar terms, Kiliç argues (2013: 87) that this episode 'reveals Gee's critique of a Eurocentric and imperial outlook, a theme dealt with more extensively in her later novels, *The White Family*, *My Cleaner* and *My Driver*'. This critique is clear throughout *Where Are the Snows*, as the global irresponsibility of Alex's and Chris's actions is constantly highlighted throughout the text.

Chris and Alex begin their travels with a sense of entitlement and romance, enjoying all that the world has to offer to rich tourists and sending back travel pieces to newspapers in England that are enhanced by untruths, 'Alex's carefree fictional geography' (*WS*, 35). But sunny Toledo and the flower-carpeted Algarve give way to more disturbing, often urban, spaces, such as the excessive consumption of Manhattan at the Millennium and the decline of Paris when Alex revisits. The city comes to figure in the novel as a representation of the changing world (and Alex's and Chris's changing awareness of their responsibilities), much in the way Philip Tew describes the city in contemporary fiction:

> As a site of narrative and culture the city is mobile, existential and yet perversely monumental, combining in contemporary fiction the globalized economy with both the localized dynamics of intersubjectivity and a sense that culture always creates a sense of loss through its very ongoing adaptation, or evolutionary survival. (Tew, 2004: 90)

In particular, Mexico City – the place Alex acknowledges as her only real home when she is dying in Paris – functions as this monumental and mobile place that is founded upon loss. Alex relies upon local knowledge to help her live (for shopping and friendship, for example) in this vast urban space that presents significant threats and dangers to a foreigner.[6] Mexico City is a place where survival is not guaranteed, a city of constant change – even its park is under threat – where the pressures of industrialization, globalization and environmental damage are felt every day.

There is a fabulist quality to this novel in the way that Alex and Chris end up either desiring or suffering from exactly what they tried to escape. In this sense, *Where Are the Snows* is cyclical in narrative structure, as the couple end up back where they started, though older and (somewhat) wiser. Having left grey London, they both settle in cities damaged by different environmental pressures: Mexico City by inward migration and pollution, Venice by rising seawater. In the absence of home, Alex tries hard to find meaning in the geography of her travels:

> Together we travelled all over the world, a glittering, shifting mosaic of places. Odd how few end up meaning anything. And so I come back again and again to the same ones, because they have meaning. Not because they are exotic, or strange. Because I loved them. Because life was here. (*WS*, 378)

In the final chapter, they are both back in London, returned to the home and family they rejected decades ago. This is part of Alex's realization that what she craves is exactly what she has given up: children, family and home. She even misses the house in Islington (*WS*, 378), though there is an element of self-deception and nostalgia in this sentiment. Alex comes to realize what her life has been and the impact of the decisions she has made. In doing so, she acknowledges the way that she and Chris tried, unsuccessfully, to live outside time and space: 'We travelled to escape ourselves, I think. We travelled to escape our littleness. If we kept moving we would never die. We left the world to die instead' (*WS*, 399). Here, she finally brings together time, death and environmental disaster, but it takes her the full novel and her impending death to come to this realization.

Locked into a cycle of consumption and the pursuit of both newness and youth, Chris and Alex are, in the end, presented as unable to escape time, ageing and death. What this novel makes clear is the danger of trying to live out of time: to deny ageing, death, society, familial and environmental responsibility. The novel does not deny the restrictions of these things – Mary Brown, for example, clearly feels frustrated by aspects of her time-bound and appropriate way of life, and ageism operates as a restrictive force on both her and Alex – but it emphasizes the recklessness of choosing selfish desire over social responsibility. In trying to escape time, Chris and Alex refuse ageing and generational identity; this leaves them homeless, without a social and familial network, and a geographical place to call their own. Maggie Gee stated in an interview in 1997 that she was looking 'at this idea about the novel being the form of transcendental homelessness' when writing *Where Are the Snows* (cited in McKay, 1997: 215). And it is clear that this is a novel of homelessness on many levels: narrative, geographical and temporal. In the end, ageing and death become unavoidable for Chris and Alex, and Alex experiences self-awareness and the connection with others that she has always denied. As Kiliç notes (2013: 85), the image of the hut in the mountain in the final chapter 'becomes a sign of transgression, a life beyond the consumer culture', where Alex is able to see 'all the faces I failed to see, all the lives I failed to notice' (*WS*, 400). The hut sees Alex finally reach the end of her time and the end of her homelessness.

Notes

1 See Joseph Brooker (2010: 16–9) on the 'contradictions' of Thatcherism. Here he outlines the tension between radicalism and retrospection in Thatcher's policies and statements.

2 Guilt is expressed by Alex (and Chris) at points throughout the novel, more and more so as the story progresses. Even in the second chapter, Alex expresses some, albeit easily dismissed, concern about leaving the children (*WS*, 11, 15). The reunion with Isaac prompts more guilty feelings (*WS*, 146–57). And, in the latter part of the book, this contrition is more fully realized (for example, on pp. 323–5).

3 The same trope of naturally red hair as the symbol of youth and vitality is repeated in Gee's *The Ice People* when the narrator Saul meets with his wife, Sarah, after years of separation. From a distance, in the gentle lighting of a London gallery, 'I recognised her without difficulty because, from above, I saw her hair. It looked, from that distance, shockingly unchanged from the hair she had on the day we first met. It was long again, down past her shoulders, it was that chestnutred I'd loved' (*IP*, 306-7). In the cold light of day, however, his realisation that her hair colour is unnaturally retained is a stark reminder of her ageing: 'She looked older, so much older out here [...]. The colour of her hair was flat, unnatural' (*IP*, 312).

4 There are, of course, examples that do not conform to this trend. Challenges to the asexuality of the older woman are found in novels as diverse as Angela Carter's *Wise Children* (1991), Doris Lessing's *Love, Again* (1996), Fay Weldon's *Rhode Island Blues* (2000), Deborah Moggach's *These Foolish Things* (2004) and Louise Dean's *Becoming Strangers* (2004). The recent burgeoning of the subgenre of the 'ageing memoir' has also involved detailed explorations of sexuality in older age: for example, Diana Athill's *Somewhere Towards the End* (2009), Jane Miller's *Crazy Age: Thoughts on Being Old* (2010) and Jane Juska's *A Round-Heeled Woman: My Late-Life Adventures in Sex and Romance* (2003). In film, the representation of female sexuality into and beyond middle age is still problematic, but is certainly more prominent than in the past, as seen in *The Mother* (2003) and *Still Mine* (2012).

5 The possibility of evading ageing, whether through technological means or other kinds of Faustian pacts has a strong literary history, from

Oscar Wilde's *The Picture of Dorian Gray* (1891) to Rider Haggard's *She* (1887). This continues in much recent speculative fiction, from Margaret Atwood's Children of Crake in *Oryx and Crake* (2003) to Drew Magary's *The Postmortal* (2011). Film also has its own tradition here, with recent examples including cinematic immortality in *The Congress* (2013) and characters with a determined lifespan in *In Time* (2011).

6 This is apparent during the carnival in the park outside of her flat, when Alex is asked for money by a man dressed as a skeleton and, after giving him cash, runs away in fear (*WS*, 329–30).

Works Cited

Athill, Diana (2009) *Somewhere Towards the End*. London: Granta.
Atwood, Margaret (2003/2004) *Oryx and Crake*. London: Virago.
Brennan, Zoe (2005) *The Older Woman in Recent Fiction*. Jefferson, North Carolina: McFarland.
Brooker, Joseph (2010) *Literature of the 1980s: After the Watershed*. Edinburgh: Edinburgh University Press.
Butler, Robert N. (1963) 'The Life Review: An Interpretation of Reminiscence in the Aged', *Psychiatry* 26(1): 65–76.
Carter, Angela (1991) *Wise Children*. London: Chatto and Windus.
Congress, The (2013) Dir. Ari Folman. Germany: Bridgit Folman Film Gang.
Dean, Louise (2004) *Becoming Strangers*. London: Scribner.
Gilleard, Chris and Higgs, Paul (2003) *Ageing, Corporeality and Embodiment*. London: Anthem Press.
Gullette, Margaret Morganroth (1999) 'The Other End of the Fashion Cycle: Practicing Loss, Learning Decline', in Kathleen Woodward (ed.) *Figuring Age: Women, Bodies, Generations*, pp. 34–55. Bloomington: Indiana University Press.
Gullette, Margaret Morganroth (2004) *Aged by Culture*. Chicago: University of Chicago Press.
Gullette, Margaret Morganroth (2011) *Agewise: Fighting the New Ageism in America*. Chicago: University of Chicago Press.
Haggard, H. Rider (1887/2008) *She*. Oxford: Oxford University Press.
In Time (2011) Dir. Andrew Niccol. USA: Regency Enterprises.
Juska, Jane (2003/2004) *A Round-Heeled Woman: My Late-Life Adventures in Sex and Romance*. London: Vintage.

Katz, Stephen and Marshall, Barbara (2003) 'New Sex for Old: Lifestyle, Consumerism, and the Ethics of Ageing Well', *Journal of Aging Studies* 17(1): 3–16.

Kiliç, Mine Özyurt (2013) *Maggie Gee: Writing the Condition-of-England Novel*. London: Bloomsbury.

Lessing. Doris (1996/1997) *Love, Again*. London: Harper Perennial.

McKay, Margaret (1997) 'An Interview with Maggie Gee', *Studia Neophilologica* 69(2): 213–21.

Magary, Drew (2011) *The Postmortal*. New York: Penguin.

Miller, Jane (2010) *Crazy Age: Thoughts on Being Old*. London: Virago.

Moggach, Deborah (2004/2005) *These Foolish Things*. London: Vintage.

Mother, The (2003) Dir. Roger Michell. UK: BBC Films.

Russo, Mary (1999) 'Ageing and the Scandal of Anachronism' in Kathleen Woodward (ed.) *Figuring Age: Women, Bodies, Generations*, pp. 20–33. Bloomington: Indiana University Press.

Still Mine (2012) Dir. Michael McGowan. Canada: Mulmer Feed Co. Production.

Tew, Philip (2004) *The Contemporary British Novel*. London: Continuum.

Twigg, Julia (2004) 'The Body, Gender and Age: Feminist Insights in Social Gerontology', *Journal of Aging Studies* 18(1): 59–73.

Wearing, Sadie (2007) 'Subjects of Rejuvenation: Aging in Postfeminist Culture' in Yvonne Tasker and Diane Negra (eds) *Interrogating Postfeminism: Gender and the Politics of Popular Culture*, pp. 277–310. London: Duke University Press.

Weldon, Fay (2000) *Rhode Island Blues*. London: Flamingo.

Wilde, Oscar (1891/2006) *The Picture of Dorian Gray*. Oxford: Oxford University Press.

Woodward, Kathleen (1997) *Telling Stories*. Doreen B. Townsend Center Occasional Papers, 9.

Woodward, Kathleen (1999) 'Introduction', in Kathleen Woodward (ed.) *Figuring Age: Women, Bodies, Generations*, pp. ix–xxix. Bloomington: Indiana University Press.

5

LITERARY EQUIVOCATION
REPRODUCTIVE FUTURISM AND *THE ICE PEOPLE*

Sarah Dillon

On 4 November 2008 voters in California, USA, approved Proposition 8, a State constitutional amendment that defined marriage as only between one man and one woman, thereby rendering same-sex marriage illegal. In 2014, directors Ben Cotner and Ryan White released *The Case Against 8*, a film that documents the long legal battle that successfully overturned Proposition 8. Beginning in August 2010, when two same-sex couples filed a law suit against the proposition in the United States District Court for the Northern District of California, the film follows these couples and their legal team until June 2013, when the case was finally settled in the American Supreme Court and the couples were able to legally wed. The film demonstrates the remarkable fact that both the team acting on behalf of the couples (supported by the American Foundation for Equal Rights), and those defending Proposition 8, similarly appeal to the figure of the Child to justify their cause. Political action is necessary, say both sides, in order to defend the innocent Child and secure its future. This is the case, whether it be to protect the gay child from feelings of exclusion and from discrimination, or to protect all children from the allegedly moral, spiritual and other corrupting effects of allowing gay marriage. Clearly evident here is what the queer theorist Lee Edelman calls *reproductive futurism* – a new theoretical concept that describes the way in which all politics is determined by the belief that the future will give meaning to the present; a fantasy of the future most often represented by the figure of the Child.

Edelman's account of reproductive futurism in his seminal work *No Future: Queer Theory and the Death Drive* (2004) is compelling and problematic, in equal parts. This chapter arose as an attempt first to understand Edelman's arguments – they are unashamedly complex – and then to put pressure on the fault lines exposed by that close attention. While this chapter is in no way the first to critique Edelman, its method of applying pressure is not one that has been employed previously. Here, Edelman's theory is put into dialogue with literary texts concerned with population, known as 'demodystopias'. The most detailed conversation is developed with Maggie Gee's novel *The Ice People* (1998), in order to demonstrate the way in which literature's specificity and essential equivocity exposes the precarious universalism and absolutism of Edelman's theory. *The Ice People* does this primarily through the disruptive force of irony: firstly, the ironic revolt of the queer child against the figurative weight placed upon it by reproductive futurism; and, secondly, the dramatic irony through which the narrator, Saul, repeatedly exposes the problems with his own investment in reproductive futurism. The conclusion reached is that both Edelman's concept of reproductive futurism, and Saul's narrative commitment to it, are *sinthomes* – a word that comes to us via Jacques Lacan, Edelman's primary theoretical source, and which names the compulsion which holds the subject together. The only defence against the fantasy of the sinthome is the equivocation that Saul and Edelman lack, but which *The Ice People*, and the critical act of placing it in dialogue with Edelman, brings to the fore.

Reproductive Futurism

Edelman prefaces, *No Future* with two epigraphs, the first of which considers the possibility of renouncing a commitment to futural continuance, and the second of which states that we already exist without a future:

> 'Isn't there something in analytic discourse that can introduce us to the following: that every subsistence or persistence of the world as such must be abandoned?' (Jacques Lacan cited in Edelman, 2004)

> 'Yes, I was thinking: we live without a future. That's what's queer...' (Virginia Woolf cited in Edelman, 2004)

The first of these quotations, from Jacques Lacan, is theoretical; the second is literary, from Virginia Woolf. Together, they establish both the terms of Edelman's discussion, the question of our commitment to the future, and its methodology. Edelman's text proposes that there is an intimate and necessary relationship between politics, reproduction (especially the Child that figures it) and the future. He calls this essential relationship, *reproductive futurism*. *No Future* both outlines this idea of reproductive futurism, and develops a critique of it: theoretically, from a Lacanian standpoint; and critically, via close readings of selected literary and filmic texts. For Edelman, reproductive futurism has two key elements: the first is faith in the future, as the endpoint, which will provide the meaning lacking in the present. Edelman (2004: 8) argues that all politics, of the left or the right or anywhere in between, partakes of, and is structurally defined by, reproductive futurism: 'politics...names the struggle to effect a fantasmatic order of reality in which the subject's alienation would vanish into the seamlessness of identity at the endpoint of the endless chain of signifiers lived as history'. Futurism is invested in generational succession – hence its intrinsic connection to reproduction – as well as linear temporality and narrative sequence. It is structurally conservative, 'perpetuating sameness' rather than 'enabling change' (Edelman, 2004: 60). And, linking the political and the psychoanalytic, as Edelman's argument does, reproductive futurism's fantasy of a future that will confer meaning retrospectively on the present is dependent on the futural temporality of desire, 'the production of narrative sequence moving towards an always unrealized end' (Edelman, 2004: 91).

The second element of reproductive futurism is the investment of this faith in the future in the emblematic figure of the Child: 'we are no more able to conceive of a politics without a fantasy of the future than we are able to conceive of a future without the figure of the Child' (Edelman, 2004: 11). According to Edelman, politics holds up the Child (representing both children in the present and children as yet unborn) as the innocents in defence of whom politics must act. As 'the perpetual horizon of every acknowledged politics' (Edelman, 2004: 3), the welfare of the Child determines all political decisions and interventions. A prime example of this, although not one Edelman gives directly, is the legal battle over California's Proposition 8, referred to earlier.

In an argument as old as that of the scapegoat, Edelman proposes that politics as reproductive futurism can only shore itself up by excluding an Other.[1] For reproductive futurism, this Other is the Queer, regularly figured as posing a threat to both the future and to the child. Contemporary liberal identity politics has sought to deny this negative figuration, often making its arguments instead from within the logic of reproductive futurism (again, *The Case Against 8* demonstrates this perfectly). But Edelman's response to the political hegemony of *reproductive futurism* is to propose that, precisely because it has been excluded, the queer can be reclaimed as a site of radical resistance. Rather than denying its negative figuration, he believes that the queer should embrace it, that it should in fact derive its power from its excluded position.[2] Edelman (2004: 4) stakes his own faith in 'the impossible project of a queer oppositionality that would oppose itself to the structural determinants of politics as such'. In this negativity, the queer is not offering the utopian hope of an alternative future, since such hope would only reproduce the logic of futurism, which the queer rejects. What it offers instead, and this is where Lacan's thought becomes significant for Edelman, is a death-drive embracing *jouissance*: a defiant transgression of the social limits placed on enjoyment, 'a jouissance indifferent to social survival' (Edelman, 2004: 140), 'a violent passage beyond the bounds of identity, meaning and law' (Edelman, 2004: 25). The queer must celebrate its position as the excluded other and absolutely deny the teleology, the deferral of meaning, and the reproductive futurism that defines politics as such.

The Universal vs. The Particular

Edelman's polemic is engaging and persuasive – the idea of *reproductive futurism* has astonishing memetic power. Once one has read Edelman, one does indeed see it everywhere. But in the years since he first proposed his queer response to reproductive futurism, many issues with Edelman's arguments have been highlighted. These include, for example, complicating his structural opposition between the queer and the child (Stockton, 2009), or problematizing the methodology of deriving a political theory from psychoanalysis (Brenkman, 2002a,b). He has been accused of developing a theory that is the privilege only of the middle-class gay white male who is 'always already guaranteed a future and so can afford to jettison the idea of one' (Freeman, 2007: 167; Muñoz, 2006, 2009), and his theoretical arguments have been set against the actual plights of queer subjects (Leap et al., 2007). Putting these and other such important and effective critiques aside for a moment, even if we were 'to assent to his argument' entirely, even Leo Bersani finds we might reproach Edelman 'for not spelling out the mode in which we might survive' (Edelman, 2004: book jacket) this assent. Edelman, of course, does not care about survival ('no future'), but Bersani's comment exposes the predicament in which Edelman places us – his is a totalizing, universalizing thesis which leaves us, if we take Edelman at his word, nowhere.[3] If one wants to go somewhere other than nowhere, is his logic, one can only be subsumed back into a politics always structurally determined by reproductive futurism and its queer exclusions. The most important challenge to Edelman's thesis, then, lies in proving the specificity, rather than the universality, of his argument. If it is only *some* politics that is embroiled in homophobic reproductive futurism, rather than the political as such, then this means that one can both agree with Edelman in his reading of a certain type of politics, for example, that of the American Christian Right, while at the same time freeing up other political spaces in which the queer can still go somewhere, can still do something.[4]

This is the approach taken in two important responses to Edelman's polemic: John Brenkman (2002b) argues that Edelman mistakes totalitarianism for politics, and offers a different understanding of the political via the work of Hannah Arendt; while Nina Power (2009) proposes Jacques Rancière's conception of politics in compelling opposition to Edelman's. Both thinkers challenge the universalism of Edelman's thesis by offering competing understandings of the political. Other commentators, such as Michael Snediker (2006), warn more generally about the stunning 'ubiquity of "always" and "every" in Edelman's argument' (para. 37), in response to which we ought to be 'wary of the seductions of absolutes over the comparably vulnerable values of particularity' (para. 44). For Edelman (2004: 6), the value of the antisocial queer may lie in 'stubborn particularity', but in the process of developing this argument Edelman does not just embrace the figuration of the queer provided by the politics to which he is so opposed, he also inherits its habits of 'coercive universalisation' and 'stereotypical generality' (Edelman, 2004: 11, 14). These are habits that are designed, as he well knows, to close down opposition, reasoned or otherwise. There is no doubt of Edelman's methodology: he develops a general argument out of specific examples, such as the politics of Clinton's family photograph, or the rhetoric of *one* form of pro-abortion rhetoric. These examples are not only specific but also selective – they have been chosen precisely to support, rather than undermine, his thesis. We can see this method also in a more careful consideration of the key literary text out of which Edelman develops his thesis: P. D. James's *The Children of Men* (1992).[5] If Edelman's (2004: 3) work is, as he avows, a 'polemical engagement with the cultural texts of politics and the politics of cultural texts' it matters greatly which texts and which politics are singled out for examination.

Edelman reads *The Children of Men* in order to prove his theories and demonstrate reproductive futurism in action. He cites the narrator, Theodore Faron, who 'gives voice to the ideological truism that governs our investment in the Child as the obligatory token of our futurity' (Edelman, 2004: 12). *The Children of Men* imagines a future in which humans have lost the capacity to reproduce. It is undoubtedly a reproductively futural novel, as Edelman's well-selected citations show. But its investment in reproductive futurism is inseparable from that fact that it is also a Christian novel.[6] This imbrication of political reproductive futurism and Christianity is not one that Edelman directly addresses. The novel's Christian imagery and plot is less than subtle: a group calling themselves 'the five fishes', which includes a priest and a devout Christian woman, Julian (whose name recalls the important Christian female mystic Julian of Norwich) rise up against oppression. Julian, bearing a deformed hand, is blessed with a 'miracle child' (James, 1992: 179), a son (of course) to save mankind, who is born safely only after his father, Luke, has been ritually sacrificed 'to save us all' (James, 1992: 215). The novel ends with the murder of the evil leader and the christening of the new baby in a woodshed with the equivalent wise men and women waiting outside. The novel is a tale of mankind's redemption, but also of one man's redemption. It is narrated, in part, by Theodore, an ageing Oxford historian who opens the novel by beginning a diary, a record for himself alone of the last part of his life. These diary entries, however, are interspersed with chapters narrated by an omniscient third-person narrator, which eventually take over from the diary entries. In the journal, Theodore is almost a caricature of the antisocial, anti-reproductive, anti-futurist male: 'he has been more ready to hurt his wife's feelings and deprive his daughter than inconvenience a pub bar full of strangers' (James, 1992: 82). He is a historian living in the past, with no sense of the future, who likes to fuck his students and who – in a moment so fitting with Edelman's theories it is surprising he does not mention it – has actually, literally, killed his child. He accidentally runs over his daughter in his car when she is fifteen months old, while he is reversing (that is, going backwards): 'I killed not only her [his wife's] beloved daughter but all hope of another child' (James, 1992: 35). The dual narrative structure gives the reader access, in the diary entries, to the 'horrors' of this man's mind, while the omniscient narrative charts his redemption, that is, his journey from antisocial child-murderer to loyal husband and father (although, literally, he is neither) who delivers the saviour child: 'It was to Julian and her unborn child, and to them only, that he owed allegiance' (James, 1992: 186). If the plot was not clear enough to signal this journey, it is indicated in the final diary entry in which Theo records an edenic day in 'the glade of a beechwood' (James, 1992: 203) and his final abandonment of the 'self-regarding, sardonic and solitary man' (James, 1992: 204) he used to be.

A similar pattern of redemption can be seen in relation to another character in the novel, Theo's mentor, Jasper Palmer-Smith. For Theo is not the only child-hating male academic in the novel. Jasper is yet another, whose 'dislike of children has been legendary and they were always kept well out of sight and sound on the rare occasions when he condescended to accept a private dinner invitation' (James, 1992: 50). Jasper's response to the species crisis of the novel is sanguine:

> It doesn't worry me particularly. I'm not saying I hadn't a moment of regret when I first knew Hilda was barren; the genes asserting their atavistic imperatives, I suppose. On the whole I'm glad; you can't mourn for unborn grandchildren when there never was a hope of them....If man is doomed to perish, then universal infertility is as painless a way as any. And there are, after all, personal compensations. For the last sixty years we have sycophantically pandered to the most ignorant, the most criminal and the most selfish section of society. Now for the rest of our lives we're going to be spared the intrusive barbarism of the young, their noise, their pounding, repetitive, computer-produced so-called music, their violence, their egotism disguised as idealism. My God, we might even succeed in getting rid of Christmas, that annual celebration of parental guilt and juvenile greed. I intend that my life shall be comfortable, and, when it no longer is, then I shall wash down my final pill with a bottle of claret. (James, 1992: 52).

One cannot but suspect that Edelman would gladly toast with him. Unfortunately, even Jasper is not safe from redemption: despite having committed suicide, it is his car and his provisions that enable the group of rebels to make their escape. In death, he is redeemed. Moreover, Theo suspects that Jasper's reproductive futurism has merely been transferred to his students, in particular the favourite he adopts each year. Theo wonders 'whether this wasn't his way of confronting age, time, the inevitable blunting of the mind's keen edge, his personal illusion of immortality' (James, 1992: 51). *The Children of Men* is thus both explicitly invested in the politics of reproductive futurism, *and* charts the narrative of redemption for the antisocial male who seeks to resist that politics. Edelman could not have chosen a more appropriate text as grist for his mill.

Demodystopias

The Children of Men is part of a whole sub-genre of speculative and science fiction that is primarily or predominantly interested in the role of reproduction, fertility, and the place of the child in our future societies. These texts have been called 'demodystopias' (Domingo, 2008) or 'demografiction' (Kuijsten, 1999) and can be divided into texts concerned with under-population, those concerned with over-population and, according to Lionel Shriver's (2003) categorization, those concerned with population professionals. James's novel belongs to the first category, whose early twentieth century origins can arguably be traced back to Charlotte Perkins Gilman's *Herland* (1914). While *Herland* concentrates on outlining a feminist utopia, this utopia arose due to the women having to rebuild society after many of the men are killed in an accident and the surviving men have to be put down by the women in order to suppress a resurgent and violent patriarchy. Katharine Burdekin's *Swastika Night* (1937), meanwhile, imagines a Europe governed by the Nazis in a weirdly feudal system which is both class and gender-riven, women being kept in a ghetto or 'cage', considered less than animals and used only for breeding purposes. This system is effective until the women stop producing female babies, threatening the continuation of the species. In Brian Aldiss's *Greybeard* (1964), an interesting comparative text in relation to *The Children of Men*, a nuclear accident has rendered humankind sterile. A different demodystopian vision is offered by Zoe Fairbairns's *Benefits* (1979), which creates an England in which political power has fallen into the hands of those who want to undo the work of feminism and return women to the home. This government is thrown into crisis when the women resist and fertility is threatened. Perhaps the most famous under-population demodystopia is Margaret Atwood's *The Handmaid's Tale* (1985), which imagines a totalitarian Christian theocracy created after a military coup overthrows the US government. Again, fertility issues are at the centre of this tale's segregation and control of women and reproduction. Published in France the same year as *The Children of Men* (in English translation the following year) one might also include in this sub-genre Amin Malalouf's *The First Century After Beatrice* (1992/1993) followed by the novel to which I will turn in a moment, Maggie Gee's *The Ice People* (1998).[7] A more recent example is Jane Rogers's *The Testament of Jessie Lamb* (2011).

Edelman's work provides a productive context in which to consider such a body of novels, since both his theories and these literary texts are explicitly concerned with the future, sexuality, children, and the continuation (or not) of the human species.[8] But bringing Edelman's theories into dialogue with these works – most of them distinctly anti-Christian, or at least critically reflective about religion – is not a unidirectional exercise in which one can only be enlightened by the fun, as Power (2009: 4–5) observes, of 'being able to "spot", in the wake of Edelman's analysis, reproductive futurism whenever it rears its smiling, big-eyed, irresistible head'. Rather, the literary texts speak back to the theory. Placing them in dialogue with Edelman constitutes a significant critical act, one that provides another method for challenging his claims to universalism. The complexities and uneven textures of singular literary texts rupture the seductively smooth perfection of Edelman's theoretical polemic. *Literary equivocation deranges theoretical surety.* Power (2009: 2) turns to real-world examples in order to challenge Edelman's 'overly neat... formulations', which, she argues, are 'easier to undo with reference to history and practice than he seems to think' (Power, 2009: 11).[9] To mount a similar offensive by a different method, I wish to turn to the literary as a mode of engagement with Edelman's theory. Literature provides such a productive site of critique not because it is the only place in which one finds equivocation, but because it is a discourse committed to embracing, exploring and exploiting it. Equivocation is not what plagues literature, as it does almost every other discourse, from law to philosophy to science. Equivocation is literature's life-blood and the source of its power. It confronts one with the singular, and with nuances, complexities and contradictions that it is not obliged to resolve. It forces one, in short, to slow down, and to think.

Bringing demodystopian literature to bear on Edelman's theories carries a number of benefits. In the first instance, these demodystopias highlight that the world in which we live is, in fact, very far from being one whose politics is *entirely* determined by reproductive futurism. This is the case even for a contemporary America dominated by a Right-wing Christian fundamentalism. As Power (2009: 5) observes, 'politics is so pro-child in theory because it is so anti-child (and anti-woman) in practice'. If, she continues, '"society" really cared when and how individuals had children, we would no longer regard these choices as personal decisions, but rather as factors to be understood in the context of politics more broadly' (Power, 2009: 14). This is exactly the founding conceit of Fairbairns's *Benefits* in which a domestic payment to mothers intended to reward 'responsible motherhood' (Fairbairns, 1979: 56) is just the first step on a slippery slope towards the total control of women's reproductive capacity and a politically instituted programme of eugenics. A truly reproductively futural political system would produce regimes such as that toppled at the end of *Benefits*, or Atwood's the Republic of Gilead, in which any other rights – gay, straight, women's, human or otherwise – are placed below the imperative to reproduce the species. Or we would see, as in Gee's novel *The Ice People*, the dissolution of the family – such an imperfect and insecure environment in which to raise children anyway – in favour of a Children's Commune that places the value of children above that of, for instance, the fathers who love them. Sarah, the wife of *The Ice People*'s narrator Saul, explains what such a place is:

'It means what it says. You know, a place for children. A place that's run for the children who share it. That thinks kids are important. More important than *anything else in the world*...' She was going into that overemphatic, intense mode that meant bad faith, or politics.

'Yeah well,' I said. 'We all think that. Even men think that. Well, I do anyway. So can I join this commune?' I knew perfectly well what the answer would be. (*IP*, 98, emphasis in original)

In order to wield the power of literary equivocation most effectively, it is necessary to close read, to engage in an intricate and intimate tracing of detail. So rather than place Edelman's theories in dialogue with the whole body of under-population demodystopias, I will now focus on one in particular: *The Ice People*. I want to put a singular literary imagining into detailed conversation with Edelman's universal theory, in order to do what all good theoretical criticism does: to allow the theory to explore and complicate the fiction; to allow the fiction to explore and complicate the theory.[10]

Ironic Allosemes: The Queer Child

The Ice People is set in a future Britain and Europe, some time after 2065, when governments, social order and population levels have been ravaged by a new ice age which arrived in only a few decades and reaches almost to the equator. Like *The Children of Men*, the story is narrated by an ageing divorcee, Saul, who is urgently finishing this chronicle of his life before he becomes the next meal for the primitive, cannibalistic wild boys who are currently tolerating his Old Timer presence in the remains of a former airport.[11] Unlike *The Children of Men*, though, there is no omniscient narrator to provide an alternative perspective on Saul and to provide the *deus ex machina* narrative of redemption. Rather, Saul's homodiegetic narrative is split between the present of his discourse and the past of the story he is telling, with regular metalepses occurring to move the reader from one narrative level to the other. The events of the story gradually move towards, and eventually catch up to, the fatal time of the telling: at the end, we learn that Saul has only been with the wild boys for two years since the end of the events he is narrating. The story Saul tells is of his life in the 'Tropical Time' prior to the coming of the ice, his problematic relationship with his wife, Sarah, and their struggle to conceive a child, Luke. This personal drama takes place against the social backdrop of widespread human infertility and a breakdown in relationships between the sexes, which causes women to set up separate colonies in which they raise and school the children. As the ice continues to advance, Saul rescues (or steals, depending on your point of view) his son from one of these enclaves and sets out on an epic journey to Ghana. He hopes to be able to secure his and Luke's entry to Ghana's soon to be closed borders because of his Ghanian grandfather.

In taking Luke on this journey, Saul explicitly and repeatedly justifies his actions in the language and imagery of reproductive futurism, not least in his investment in the figure of the Child which does indeed for him, as Edelman (2004: 18) writes, seem 'to shimmer with the iridescent promise of Noah's rainbow, serving like the rainbow as the pledge of a covenant that shields us against the persistent threat of apocalypse now – or later'. Facing a modern flood of frozen water, Saul places all his hope for the future in his son. This role of the child is apparent from the early stages of the story, when Saul's parents' generation start to become fearful in the face of increased segregation between the sexes and the ensuing drop in fertility:

> The screens and the newstexts were full of statistics. They didn't mean all that much to the young, who were too busy having fun to think that having children mattered, but our parents discussed it in solemn voices. They wanted grandchildren. They wanted a future. (*IP*, 23–4)

When, after ten years of trying, Sarah and Saul finally manage to conceive with the help of advanced scientific methods, the child represents futural hope: 'we heard the loud rhythm of hope in our hearts, the rhythm we heard when she took my hand and held it patiently over her belly till I felt the child kicking, quick and strong' (*IP*, 56); when Sarah goes into labour, Sarah and Saul lie there, 'electric with excitement and hope' (*IP*, 57). When Saul first has sex with Briony (a member of Sarah's women's group who travels with Saul and Luke on their journey to Africa) again he thinks in terms of the Child representing the hope of the future: 'That morning was so bright, so unforgettable. I thought, *A new life away from Sarah. Hope. Joy. Another child?*' (*IP*, 207, emphasis in original). But he is willing to sacrifice Briony's life for his current child: 'I tried to think of the future, not the past... Safety for Luke, where the ice would not come. I told myself it was all for him. I had even sacrificed Briony' (*IP*, 272). The language of sacrifice returns when he is reunited with Sarah and is frustrated by her hatred of him: 'She didn't know I had sacrificed everything to try to give Luke a life in the sun, him and his children, our grandchildren, for surely in Africa there would have been children' (*IP*, 302). Saul, in fact, sacrifices everything on the altar of this child, 'for the sake of whom... everything else in the world, by force if needed, must give way' (Edelman 2004: 49).[12] Luke thus embodies Saul's 'belief in the future' (*IP*, 251), his dream of:

> The new, fertile, temperate Africa, where Luke would be safe and have a future, where perhaps our line would go on forever, back in the land from which we came, our genes rejoining the old dark river. It was my dream, a father's dream. (*IP*, 279)

But 'sons, of course,' he finally comes to realize, 'have different dreams' (*IP*, 279). And herein lies the first of one of the deep ironies at work in Gee's text, which complicate and challenge Saul (and Edelman's) reproductive futurism.

Drawing on the theory of Paul de Man, Edelman argues that akin to the functioning of the death drive is the function of irony, any theory of which, according to de Man, 'is the undoing, the necessary undoing, of any theory of narrative' (de Man, 1996 cited in Edelman, 2004: 23):

> Words have a way of saying things which are not at all what you want them to say... There is a machine there, a text machine, an implacable determination and a total arbitrariness... which inhabits words on the level of the play of the signifier, which undoes any narrative consistency of lines, and which undoes the reflexive and dialectical model, both of which are, as you know, the basis of any narration. (de Man 1996: 179, 181 cited in Edelman, 2004: 23)

The irreducible irony of words is the text machine that produces literature's irrepressible equivocity. We are gathering here a chain of 'allosemes', words that whilst not obviously synonyms carry the same meaning in their conceptual linkage: literature, equivocation, irony.[13] To this chain, Edelman adds 'queer'. For him, the queer is the privileged figure of disruptive irony, 'that queerest of rhetorical devices' (Edelman, 2004: 23). In *The Ice People* the power of literary irony is also wielded by a queer figure. But the novel adds its own word to the allosemic chain, a figure that Edelman absolutely excludes from it: that of the Child. In the literary text *The Ice People*, the child Luke is the queer figure of disruptive irony. If irony, as Edelman notes, 'severs the continuity essential to the very logic of making sense' (Edelman, 2004: 24), here, the sense that is being shattered by Luke is Edelman's insistent and fallacious logical opposition between the Child and the Queer – an opposition foundational to his argument.[14]

Luke's queerness is first signalled in the text early on when Saul returns from work 'to find Luke and Polly in the bathroom, Polly pink and naked and laughing. Luke was dressed up in her flowered skirt, with the matching top tucked up as a bra' (*IP*, 74). Polly and Luke are both delighted by Luke's transvestism, but this is not just cross-dressing. For Luke and Polly, the change of clothes constitutes a shift in ontological status, Luke *is* now a girl:

> "He's a girl," said Polly, laughing.
> "I'm a girl, Daddy," said Luke, excited. (*IP*, 74)

As Eve Kosofsky Sedgwick's analysis in 'How to Bring Your Kids up Gay' (1991: 20) has shown, whilst revisionist ego-psychology consents to the depathologization of homosexuality, it does so only at the expense of the pathologization of childhood gender identity disorder: 'The same DSM–III that, published in 1980, was the first that did not contain an entry for "homosexuality," was also the first that *did* contain a new diagnosis…"Gender Identity Disorder of Childhood"' (emphasis in original). While girls are only pathologized if they assert that they are anatomically male, boys are pathologized merely if they display, like Luke, a 'preoccupation with female stereotypical activities as manifested by a preference for either cross-dressing or simulating female attire' (*Diagnostic and Statistical Manual of Mental Disorders*, 1980: 265-6 cited in Sedgwick, 1991: 20). The gay rights movement has been important in dismantling the traditional conflation of gender and sexuality, but it remains the case that 'for any given adult gay man, wherever he may be at present on a scale of self-perceived or socially ascribed masculinity... the likelihood is disproportionately high that he will have a childhood history of self-perceived effeminacy, femininity, or non-masculinity' (Sedgwick, 1991: 20-1). Sedgwick cites a 1981 study which concludes that 'Childhood Gender Nonconformity turned out to be more strongly connected to adult homosexuality than was any other variable in the study' (Bell et al., 1981: 80 cited in Sedgwick, 1991: 27n.7). This is a correlative, rather than a causative, relation, but its statistical dominance supports a reading of the cross-dressing Luke as a queer child.[15] This is clearly how he is perceived by Saul. Luke's queerness uncomfortably confronts Saul's gender essentialism and homophobia, prejudices that determine his hopes and expectations for his child, and which I will address further below: 'I felt upset,' says Saul, after witnessing Luke's cross-dressing, 'but knew I mustn't show it' (*IP*, 74).[16]

In *The Ice People*, the reader gains no direct insight into Luke's thoughts and feelings since our only access to him is through Saul – even Luke's rare moments of direct speech are of course reported by Saul, since this is his chronicle. Luke is thus represented to the reader only as the symbolic future-ensuring Child he signifies for Saul. But in one definitive defiant act, Luke refuses to be cast in this light – he disappears, just as Saul is about to secure transport to Africa. With this act, Luke interrupts the continuity of Saul's story and refuses the futural hope placed in him. Exposing the machinery of the signifier – the actual human child, not just the figure of one – he demonstrates the way in which that signifier is always ironically 'in the way of what it would signify' (Edelman, 2004: 24). Luke's disappearance serves as an anacoluthic rupture in Saul's narrative – Saul continues his story, recounting his fruitless search for Luke and his eventual return to England, but this is not the (narrative nor genealogical) continuance for which he was hoping.[17] In his first act of free will in the text, a queer child performs the function that Edelman so preciously reserves for the child-defying queer: Luke 'pierces the fantasy screen of futurity, shattering narrative temporality with irony's always explosive force' (Edelman, 2004: 31).

Dramatic Irony

Luke is not the only child to refuse the figural weight placed upon him by his parents' generation. Rather, as Saul attests, 'the escape of the children, all over the world, was the strangest thing about the coming of the ice' (*IP*, 227). The children run away, forming wild, roaming groups. Such groups might be considered to represent a space outside of politics, and thus a realm outside of the reproductive futurism that Edelman considers inseparable from it. But these groups appear to return to a biologically reproductive heterosexual primitivism:

> Simple is best, for the wild boys. Death excites them, and love and adventure. Love they can understand again, in their savage way, their animal fashion, love between male and female, that is, for they're mating again, the wild boys. When they find the girls, they know what to do… (*IP*, 289)

Luke, Saul believes, is attracted to the children because 'they're starting again…from scratch' (*IP*, 284), engaging in '*naked, old-style, natural fucking*' (*IP*, 289, emphasis in original), and, at least in the countryside, seem to be reproducing without problems. From the perspective of Edelman's theory, this is problematic, since the heteronormative imperatives and queer exclusions of reproductive futurism can be understood as merely having been transposed to a different social environment. But to read this moment in *The Ice People* in such a way is to be subsumed again by the universalism of Edelman's claims, specifically by his transfiguration of the banal specificity of 'reproduction' into the seductive universal concept 'reproductive futurism'.[18] 'Reproduction' and 'reproductive futurism' are not synonymous. Only if one thinks they are, as Edelman does, can the necessary structural exclusion of the queer from the latter be asserted to be an equally defining necessity of the former. *It is not.* Queer exclusion might be structurally essential to reproductive futurism, but queer exclusion is contingent, not essential, to reproduction. 'Reproduction' is a far less catchy and tantalizing idea than 'reproductive futurism'. It is embedded in the nonfigurative, and it is explicit in its bare scientific reflection of the biological practicalities – if not the politics – of species survival.[19]

Does the *'natural fucking'* of the wild boys and girls preclude wild boys fucking wild boys, and wild girls fucking wild girls (although even in Edelman's account of the queer the latter seems remarkably unimaginable)? The very question of the 'natural' is of course at issue here, and the reader must not forget who is speaking – when Saul first sees the children copulating, their gender is not specified:

> A couple, two couples, mother naked, struggling together on the ground, and others lounging by the road, watching – longhaired, slender, animal shapes of more *salvajes*, lithe, slinking, and they suddenly scattered but the couples continued, and I saw more clearly, from the corner of my eye, the moment before we shot out of the wood and back into the blinding light, they were fucking. (*IP*, 289)

It is Saul, our misogynistic, heteronormative, gender essentialist narrator, who identifies this as 'making love' (*IP*, 289).[20] It is he who connects it with the children he (perhaps) glimpses in the background: '*I saw or imagined something else*, as well. Behind them, playing on a bank where a tree had fallen and lay uprooted, three or four naked babies played, watched by two women with long black hair' (*IP*, 289; emphasis added). 'I saw or imagined' – which one is it? Saul projects his heteronormative fantasy of reproductive futurism onto the scene he witnesses, but there is no proof in his narrative that this fantasy in any way corresponds with reality. There is no evidence, let alone a structural necessity, that the *'natural fucking'* he observes is heterosexual. Even if it were, that would not preclude the presence of homosexual activity amongst the wild children as well.[21]

The fallibility and subjectivity of our narrator must also be crucially borne in mind when considering the end of Saul's story. Unable to track Luke down after his disappearance, Saul eventually returns to England for one final meeting with his estranged wife. Sarah has found a picture showing a 'tall blonde youth, a dark-haired woman, and three other white heads so small I hadn't seen them, three blonde children, playing with a black one' (*IP*, 308). In the photographs, there is no certainty that the youth is Luke – 'none of them made identification certain' (*IP*, 308) – but Saul and Sarah cling to their fantasy of continuance: 'looking at them with such passionate desire we could both see precise curves of ear and mouth in the vaguest patches of light or darkness' (*IP*, 308). Despite the anacoluthic interruption Luke causes to Saul's narrative by his disappearance, Saul will not relinquish his commitment to reproductive futurism; he merely transfers it from the child to the fantastical grandchild: '…neither of us could say anything, because this was the point of everything' (*IP*, 308–9). Saul is steadfast in his reproductively futural belief that the only thing that matters is 'whether you and your seed survive' (*IP*, 84). 'It's as if the game were extremely simple,' he says, 'yet we kept on attempting impossible moves, stupidly intelligent, frowning in the mirror' (*IP*, 84). Nothing threatens this fantasy more than the possibility Saul absolutely will not countenance, but which remains open in the text: that his queer child may well have become a boy-fucking boy. Nothing threatens Edelman's fantasy of the universal theory of reproductive futurism more than the fact that in *The Ice People* it is the children, both queer and not, who occupy the site of resistance to the political as such.

The events of the story Saul is chronicling end with the final meeting with Sarah that takes place two years before he records his narrative. Saul is writing this tale while surviving his last days amongst a group of wild boys who, the narrative repeatedly implies, live off human meat. This implication is made explicit towards the end of the novel when the only other adult living with the boys, Monsieur Chef, is spit roasted with an apple stuffed in his mouth.[22] Saul's death at the hands of the wild boys is part of the novel's persistent critique of his faith in reproductive futurism. There is no omniscient or heterodiegetic narrator in *The Ice People*, no external voice to guide the reader's response to Saul. Rather, this critique is effected through dramatic irony; Saul's words, opinions and actions betray his prejudices and beliefs to the reader. And they do so primarily in the same way as Edelman's texts do – because of their absolutism. In the end, this dramatic irony and its critique are reified in an almost parodic enaction of the logical extreme of reproductive futurism: the child literally consumes the adult; the boys eat Saul.[23] Saul's fantastic consolation that he and Sarah 'live in Luke. We can never be parted' (*IP*, 315) is macabrely undercut by his eventual consumption and ingestion by the cannibalistic wild boys.[24]

Fantastic Sinthomes

Saul initially figures his narrative, his reproductively futural tale, as a defence against his death. On the whole illiterate, the wild boys still retain a love of stories and Saul wonders if 'perhaps my story will keep me alive. Perhaps they will let me finish my story' (*IP*, 14): 'Don't you see, you boneheads,' he writes, 'I'm Scheherezade [sic.]? I'll spin out my story night after night, hamming, stalling, to save my life – ' (*IP*, 21). But stealing the time to write the story takes him away from his essential work for the boys – maintaining their fleet of Doves – rendering him inessential and thereby hastening, not deferring, his end. Saul's narrative of reproductive futurism is not a defence against his end but, in the term Edelman takes from Lacan, his *sinthome*.[25] That is, it is his compulsion, that which holds him together, that which shores up his identity: '*I tell this story because I must*' (*IP*, 14, emphasis in original).

Likewise, Edelman's story of a universal politics structurally defined by reproductive futurism is *his* sinthome, his account of the straight and the queer, the political and the personal, without which he cannot live and which is compulsively repeated across texts.[26] Saul recognizes the futility of his sinthome to secure him a future, while the rejection of the future is essential to Edelman's sinthome. But both figure the differing relations of their sinthomes to the future as a rejection of the literary myth of Scheherezade: 'Scheherezade [sic.]! Don't make me laugh,' Saul continues, 'None of them knows what I'm talking about. It's a world ago, the *Arabian Nights* my mother used to read to me...' (*IP*, 10). Edelman similarly invokes *The Arabian Nights* when he introduces his neologism – *sinthom*osexuality: 'if this word without a future seeks a hearing here,' says Edelman (2004: 33), 'it's not to play for time or, like Scheherazade, to keep at bay its all too certain doom.'[27] If we place Saul's narration in dialogue with Edelman's analysis, then, we can identify that for both of them their sinthome is a fiction occurring, as Lacan observes, where the knot between the imaginary, the real and the symbolic 'slips' (Lacan, 1975–6: 43), where it is necessary to shore up one's self. But both Saul and Edelman's sinthomes are fantastic – Edelman's queer politics might be constructed to deny the appeal of the fantasy of the future, but Edelman is just as much invested in the queer presentist fantasy of no future as Saul is invested in the reproductively futural fantasy of there being one.[28]

In a final irony, it is Lacan – whose theory is so integral to Edelman's arguments – who provides a fitting conclusion to this critique of them. 'In the end,' he says, in his seminar on the sinthome, 'we have only that as a weapon against the symptom – equivocation' (Lacan, 1975–6: 4). Equivocation is exactly what Saul and Edelman, with all their absolutes, do not have. But equivocation is the essence of literature, of theoretical criticism, and, as Edelman does not recognize, of politics too.[29] 'Bringing into play that equivocation which could free one from the sinthome', bringing Gee's novel into conversation with Edelman's theories, is a necessary and productive act of interpretation of both texts that operates, as Lacan insists, 'solely by equivocation' (Lacan, 1975–6: 4).

Notes

1 For the anthropological theory of the scapegoat see Kenneth Burke (1935/1992, 1945/1992). See also René Girard (1986). While it is not my intention here to develop a detailed comparative analysis of Edelman and Girard's theories, although it would be productive to do so, it is interesting at least to observe that both share a common method of deriving a social theory from psychoanalysis.

2 Tim Dean (2006: 826) finds this move deeply problematic, since 'the antisocial theory originates not in queer theory but in right-wing fantasies

about how "the homosexual agenda" undermines the social fabric'. There is something both politically disempowering and simply unimaginative in the idea that the queer can, even ought, do nothing other than embrace the figuration given to it by the dominant politics of reproductive futurism. Other key figures in queer theory's antisocial turn are Leo Bersani (1995), Lauren Berlant (1997) and, more problematically, Judith Halberstam (2011). See Caserio et al. (2006) for an explanation of this recent strand of queer theory.

3   It is, of course, very difficult to take Edelman at his word on this, because of the unresolved tension in his text between the figurative and the actual. Edelman brands reproductive futurism as irreducibly heteronormative, at the same time as insisting that both this heteronormativity and the queer resistance he is advocating are in no way associated with actual sexual practices, lifestyles nor identities. However, what becomes clear reading Edelman is that there is in fact only one main reason for his resistance to reproductive futurism: the latter is bad because it sacrifices a real present to an imagined, and impossible, fantasy of the future. For the sake of the Child, the imagined future, we compromise ourselves now. What becomes even clearer, however, is that this 'we' is not universal but specifically queer, queer not in the figurative sense Edelman continually invokes but in the literal sense of gay and lesbian subjects. It is in their name that Edelman opposes reproductive futurism, since his polemic is directed at certain facets of US culture that premise their persecution of and discrimination against gays and lesbians on the basis of the need to safeguard the Child and the future it represents. Edelman (2004: 11, 26) continually insists that his argument is a figurative not a literal one – 'the image of the Child [is] not to be confused with the lived experiences of any historical children', 'the subject's (hetero)normalization...is accomplished regardless of sexual practice or sexual "orientation"' – but the future-negating queer is repeatedly best represented by gay subjects who challenge heteronormativity. It is precisely in the name of those subjects, and their lifestyles, that Edelman mounts his challenge to reproductive futurism. Driving Edelman's figural queer politics, then, is actually a very traditional gay identity politics – behind his complex theory lies the fierce demand, let us live our lives in peace. In agreement, see here Brenkman (2002a: 180): 'in its poetry and protest, it makes a jarring statement of conscience – a statement that belongs to the very political realm that queer post-politics imagines it could transcend'. Brenkman develops his observation by drawing attention to

the moments when Edelman formulates his queer post-politics whilst also hesitating about dispensing with the importance of gay identity politics, moments, Brenkman argues, which highlight 'the faultlines of his theoretical position' (Brenkman, 2002a: 177). Consider for example, the following Edelman (2004) caveats: 'Without for a moment denying the importance that distinguishes many of those projects...' (Edelman, 2004: 473); '...patient negotiation of tolerances and rights, as important as these undoubtedly are to all of us still denied them...' (Edelman, 2004: 16); 'Though the material conditions of human experience may indeed be at stake in the various conflicts by means of which differing political perspectives vie for the power to name, and by naming to shape, our collective reality...' (Edelman, 2004: 7); liberalism, Edelman freely acknowledges, is 'better enabling the extension of rights to those who are still denied them (Edelman, 2004: 26).

4 See Daniel K. Williams (2010) for a lucid account of the Religious Right in America, one that addresses both its rise since 1980 and the wider historical context of Conservative Christian involvement in US politics.

5 *No Future* consists of four essays, the first of which – 'The Future is Kid Stuff' – was originally published in the journal *Narrative* in 1998 and constitutes his manifesto. The remaining three chapters develop this main argument in relation to an additional idea, that of *sintho*mosexuality (see note 27 below), and in readings of a number of literary and filmic texts, the former drawn from nineteenth century realist fiction – Dickens' *A Christmas Carol*, Eliot's *Silas Marner* – the latter from Hitchcock's oeuvre, specifically *North by Northwest* and *The Birds*. However, the only literary text that Edelman reads in any detail in 'The Future is Kid Stuff' is James' contemporary dystopian novel.

6 See, for instance, Hamilton (2006) and Taylor (2006). See also Wood (n.d.) and Dalley (1992), who observes that the book is 'unfashionably Christian'.

7 In placing Gee's novel within the genre of demodystopias, rather than climate change fiction, I am no doubt yet again opening myself up to the charge placed against me by Adam Trexler and Adeline Johns-Putra (2011) with regard to my earlier reading of Gee's novel *The Flood* (2004) (Dillon 2007a). In their survey of climate change in literature and literary criticism, Trexler and John-Putra (2011: 190) observe that 'neither of Gee's climate novels has been critiqued as dealing explicitly with the current global warming crisis, although the threatened environments

of both novels would seem to invite such treatments. *The Ice People* has received little critical attention, while Dillon has read *The Flood* as a response to the 9/11 attacks and (somewhat anachronistically) the Boxing Day tsunami of 2004, but neglects the rather obvious interpretation that the flood of the novel's title has been brought about by climate change'. It does not seem to me, however, that a treatment of a novel in relation to one topic – for instance my concentration on the idea of apocalypse in relation to *The Flood*, or on reproductive futurism here in *The Ice People* – precludes it being also studied in the context of another body of texts and concerns. For explicit discussion of climate change in relation to Gee's work see Johns-Putra's (2014) recent essay on *The Ice People* and Christopher Maughan's chapter in this volume on *The Flood*. It might also be useful to note that, in my discussion of *The Flood*, reference to the Boxing Day tsunami does not confuse the chronology of 2004 (in which the tsunami took place after the publication of *The Flood*) but talks about the tsunami precisely in relation to the idea of literature and prophecy.

8   In his account of demodystopias Domingo (2008: 735) unintentionally provides a link between these texts and Edelman's theory via the title of Edelman's polemic, 'no future': 'One of the contributions made by these demodystopias is to take account of economic context in explaining demographic changes then occurring [...]. Nevertheless, the authors maintained, these changes could not be understood without acknowledging the effects, both material and political, of the straitened economic conditions of the 1970s and 1980s on nuptuality and fertility behavior – effects encapsulated in the dystopic slogan "no future"'. In the context of Edelman's pro-queer polemic, the name of the Sex Pistol song from which his title derives takes on an ironically different connotation: 'God Save the Queen'.

9   In challenging Edelman's universalisms, Power (2009: 3) draws 'on empirical historical examples of certain left-wing and alternative political movements, such as the kibbutzim movement in Israel, which explicitly refused reproduction but were nevertheless most definitely political, and quite often "queer" from the standpoint of the norms of the social order'.

10 For an elaboration of my understanding of the term 'theoretical criticism' see Dillon (2007b: 2–3).

11 The chronicler is a recurrent narrative device in demodystopian fiction beginning with Vandyck Jennings who writes the tale of *Herland* 'from memory' (Gilman, 1914/1998: 1). Such chroniclers are often working

under constraint or threat. Consider, for instance, Offred's secretive recording of her Handmaid's Tale, with the cassettes hidden at a prominent way-station on The Underground Femaleroad, or Jessie Lamb's scribbled testimony of her struggle against her father in order to sacrifice herself in order to reproduce. Comparing *The Children of Men* to *The First Century After Beatrice*, Anton C. Kuijsten (1999: 92) observes a parallel between this narrative device in fiction and in demographic science. He observes that 'in both books the main character is acting as a chronicler, having kept a diary from the time when "it all started", "round about the year with three noughts" and now writes it all down helped by hindsight. It reminded me of the fact that exactly the same procedure was chosen by Dirk van de Kaa in his inauguration speech as Professor of Demography at the University of Amsterdam in 1981...He created a time distance towards his topic, by pretending to deliver his speech in the year 2081 instead of 1981, and by acting as a historian and narrator explained the demographic developments of the century by looking back at "how it all started" in the 1960s and 1970s'.

12 Further examples of Saul's reproductively futural investment in the figure of the child abound in the text. See, for example: 'I would do it for Luke. I was no longer depressed. I was a man, a father, not some godforsaken wimp' (*IP*, 165); 'I had escaped. I had stolen the future' (*IP*, 207–8); 'I learned staying alive mattered more than anything, staying alive to protect my son' (*IP*, 210); 'I could not die, because of my son' (*IP*, 231); 'All that I did, I did for him' (*IP*, 252); '...maybe he genuinely didn't realise that I'd thrown everything up for him. / My choice, not his. I don't reproach him –' (*IP*, 291); 'But I knew I would never let anyone kill me while Luke was alive and needed me' (*IP*, 292).

13 See Jacques Derrida (1986) for an exploration of allosemes in relation to Nicolas Abraham and Maria Torok's theories of the crypt and cryptonymy. The term comes from the Greek 'allo' meaning 'other, different' and 'seme' meaning 'sign'.

14 Much recent work of course supports Snediker's (2006: n.18) observation regarding the unfathomability of Edelman's persistent opposition of the queer and the child: 'such claims seem so patently misguided and foreclosing that it's difficult to know how to respond, beyond the obvious fact that *there's nothing queerer than childhood*'. For work on the queer and the child see Stockton (2009) and Bruhm and Hurley (2004).

15 Luke is not the only queer child in Gee's fiction. In her most recent novel, *Virginia Woolf in Manhattan* (2014), one strand of the narrative is focused through Gerda. Readers of Gee will remember first encountering Gerda as a young child in *The Flood*. Here we meet her again, on the cusp of her fourteenth birthday, and Gerda is explicitly queer. Against the backdrop of the reincarnated Woolf's queerness, Gerda explores her developing sexuality through sex with another girl: 'Gerda reached forward and kissed the other girl full on the mouth, and felt Lil pull away, and then kissed her again, and they stood on the rock like two gladiators, half-kissing and half-wrestling' (*VW*, 320); later, they make love (*VW*, 390). Echoing the *salvajes* of *The Ice People*, Lil is the leader of a pack of wild children who live in New York's Central Park. Despite being 'an inside girl mostly' (*VW*, 410), in the time Gerda spends with the wild children, she realizes the kinship of youth and the unavoidable affinity between the young and the future they will inhabit: 'We were the young, alone with the future, while the parents would slip away into the past' (*VW*, 330).

16 Evidence of Luke's queerness builds throughout the text. A little later – when their first Dove (a family robot) is delivered – the question of its gender arises. Luke wants it to be a girl like him (*IP*, 92). When the Dove meets an untimely end in a stream, Luke explains that he 'was pretending we were boys, fighting' (*IP*, 104). The comma is carefully placed here, to emphasize that the verb 'pretending' relates to the 'being boys', rather than to the 'fighting'. Luke's queer gender non-conformity may be artificially enhanced by the female hormones given to him in the women-run Children's Commune, but it is manifest in the text before this occurs.

17 Edelman (2004: 24) notes that de Man likens the effect of irony 'to the syntactical violence of the anacoluthon'. The *anacoluthon* is a substantivized figure derived from the grammatical term *anacoluthia*: literally, a want of grammatical sequence, the passing from one construction to another before the former is completed. It has a modern history in literature and theory that passes from Marcel Proust, to Paul de Man to J. Hillis Miller to Jacques Derrida. See Dillon (2006) for an exegesis of this history and a further theorization of the anacoluthon as a figure for the process of reading, writing and thinking after Derrida.

18 See Snediker's (2006) crucial critique of Edelman which he constructs with reference to the theories of D. W. Winnicott: 'Winnicott's polemic distinguishes helpfully between the existence of a range of energies or pulsions and the denomination of that range as one "concept." My

reservation regarding works such as Cvetkovich's [one might insert Edelman here too] has less to do with any given set of "speculations," which (as Winnicott suggests) are often innovative and adriot, than with their resigned gravitation to a single concept, which can't possibly do speculations as such justice. The more one can transform speculations into concepts, the more likely one is to turn observations into figurations. Easy enough, as Eng and Kazanjian demonstrate, to wax lyrical on melancholy. Harder to wax lyrical about "doldrums," and thus "doldrums," for all its banality, retains a useful nonfigurative (or at least differently figurative) specificity' (para. 23).

19 See Edelman's (2002: 176) response to Brenkman's criticism on this point, in relation to which he persists in the conflation of 'reproductive futurism' and 'reproduction': "'A society's survival," Brenkman writes, certainly not without reason, "depends upon, among many other things, the fact that its members reproduce". He doesn't, of course, intend this as anything *but* such a statement of fact. Its expropriability, however, for the purpose of heteronormative regulation, or even as a justification for violence (in the name of self-defence) against those who might be identified with nonreproductive forms of sex ("society's survival," after all, is at stake), cannot be explained as merely a contingent aspect of this formulation' (Edelman, 2002: 182).

20 Saul was first attracted to Sarah because 'she was *womanly*, that was the only word, old fashioned though I knew it was. So I could be manly, as I wished to be' (*IP*, 32). His gender essentialism is absolute and entrenched, characterized by repeated generalizations about 'woman's' nature: 'Women are sometimes very slow' (*IP*, 258); 'but women always find things for you to do' (*IP*, 263); 'women always have to move things around' (*IP*, 265); women, he thinks, are 'so practical...knowing from a baby's congested face what type of thing had just leaked from its bottom...and they enjoyed it, surely. It was what women liked' (*IP*, 139).

21 It is possible to have recourse to the now plentiful scientific studies which prove that homosexuality (as well as oral sex, masturbation and other non-reproductive sexual activities) are a 'natural' part of the animal kingdom, to dissociate the 'natural' from the heterosexual. (The Wikipedia entry under 'Homosexual behaviour in animals' provides an extensive preliminary reading list.) But the very idea of the natural is also one that is continually put into question throughout Gee's novel. It is semantically malleable enough to be called to the defence of even mutually exclusive

positions: "'... It's natural that men don't want to lose their children." (But she said it as though it were inevitable; as if it were natural that the women should steal them' (*IP* 99). To adopt for a moment Edelman's theoretical progenitor, one might usefully pay attention to Jacques Lacan's (1975–6: 1–2) problematization of the natural at the opening of his seminar 'The Sinthome'.

22 It is too tempting not to read into this the sexual activity that the slang 'spit roasting' denotes, in which case, Chef is fucked by the boys in more than one figurative sense.

23 Reproductive futurism taken to its macabre logical extreme of the sacrifice of the adult to the cannibalistic child is also seen in Tomas Alfredson's horror film *Let the Right One In* (2008) in which Håkan, the adult carer of the eternally child vampire Eli, eventually offers up his own body for her sustenance.

24 Note that the other option Saul is offered for his death – that he order his Dove, Dora, to paralyse and consume him – does not in fact represent an alternative since the Doves are repeatedly figured throughout the novel as surrogate children: see, for instance (*IP*, 93, 94, 97, 100, 103, 107, 109, 110, 122, 126). But, like Luke, the Doves are of course queer children, artificially intelligent robots that eventually mutate in order to become a radically antisocial threat to the political order, one that must be combated in the reproductively futural politics of the Wicca women in the name of the 'real' children the mutant Doves are killing and eating: 'the Speakers came on to promise us that they would "save us from the Doves," shield our children from "robot perverts"' (*IP*, 150).

25 The idea of the 'sinthome' is introduced by Lacan in his seminar *Le sinthome* (1975–6), as a fourth term to be added to his original triad of the imaginary, the real and the symbolic. Put simply, 'a sinthome is what allows the symbolic, the imaginary and the real to be held together' (Lacan, 1975–6: 42). It is situated at precisely the point where there is a weakness in the knot between these three, 'where there is a lapsus of the knot' (Lacan, 1975–6: 43).

26 For the compulsive unequivocal repetition of the same argument see Edelman (1998, 2002, 2004, 2006, 2007).

27 Edelman introduces the idea of *sinthomo*sexuality in the second chapter of *No Future*, in order to name this queer politics that embraces *jouissance* and the death drive in opposition to reproductive futurism. The neologism grafts together Lacan's idea of the *sinthome* and the

homosexuality which reproductive futurism casts out. *Sinthom*osexuality endangers reproductive futurism's fantasy of survival by replacing the futural temporality of desire, upon which it depends, with an insistence on the mechanistic and continuous satisfaction of the drive.

28 At the heart of Edelman's idea of *sinthom*osexuality is a fantasy of the present, of the possibility of an immediate present moment in which there can be a constant access to *jouissance* via the immediacy of the drive. The philosophical problems with Edelman's ideas of temporality have been another site of criticism of his work: see, for example, Michael O'Rourke's (2011) Derridean critique, informed by Derrida's deconstruction of the idea of the 'present' which is in fact always already inhabited by the past and by the future to come; and José Esteban Muñoz (2007: 364) who comments on the 'weirdly atemporal' aspect of Edelman's theories.

29 I am grateful to one of my readers, Alexander Beaumont, for suggesting this final point regarding the equivocity of politics. Beaumont would no doubt agree with John Brenkman's (2002b: 188) Arendtian rejoinder to Edelman in which he argues that 'the political frame of laws and rights, and of debate and decision, is intrinsically inadequate to the plurality of projects and the social divisions within society – there is always a gap in its political representation of the "real" of the social – and for *that* very reason the political realm itself is open to change and innovation'.

Works Cited

Aldiss, Brian (1964) *Greybeard*. London: Gollancz.
Atwood, Margaret (1985/1996) *The Handmaid's Tale*. London: Vintage.
Bell, A.P., Weinberg, M.S. and Hammersmith, S.K. (1981) *Sexual Preference: Its Development in Men and Women*. Bloomington: Indiana University Press.
Bersani, Leo (1995) *Homos*. Cambridge: Harvard University Press.
Berlant, Lauren (1997) *The Queen of America Goes to Washington City: Essays on Sex and Citizenship*. Durham and London: Duke University Press.
Brenkman, John (2002a) 'Queer Post-Politics', *Narrative* 10(2): 174–80.
Brenkman, John (2002b) 'Politics, Mortal and Natal: An Arendtian Rejoinder', *Narrative* 10(2): 186–92.
Bruhm, Steven and Hurley, Natasha (eds) (2004) *Curiouser: On the Queerness of Children*. London and Minneapolis: University of Minnesota Press.
Burdekin, Katharine (1937/1985) *Swastika Night*. New York: Feminist Press.

Burke, Kenneth (1935/1992) *Permanence and Change: An Anatomy of Purpose*, 3rd edn. Berkeley: University of California Press.

Burke, Kenneth (1945/1992) *A Grammar of Motives*. Berkeley: University of California Press.

Case Against 8, The (2014, dir. Ben Cotner and Ryan White).

Caserio, Robert L. Lee Edelman, Judith Halberstam, José Esteban Muñoz and Tim Dean (2006) 'The Antisocial Thesis in Queer Theory', *PMLA* 121(3): 819–28.

Dalley, Jan (1992) Interview / Mistress of morality tales: P. D. James', *The Independent*, 20 September, URL (consulted 20 July 2014): http://www.independent.co.uk/voices/interview--mistress-of-morality-tales-p-d-james-jan-dalley-meets-the-celebrated-crime-writer-whose-latest-novel-examines-evil-from-a-very-different-perspective-1552435.html

de Man, Paul (1996) *Aesthetic Ideology*, ed. Andrzej Warminski. Minneapolis: University of Minnesota Press.

Dean, Tim (2006) 'The Antisocial Homosexual', Forum: Conference debates. The anti-social thesis in queer theory. *PMLA* 12(3): 826–8.

Derrida, Jacques (1986) '*Fors*: The Anglish Words of Nicolas Abraham and Maria Torok', trans. Barbara Johnson, in Nicolas Abraham and Maria Torok, *The Wolf Man's Magic Word: A Cryptonymy*, trans. Nicholas Rand, pp. xi–xlviii. Minneapolis: University of Minnesota Press.

Diagnostic and Statistical Manual of Mental Disorders (1980) (3rd edn). Washington: The American Psychiatric Association.

Dillon, Sarah (2006) 'Life After Derrida: Anacoluthia and the Agrammaticality of Following', *Research in Phenomenology* (36): 97–114.

Dillon, Sarah (2007a) 'Imagining Apocalypse: Maggie Gee's *The Flood*', *Contemporary Literature* 48(3): 374–97.

Dillon, Sarah (2007b) *The Palimpsest: Literature, Criticism, Theory*. London: Continuum.

Domingo, Andreu (2008) '"Demodystopias": Prospects of Demographic Hell', *Population and Development Review* 34(4): 725–45.

Edelman, Lee (1998) 'The Future is Kid Stuff: Queer Theory, Disidentification, and the Death Drive', *Narrative* 6(1): 18–30.

Edelman, Lee (2002) 'Post-Partum', *Narrative*, 10(2): 181–5.

Edelman, Lee (2004) *No Future: Queer Theory and the Death Drive*. Durham and London: Duke University Press.

Edelman, Lee (2006) 'Antagonism, Negativity, and the Subject of Queer Theory', Forum: Conference debates. The anti-social thesis in queer theory, *PMLA* 12(3): 821–3.

Edelman, Lee (2007) 'Ever After: History, Negativity, and the Social', *South Atlantic Quarterly* 106(3): 469–76.
Fairbairns, Zoë (1979) *Benefits*. New York: Avon.
Freeman, Elizabeth (2007) 'Introduction', *GLQ* 13(2–3): 159–76.
Gilman, Charlotte Perkins (1914/1998) *Herland*. Mineola, NY: Dover Publications.
Girard, René (1986) *The Scapegoat*, trans. Yvonne Freccero. Baltimore, MD: The Johns Hopkins University Press.
Halberstam, Judith (2011). *The Queer Art of Failure*. Durham: Duke University Press.
Hamilton, J.M. (2006) 'Great Christian Literature', *For His Renown*, 18 December, URL (consulted 20 July 2014): http://jimhamilton.info/2006/12/18/great-christian-literature-p-d-james%E2%80%99s-the-children-of-men/
James, P.D. (1992) *The Children of Men*. London: Faber and Faber.
Johns-Putra, Adeline (2014) 'Care, Gender, and the Climate-Changed Future: Maggie Gee's *The Ice People*' in Gerry Canavan and Kim Stanley Robinson (eds) *Green Planets: Ecology and Science Fiction*, pp. 127-42. Middletown: CT: Wesleyan University Press.
Kuijsten, Anton C. (1999) 'Demografiction' in Anton Kuijusten, Hans de Gans, and Henk de Feijter (eds) *The Joy of Demography ... and Other Disciplines: Essays in Honour of Dirk van de Kaa*, pp. 83–102. Amsterdam: Thela Thesis.
Lacan, Jacques (1975–6) 'Le Sinthome', Seminar XXIII, *Ornicar?* 6–11 (1976–7): 1-65, ed. J.-A. Miller, trans. Luke Thurston. URL (consulted 10th July 2014): http://www.scribd.com/doc/97204361/Seminar-of-Jacques-Lacan-Book-XXIII-Le-Sinthome
Leap, William L., Lewin, Ellen and Wilson, Natasha (2007) 'Queering the Disaster: A Presidential Session', *North American Dialogue* 10(2): 11–14.
Let the Right One In (2008, dir. Tomas Alfredson).
Malalouf, Amin (1992/1993) *The First Century After Beatrice*. London: Abacus.
Muñoz, José Esteban (2006) 'Thinking beyond Antirelationality and Antiutopianism in Queer Critique', *PMLA* 121: 825–26.
Muñoz, José Esteban (2007) 'Cruising the Toilet: LeRoi Jones/Amiri Baraka, Radical Black Traditions, and Queer Futurity', *GLQ* 13(2–3): 353–67.
Muñoz, José Esteban (2009) *Cruising Utopia: The Then and There of Queer Futurity*. New York and London: New York University Press.

O'Rourke, Michael (2011) 'The Afterlives of Queer Theory', *Continent* 1(2): 102–116.
Power, Nina (2009) 'Non-Reproductive Futurism: Rancière's rational quality against Edelman's body apolitic', *Borderlands* 8(2): 1–16.
Rogers, Jane (2012) *The Testament of Jessie Lamb*. Edinburgh: Canongate Books.
Sedgwick, Eve Kosofsky (1991) 'How to Bring Your Kids up Gay', *Social Text* 29: 18–27.
Shriver, Lionel (2003) 'Population in Literature', *Population and Development Review* 29(2): 153–162.
Snediker, Michael (2006) 'Queer Optimism', *Postmodern Culture* 16(3): no pagination.
Stockton, Kathryn Bond (2009) *The Queer Child, Or Growing Sideways in the Twentieth Century*. Durham and London: Duke University Press.
Taylor, Justin (2006) 'P. D. James and The Children of Men', *The Gospel Connection*, 20 December, URL (consulted 20 July 2014): http://thegospelcoalition.org/blogs/justintaylor/2006/12/10/pd-james-and-children-of-men/
Trexler, Adam and Adeline Johns-Putra (2011) 'Climate change in literature and literary criticism', *Wiley Interdisciplinary Reviews: Climate Change* 2(2): 185–200.
Williams, Daniel K. (2010) *God's Own Party: The Making of the Christian Right*. Oxford: Oxford University Press.
Wood, Ralph (n.d.) 'A Case for P. D. James as a Christian Novelist', *Bear Space*, URL (consulted 20 July 2014): https://bearspace.baylor.edu/Ralph_Wood/www/james/PDJamestheChristian.pdf

6

'One and Indivisible, a Seamless Web'
Climate Change as Historical Process in *The Flood*

Chris Maughan

> The two girls stared riveted, for a moment, at a computer simulation of a tidal wave. Tiny people struggled like ants. Something big and important at last. Something marvellous that would sweep them away [...] Something massive, sexual, final. (*TF*, 57)

A common claim made by cultural and social theorists has been that our representational engagements with climate change have, thus far, been inadequate. In *Slow Violence and the Environmentalism of the Poor* (2011), for example, Rob Nixon writes:

> We need, I believe, to engage a [...] violence which is neither spectacular nor instantaneous, but rather incremental and accretive [...] In so doing we need also to engage the different representational, narrative and strategic challenges posed by the relative invisibility of slow violence. (Nixon, 2011: 2)

In the arts, where the need to address these 'representational, narrative and strategic challenges' possesses an obvious pertinence, the response to climate change has been relatively slow to gather pace. As late as 2005, the writer Robert MacFarlane asked, incredulously:

'Where are the novels, the plays, the poems, the songs, the libretti, of this massive contemporary anxiety?' (MacFarlane, 2005). In recent years, however, there has been a conspicuous change in this trend. In a 2013 article, writer Rodge Glass noted the new currency of the term 'cli-fi', now used, allegedly, to denote the sizeable corpus of literary and filmic engagements with climate change. It remains to be seen, however, whether any of the more recent attempts to engage with climate change via creative literature are (or will be), as a number of commentators have hoped, 'capable of revealing what conventional forms obscure' (Kerridge, 2013: 361).

As some critics have suggested, the problems with representing climate change may be suggestive of more than just the shortcomings of the literary imagination, but rather the culture industry as a whole. Marxists, for instance, have long been sceptical of the capacity of the culture industry to offer genuinely revolutionary impetus. Theodor Adorno's famous insistence on the impossibility of a positive representation of 'an emancipated society' was predicated on the idea that such representations foster passivity, and 'the falling away of that imperious drive towards self-preservation' otherwise pursued outside the literary frame (Adorno cited in Jameson, 2004: 51). Adorno's concerns regarding the symbolic problems of representing revolution are, of course, compounded yet further by idea that 'the triumph of invested capital' provides 'the meaningful content of every film, whatever plot the production team may have selected' (Adorno and Horkheimer, 1944/1987: 124). Where these critics are at all optimistic is in suggesting new ways to approach our cultural output in order to uncover revolutionary sentiment hiding within them. In short, the only way to transcend the totalizing and distorting influence of invested capital – in the twenty-first century as in the mid-twentieth century – is to expose its contradictions and thereby to enlarge, via the partially suppressed voices in already existing texts, a robust and mobilizing politics.

Nixon's appeal for new representational forms is, at times, puzzling, especially given that the examples he goes on to explore – writing from across the globe in numerous formats – sketch a corpus which often explicitly unearths, or is at least deeply haunted by, what he calls 'a robust national memory of popular resistance to colonialism' and its more egregious environmental impacts (Nixon, 2011: 137). Given the availability of relevant material, to lament a perceived representational poverty with regard to environmental issues in contemporary culture is no longer a tenable position for literary critics. Such a situation invites an engagement less with how we represent climate change than with how we read narrative in a time of environmental anxiety. This approach is vital, moreover, in better establishing the value of literary and cultural criticism in a time when such activity is often overlooked in favour of more instrumentally rationalized interventions. In short, what is required is not merely 'good' or 'better' literature – that which, as Nixon argues, at least approaches a representational depth commensurate with climate change – but also the most appropriate hermeneutic with which to explore and better understand our existing cultural output, as well as the broader context of its production.

Maggie Gee has undertaken a number of explicit engagements with environmental issues in her work. In her early novel, *Grace* (1988), Gee explored the difficulty of taking direct action against the environmental dangers of nuclear energy; in *The Ice People* (1998) she depicted the impact and aftermath of abrupt climate change; in *The Flood* (2004) (the novel under examination in this chapter) her focus moved to that of a near-future London straining under the pressure of chronic flooding shortly before a devastating meteor impact. Despite an apparent appetite for the sensational aspects of environmental problems, *The Flood* – if read according to an updated representational hermeneutic appropriate to understanding contemporary climate change – can help us understand the sort of environmental problems with which we can and must engage; namely those, like climate change, which are slow to manifest and bound up in human activity. By juxtaposing sensational and non-anthropogenic forms of natural disaster (for example, the meteor) with socially embedded environmental problems, *The Flood* permits a confrontation with a real-world environmental discourse which often foregrounds the former at the expense of the latter. As I will demonstrate later, *The Flood* mirrors the problems of this real-world discourse in its literary form offering, on the one hand, a climate in the process of slow and creeping change and, on the other, the gripping sensation of an event 'external' to the production and influence of social relations. In doing so, *The Flood* deconstructs the idea of an unforgiving, extra-societal 'nature' to reveal environmental problems that are part of a vast environmental history in ceaseless motion, a history which humankind has helped (and continues in ever more substantial ways) to create.

The Flood's engagement with environmental problems as dynamic, historical processes has, crucially, implications beyond those pertaining to Gee's literary stature. Such characteristics make it much easier to engage in the type of reading offered here, one which goes beyond the text as an 'individual utterance' (Jameson, 1981: 85) to a consideration of the historical and social context in which *The Flood* was composed: principally, that of widening social inequalities in the early years of the twenty-first century and intensifying environmental threats. Making this move, I argue, is essential not only for understanding climate change as an anthropogenic phenomenon (as part of the environment we produce), but also for literary criticism in general, as a discipline which scrutinizes and, in turn, influences the stories we tell about ourselves, not least those concerning our engagement with the environment. The aim here is to offer a hermeneutic which gives one the ability to do two things: firstly, to see *The Flood* as a text which represents environmental history via its effects but also, secondly, to see that text as active within broader historical processes.

Marxism and Ecocriticism

The engagement with the kind of 'representational obstacles' Nixon identifies has a considerable legacy, one much older than the environmental discourse within which Nixon (and Gee) are often placed. In *Capital Vol. I*, Karl Marx (1867/1990) compares his own methodology of 'historical materialism' to the efforts of contemporary biologists (namely, Charles Darwin) to compile a 'natural history', a project Marx believed to be far more ambitious than his own. 'Natural history', Marx claims, makes definitive recourse to abstraction because it is not history we have 'made'. As such, natural history excludes 'the historical process'; that is, one which 'lays bare [...] the production of [...] social relations' (Marx, 1867/1990: 493). Marx's understanding of history – as a process in which humans are dialectally intertwined – is the one that I am interested in exploring in this chapter. As Marx (1852/1972: 10) famously wrote, people 'make their own history, but [...] not under self-selected circumstances'. In doing so, Marx offered a way to collapse the vexing opposition of 'produced' human and 'received' natural histories into an inclusive, ecological analysis; one capable of considering forces acting on us from the past, as well as our active production of all subsequent history.

As the physical sciences have developed, and awareness increases as to the extent of our own far-reaching influence (a paradigm Bill McKibben [2003] describes as 'the end of nature'), the methodological gap between human and natural historiography has narrowed. This development is perhaps most evident in the environmental sciences where a consistently high priority has been to describe the consequences of, in Marx's words (1867/1990: 493), 'the active relation of man to nature'. Indeed, there have already been robust attempts to bring the disciplines of natural and human historiography together. Jason W. Moore (2012: 227, emphasis in original), for example, argues for a '[move] from the "environmental history *of*" modernity, to capitalism "*as* environmental history"', where we move from seeing capitalism as *having* 'an ecological regime' to seeing it *as* 'a world-ecological regime – joining the accumulation of capital and the production of nature as an organic whole'. Timothy Morton, too (along with numerous others), has argued for the pressing need to move beyond a dualistic conception of nature and society – literally, as his book's title suggests, an *Ecology without Nature* (2007) – if we are seriously to address the problems which underpin environmental crises like climate change. Surmounting the 'representational obstacles' of phenomena like climate change, then, requires not only an ability to represent our 'natural' and cultural history as coterminous and co-constitutive but, more urgently, an ability to *read* that history. This is where I believe literary criticism currently finds its most urgent function and necessity.

The Flood and the 'political unconscious'

In *The Political Unconscious* (1981), Fredric Jameson writes (1981: 28) that the main issue for Marxist criticism remains 'the representation of History itself', where history, whether 'natural' or 'cultural,' is understood as 'fundamentally non-narrative and nonrepresentational' (Jameson, 1981: 82). This apparently self-defeating – though, in reality, supremely rigorous – approach to historiography marks a crucial point of intersection between environmentalists and historical materialists today. Such a vision is valuable only if, like Jameson, we understand that 'history is not a text, not a narrative, master or otherwise' but that, nonetheless, it is 'inaccessible to us except in textual form' (Jameson, 1981: 35). For Jameson (1981: 20) the primary object for literary analysis is that which provides a glimpse of what Marx called 'concrete history', by 'restoring to the surface of the text the repressed and buried reality' of class struggle. If climate change, as a phenomenon occurring within history, currently evades representation in the ways Nixon has outlined, one option is to look at how it is already (mis)represented 'in textual form'. Contemporary narratives of all kinds (not just those explicitly about climate change) can thus be read as 'mythic resolutions of issues [like climate change] that [we] are unable to articulate conceptually' (Jameson, 1981: 79). An awareness of narrative's capacity to '[invent] imaginary or formal "solutions" to unresolvable social contradictions' (Jameson, 1981: 79, 102), argues Jameson, pushes one into an encounter with an expansive conception of history (and ecology), which 'refuses' simplification. As far as comprehending current environmental conditions demands understanding, as Jameson (1981: 101, 19) puts it, 'why what happened [...] had to happen the way it did', both environmentalists and historical materialists seek to engage in historical enquiry in order to retrieve 'the essential mystery of the cultural [and, I argue, environmental] past'.

Jameson's theory of the 'political unconscious' is not, it must be stressed, entirely fit for purpose within environmental literary criticism (or 'ecocriticism'). Environmental discourses have developed significantly since the publication of *The Political Unconscious* in 1981 and many aspects of Marxism and environmentalism remain at odds.[1] Chief among these would be the unwitting exclusion from Jameson's (1981: 20) concept of a 'single vast unfinished plot', of not only the human-felt consequences of an increasingly unstable and toxic environment, but also the non-human animals, plants, and even non-living ecological phenomena (nutrient cycles, mineral deposits, and other geological features) whose continued existence within the environment is also under threat. The aim of a Marxist environmentalism, in short, is to argue that instances of environmental injustice result from the same conditions of inequality, exploitation, and oppression as instances of class injustice, and to find evidence for this in narrative. Ecocriticism has not thus far either adequately demonstrated this type of interconnectivity, or even consistently aspired to promote it as a critical priority. As Joshua Dolezal (2008: 12) suggests, many western writers 'have not addressed the story [of the connections between global poor and environmental damage] in their own work, focusing instead on what he calls 'the preservation of roadless areas and wildlife refuges'. Indeed, it has been further suggested that 'pretending to isolate the environment [from social issues] ... has severely limited the appeal of environmentalist thought' (De Loughrey et al., 2005: 27). This chapter is accordingly an attempt to bring together an ecocritical focus and Jameson's theory of the political unconscious that will not only 'update' Jameson's theory and demonstrate its applicability in ecocritical directions, but also help to address some of the shortcomings and contradictions which have hampered ecocriticism to date.

As writers like Nixon (2011: 5) eloquently demonstrate, environmental and social connections are invariably inscrutable, presenting 'the writer-activist' with a 'challenge of visibility'. As Jameson (1981: 40, 95) himself sees it, 'social life is in its fundamental reality one and indivisible, a seamless web, a single inconceivable and transindividual process'; one 'crisscrossed and intersected by a variety of impulses from contradictory modes of cultural production all at once'. Jameson's method for realizing such a critique begins by envisaging 'a series of enlarging theoretical horizons' that would guide the analysis 'toward one particular order of textual phenomena' (Jameson, 1981: 91, 71). The analysis that follows in this chapter reflects Jameson's (1981: 102) approach by rehearsing a general movement from individual text to the 'untranscendable horizon' of the text in the context of its historical production. Such an approach achieves the ideal situation, as Jameson (1981: 45) puts it, of 'the idea of textual production' as one that 'helps us break the reifying habit of thinking of a given narrative as an object, or as a unified whole, or as a static structure'. Jameson's political unconscious invites us, therefore, to challenge the habits of cognition that keep us returning to the kind of synchronic analyses which either see climate change as not happening, as an inevitability, or as actively desirable as a means to provide a cleansing moment – much like the '[s]omething massive, sexual, final' (*TF*, 57) that Lola and Gracie anticipate in the computer-simulated image of a tidal wave. Seen through the political unconscious, climate change can be apprehended, in contrast, as *happening everywhere now*, and being inextricably bound up in social relations.

The Political Unconscious I: The Political Horizon

The Flood's many characters and convoluted storylines are spun in a slowly accumulating complexity, set against a backdrop of social inequality and looming environmental crises. The flooding, in particular, provides the lens through which we view all these lives, each affected in unique ways – sometimes almost imperceptibly, though at others severely – as whole communities such as those in 'the Towers' (*TF*, 21) are left to cope in whatever way they can. As its title suggests, *The Flood*'s chief focus is the impact of the flooding as it begins to shape what Adeline Johns-Putra and Adam Trexler (2011: 196) call the 'inner and outer lives' of its protagonists. As Johns-Putra and Trexler continue (2011: 190), one of the few critical engagements with the novel to date (Dillon, 2007) does not focus on climate change, but reads the text instead 'as a response to the events of September 11' (Dillon, 2007: 374). Though climate change indeed looms large over *The Flood*'s storyline, it is never mentioned as such; however, as I will go on to explore in later sections, this provides a depressingly accurate portrayal of climate change in popular discourse, especially the muted nature of reporting on it in the mainstream media (Hulme, 2009; Specter, 2009).

The first horizon of analysis within Jameson's (1981: 76) political unconscious positions the 'object of study' as an 'individual literary work or utterance' to be considered purely as a 'symbolic act'. Viewed as just such an individual utterance, *The Flood*'s chief motif is the localized preoccupations of its various characters. Overwhelmingly, the themes of these preoccupations concern negative emotions – particularly feelings of loneliness, alienation, confusion, misunderstanding and loss, repeatedly dramatized in the disharmonious and dysfunctional interaction of its numerous characters. The first character to appear in the novel is May, both widowed and retired. Her experience is exemplary of this kind of isolation. Events of recent years have torn May's family apart: her son Dirk is sent to prison for murdering his sister's brother-in-law and her husband dies shortly afterward (the events which form the central narrative of Gee's earlier 2002 novel, *The White Family*). The result is an abrupt end to communication between the respective family members. With her husband and son-in-law, Winston, dead and Dirk in prison, May is left alone, eventually ceasing her visits to see her son altogether because 'Dirk barely talked to her' when there and 'never replied' to her letters (*TF*, 179–80).

Dirk, too, seems resolutely isolated, atomized, and deeply frustrated by his lifelong inability to connect with anything, despite long feeling 'that he wanted something, he wanted anything [...] it was like hunger, pressing him on' (*TF*, 24). Immediately after his release from prison, Dirk turns to religion joining the millennial 'One Way' group, where he is 'accepted at last', though only because 'no one actually turned him away' (*TF*, 25). A similar loneliness characterizes Moira, a one-time literary critic, who finally abandons her six-year project on author Angela Lamb to join the same religious group as Dirk. During Angela and Moira's first meeting in years it is clear that author and critic 'hated each other' (*TF*, 62) and the book will never be published. The meeting soon erupts into a full-blown confrontation, with Angela detecting 'something new in the scale of hostility', and ends with Moira 'shrieking' scripture in prophesy '"that everything on earth shall perish"' (*TF*, 67). Her prophesying has no apparent effect on those around her beyond the momentary startled concern of onlookers; the hustle and bustle of early evening London life soon resumes (*TF*, 68). Moira's disquieting behaviour, we are led to believe, is the product of some form of mental illness, into which she stumbles ever further, 'alone, unaccommodated' (*TF*, 145).

Much like Moira's shrieking, political messages are regularly delivered in *The Flood* through faltering and (sometimes) alienating (that is, messianic, sensational, or fanatical) ways. Lottie's daughter, Lola, for example, and her friend, Gracie, repeatedly garble their anti-capitalist messages, at one point misspelling a political slogan (*TF*, 238). Ian, a satirical painter, is also rarely understood – when he asks Lola and Gracie what they think of his painting lampooning the guests at a lavish 'Gala' event organized by the government to distract its citizens from the foreign war that it is waging, they fail to make the connection between 'his picture of a troupe of monkeys, capering across the stage, grinning' and the celebrities gathered for the event (*TF*, 237–8). This difficulty is perhaps more acutely felt by the most desperate and marginalized in society. At the same event, a protester is described holding up a sign saying 'NO HOME. NO MONEY. NO HOPE' (*TF*, 234). While no one registers her presence, the protester is similarly unable to relate to anyone else, and has perhaps an exaggerated impression of the true extent of the surrounding guests' wealth and happiness:

> She *thinks* that the people invited to the Gala must all have nice homes, and hope and money, she *believes* they are smiling, not just for the cameras [...] but at themselves, in invisible mirrors that whisper to them what their lives amount to; theirs are enormous, hers is nothing (*TF*, 234–5, emphasis added).

Though the protestor is not necessarily mistaken regarding the Gala's display of wealth, she is unable to imagine the alienation and isolation that nonetheless afflicts the lives of all *The Flood*'s characters.

The Political Unconscious II: The Social Horizon

In the words of Hans-Georg Gadamer (1960/2006: 304), Jameson's theoretical precursor for his concept of 'horizons' in *The Political Unconscious*, '[to] acquire a horizon means that one learns to look beyond what is close at hand – not in order to look away from it but to see it better, within a larger whole and in truer proportion'. In the second Jamesonian horizon of our hermeneutic for reading *The Flood* we apprehend this 'larger whole' by re-encountering the disharmony experienced by the novel's characters as part of that same 'single vast unfinished plot' of class antagonisms, revealing what Jameson describes (1981: 42) as 'structural oppositions and contradictions' inherent in any given mode of production. *The Flood's* presentation of social relations are, fittingly, antagonistic; that is, as Jameson understands it, 'two opposing discourses [fighting] it out within the general unity of a shared code' (Jameson, 1981: 84). The narrative of *The Flood* repeatedly highlights these antagonisms, moving discursively through its diverse cast to reveal a community of stark inequality. A key figure in this dynamic is the affluent, middle-aged Lottie, completely oblivious to the relative hardship endured by poorer demographics, let alone poverty's historical contingency. The degree of Lottie's obliviousness is both ridiculous and ridiculed in Gee's third-person narrative presentation: at one point Lottie muses that '[t]he Tower-dwellers did keep making a fuss, but life had definitely been worse for her' (*TF*, 95).

Crucially, the plot of *The Flood* goes beyond 'class' in the traditional sense of a socio-economic designation. Many Marxists, including Jameson himself, anticipated this need to extend an understanding of 'class antagonism' to various other identifiable oppositions within society. 'Sexism and the patriarchal,' Jameson (1981: 99) suggests:

are to be grasped as the sedimentation and the virulent survival of forms of alienation specific to the oldest mode of production of human history, with its division of labor between men and women, and its division of power between youth and elder. (Jameson, 1981: 99)

The Flood, in turn, presents a comprehensive range of oppositional relationships. Discrimination on the basis of race and sexual orientation is perhaps best represented by Dirk, who has already served time for murdering Winston, whom he describes as 'the pansy fucking brother of [his sister's] black boyfriend', Elroy (*TF*, 24). Dirk's very opposition is framed as a violent and ugly opposition to difference, one we are encouraged to see as a misplaced utopian impulse to resolve antagonisms. Dirk's vision of heaven is a nightmarish purgatory, 'a mount of blood and gold and glory, a place where his enemies will burn like straw' (*TF*, 23).

Each set of antagonisms plays a crucial role in describing a view of social life as 'crisscrossed and intersected by a variety of impulses' (Jameson, 1981: 95). Such impulses, it is clear, are not limited to those of 'class' in the narrow sense; rather, they are 'the sedimentation and the virulent survival of forms of alienation', which afflict almost every sphere of life (Jameson, 1981: 99). Despite the proliferation of antagonisms among, and between, its characters we rarely see any outward confrontation regarding the problems which cause these inequalities, least of all over the novel's most visible symptom of a dysfunctional mode of production; that is, the rampant capitalist degradation of the environment which, it is implied, is responsible for the flooding. Instead, a social discourse of denial pervades the severity of the floods, as well as an active readiness to accept at face value any sign or claim that the floods are abating. On the day of the Gala, for example, despite significant evidence to the contrary this readiness to accept the narrative of 'recovery' is obvious. As Gee's omniscient narrator states: 'probably not much was different today, except the sun and the government statement. But that was all they needed: hope' (*TF*, 198). It is a strong force, matched only by the accompanying effort to conceal the impact of the floods. 'Soldiers had been working for seventy two hours', we are told, 'and the worst of the mud had been jetted off the buildings, scrubbed off the kerbs' (*TF*, 199).

Despite collective denial, disaster lingers insistently at the edges of the novel's presentation of renewed optimism. Indeed, the citywide credulity concerning recovery complements earlier failures to communicate effectively, borne along by the impulses of 'a city recovering from chaos, a city eager to be normal again' (*TF*, 213). However, the assertions that the city 'has been reclaimed from the edge of disaster' (*TF*, 214) are chillingly undermined, for, we are told, '[a]t six p.m., the end would begin' (*TF*, 216). Not all characters, it has to be said, are entirely confident of recovery. At a swimming pool a couple worry over rumours that 'they're shutting down the city pools ...There's talk about some virus, too. And people are saying it's waterborn'" (*TF*, 224). Prompted by this rumour incredulity resurfaces: "'But the floods are over [...] That's why they've gone ahead with the Gala'" (*TF*, 224).

The Gala is indeed a fitting focus for *The Flood*'s handling of concealed antagonisms as a set piece of political misdirection, the city and national government 'knowing a show was what they needed' (*TF*, 200). For the Gala is not just a distraction from the flooding, but also from many other forms of social conflict. The event is a tour de force of wilful decadence and ignorance – '[o]nly the *crème de la crème* have been chosen, the people the city defines itself by, the rich, the celebrities, the people who count' (*TF*, 235, emphasis in original) – an attempt to mythologize social inequality. In spite of itself, the event is as much characterized by the people it excludes as by those to whom it actively allows entry. Our attention in drawn, for example, to the significance of the claim that 'everyone was there' (*TF*, 242) by, only pages later, the admission by Gee's narrator that of course 'so many of the city's people weren't there. The builders' labourers, the rat-catchers ...the hospital auxiliaries, the midwives' (*TF*, 245). Far from achieving a successful glossing over of difference and disharmony, the Gala acts as an amplification of the city's problems. Dysfunctional communication at the level of character is mirrored by a social discourse unable to handle and confront the sheer magnitude of unfolding environmental and social crises. Applying Jameson's (1981: 79) terms, we can read the Gala as one of our 'mythic resolutions of issues [like climate change] that [we] are unable to articulate conceptually'.

The Political Unconscious III: The Historical Horizon

While Jameson is interested in 'mythic' (rather than real-world) resolutions, his ultimate aim is not to argue for the unresolvable nature of social antagonisms, but rather, in Gadamer's (1960/2006: 304) terms, 'to look beyond what is close at hand' to the widest possible horizon of interpretation: he identifies this as 'history', that is, 'the ultimate ground as well as the untranscendable limit of our understanding' (Jameson, 1981: 100). Insofar as it is an *inclusive* analysis, environmental research provides a fitting accompaniment to a Marxist historical methodology as an approach, as the ecologist Barry Commoner (1972: 33) famously put it, which understands that 'everything is connected to everything else'.

In contrast to its broad social sweep, *The Flood*'s action is geographically confined to one city: London (although it is never named as such). While the resolution *The Flood* moves towards is one of localized social harmony, this movement takes place against the backdrop of global environmental crises, which dwarf the concerns of individuals and nations. The physical environment of *The Flood* becomes, as Jameson (1981: 210) would call it, a 'privileged place of the strategy of containment' for highlighting both environmental and geopolitical dynamics less easy to identify at the surface level of the text. *The Flood*'s environmental and geopolitical backdrop nonetheless struggles to contain the 'shared codes' (Jameson, 1981: 84) of ideological narratives such as nationhood and class. The Gala, for example, projects an image of an event that 'everyone' (*TF*, 242) will attend. Yet, ultimately, as the narrator concedes, '[s]o many of the city's people weren't there [...] Actually, most of the world isn't here' (*TF*, 245–7).

As the work of various Marxist ecologists have argued, a truly ecological analysis is incompatible with thinking about geographical locales in isolation.[2] As writers such as Neil Smith, Jason W. Moore, and Jameson himself have pointed out, it is via an understanding of space (as much as – or even more so than – 'history') that the most subversive politics emerges. Indeed, some of the most politically charged moments in Gee's novel are those that gesture towards what Moore describes (2003: 434) as, a 'geographical division of labor', through which an oppressed or marginalized global majority begins to affect and disrupt the political realism of *The Flood*'s capitalist world system. For example, the descriptions of the '[p]rotests in Varna where a massive new dam was said to be threatening the whole coastline [...] Eco-protesters envisaged tidal waves, global disaster, millions drowned' (*TF*, 57), echo the manifold and dynamic (though often overlooked) sites of resistance around environmentally 'destructive hydrological regimes' (Nixon, 2011: 171) from across the globe. In their turn, *The Flood*'s depictions of resistance from the periphery are not easily visible, half-manifesting at the margins of the text in muddled or discontinued conversations. Davey (a television astronomer) tells Lola and Gracie: '"There are real things to worry about, you know, girls. The war, for example. The floods, for another"' (*TF*, 86). As Davey himself soon discovers, however, successfully identifying the 'real things to worry about' remains an ongoing and elusive prize. Upon learning about the imminent meteor impact, for example, Davey is noticeably troubled by his previous complacency, exclaiming '"if this object hits [...] there will be massive tsunamis [...] ironically just as our programme predicts. But this time it's real. It's serious. Thousands of people will die on the coasts"' (*TF*, 283).

Of course, no character in *The Flood* really knows what is happening. Indeed, the more sensational forms of environmental threat – not least the meteor impact itself or the threat of astronomical 'Planetary Pile-up' (*TF*, 180) – work against attempts to uncover a history of the destructive aspects of 'the active relation of man to nature' (Marx, 1867/1990: 493), namely, the socially embedded environmental threat of the floods. As Jameson's theory (1981: 217) suggests, an 'ostensible or manifest "theme" of the novel is no more to be taken at face value than is the dreamer's immediate waking sense of what the dream was about'. Unearthing the political unconscious in a literary text, it must be emphasized, is in no way intended pre-emptively to condemn engagements with text or history to failure, rather, it is suggested precisely in order 'to resist [the] thematization or reification [of history]' and its 'transformation back into one optional code among others' (Jameson, 1981: 101). Jameson's aim is for readers to grasp history as ongoing, a dynamic and irreducible process, what he describes elsewhere – as I have already mentioned above – as 'a seamless web, a single inconceivable and transindividual process' (Jameson, 1981: 40).

As a number of commentators have observed, the process of history is one that is readable not only in written narrative but, concurrently, in the landscape around us.[3] The distribution of environmental benefits and burdens is, as studies of post-industrial landscapes have consistently uncovered, never equal. 'The real patterns of uneven development', Neil Smith (2010: 50) writes, should be seen to reside in 'the unity of capital, rather than [...] the false ideological dualism of society and nature'. The landscape presented in *The Flood* is accordingly a conspicuously 'produced' (Smith, 2010: 66) one (to borrow Smith's suggestive term), which we glimpse as the 'warm coral stain of the human animal', and which characteristically forms 'long grids of light' stretching out '[a]ll over the world' (*TF*, 89). And though this human 'coral stain' may *appear* ubiquitous – '[e]astward, southward, there are no more gardens. Every scrap of land has a building on it' (*TF*, 16) – it is one which manifests in sadly uneven ways. The overdevelopment of alluvial land to which this passage makes reference has relevance not only to the numerous environmental problems which result from such activity (flooding, water contamination, disease transmission, and so on) but also the concentration of the poor (historically confined to the southern and eastern areas of the city) within those now environmentally vulnerable areas. Areas of the city 'where people were poor', (*TF*, 22) moreover, are presented repeatedly as ecologically (as well as economically) barren – council estates and tower-blocks rise 'above the earth like a forest of dead trees' (*TF*, 22). *The Flood* reproduces in its topography a comprehensive imbrication of environmental and social deprivation.

More affluent people, conversely, are shown in the novel to be comparatively free from these risks, but disproportionately responsible for polluting behaviour. In a rare confrontation, Shirley's cleaner, Faith, complains that "'car drivers'" have "'more money than sense [...] whizzing round polluting everything'" (*TF*, 26). Altercations of this sort are infrequent in *The Flood*; more commonly, Gee's readers are merely shown the uneven distribution of environmental benefits and burdens and left to connect the dots. Like the polluting 'plane engine [that] gnawed like a distant headache' (*TF*, 32), these concerns remain banal and remote, part of those social and political antagonisms kept from immediate resolution by the distances that exist between their (often unwitting) antagonists. These distances, moreover, are as much conceptual as spatial: ecological literacy, when revealed in the novel, is pointedly arcane and difficult. A notable example of this esotericism comes via the character Harold, Lottie's husband, while he considers the temporal nature of 'simultaneity':

> [Events] Going on for ever, now, now, all across the planet [...] and even at this instant, as he lay on the floor [...] great events were breaking, somewhere else, people were burning, people were laughing, soldiers were marching across the desert, little children were learning to swim, lives were being changed for ever – and there were the ants, the bower-birds, the lizards, *the intricate cross hatchings of a thousand other species* (*TF*, 205–6, emphasis added).

The passage is perhaps the most poised and insightful in *The Flood*, certainly the one that moves most consciously and calmly towards a robust ecological understanding. It is not panic which grips Harold here, but rather a measured appreciation of the vastness of ecological interconnection. The passage, too, reflects Jameson's (1981: 95) own lucid vision of history as a spatiotemporally interconnected web, 'crisscrossed and intersected by a variety of impulses'. Just like Jameson, Harold's vision is presented as the basis from which one can engage with the world, rather than engendering political aporia. While undoubtedly insightful, other encounters with the produced environment in the novel are not always presented in such measured terms as Harold's, reminding us that ecological literacy does not result automatically from *looking* at environmental despoilment. May, for example, staring into the flood waters, has the disturbing impression that things:

> moved beneath the surface like sea monsters [...] perhaps they were only rotting car-tyres, but they looked black and slimy and warm and alive.
> What had she ever understood? What did she know about the world? [...] Suddenly May felt she knew nothing at all (*TF*, 190)

Shortly after this passage May meets Jehangir, a proponent of the 'One Way' religious group, and has an exhilarating discussion about faith. The syncretic harmony and possibility of heavenly absolution which religion apparently offers May leaves her feeling suddenly that 'life is wonderful' (*TF*, 193). The juxtaposition of these two encounters is demonstrative of the gulf between the kind of cognitive challenge of confronting and positioning oneself within the reality of a 'produced' ecosystem (which elicits an existential panic in May) versus the immediate allure of externally (and divinely) managed resolution. Indeed, *difficulty* becomes the shared quality of all these encounters, in a way that highlights the central challenges of environmental interventions in general. Bill McKibben (2003: 97) describes this feeling as the 'loneliness' of a world without external nature, which, when disaster strikes, is manifested to us as a mere 'subset of human activity'. Like the sea monsters May thinks she sees, this created aspect of the environment conjures feelings of the uncanny, but also of despair.

The difficulty of characters achieving an ecological cognition in *The Flood*, then, has urgent political implications. In a key scene with the Prime Minister, Mr Bliss, the manipulation of environmental ideology for political ends is given direct thematization. The scene centres around the discussion of Middle Eastern terror threats and provides another example of the entanglement of a difficult-to-assimilate but maddening insistence of environmental and geopolitical problems in the novel. Mr Bliss's cartoonish aspiration to destroy terror threats at their source is sardonically undermined when one advisor observes: "'We've been bombing them for years [...] it hasn't made them any nicer'" (*TF*, 38). The environmental threat posed by the flooding (the novel's faintly – though relentlessly – articulated emblem of anthropogenic climate change) poses a similar problem for the politicians to that of the terrorists, as threats which those in power know will be difficult to handle if allowed to manifest with any degree of complexity. The confrontation with the lived reality of environmental decline brings with it the threat of civil unrest. "'If the rains continue,'" another advisor warns "'we [will] have to do something. The people are restless around the Towers'" (*TF*, 38). In its place, therefore, Mr Bliss moves to construct a simple and distracting narrative: the "'common enemy'" (*TF*, 38) of the terrorist. The pursuit of such political misdirection is given its due historical context. Mr Bliss, 'his eyes [...] bright,' gleefully anticipates that '[s]omething enormous was going to happen': in his words a "'Historic opportunity'" (*TF*, 38) to reify (as Jameson would say) environmental and geopolitical problems. The scene is key, setting up a troubling precedent for the simplified direction in which popular understandings of the environment can be manipulated. Indeed, despite direct experience of environmental decline, many are shown to be only too willing to accept this narrative of 'business as usual':

> Trapped motorists listened to their radios; more rains predicted; demonstrations in the south and the east, where the populace claimed they were being neglected, their basements left flooded, their drains left blocked. Business as usual. They sighed and switched off (*TF*, 81).

As well as the hints here of a jaded acceptance of environmental injustices visited upon a 'neglected populace', the passage is interesting more for its juxtaposition with the description of 'the end of the world spectacular'; a two-hour special TV show which Lottie's son, Davey (the TV astronomer), will present, covering the unique astronomical event in which the planets 'were due to line up in the heavens' (*TF*, 82). In contrast to the slow violence of the floods described above, the 'Planetary Pile-up' threat is presented in morbidly lurid terms. The 'repercussions,' we hear, 'could be cataclysmic. The footage, [the] producer promised would be stunning. "Hope you're as excited about this as we are"' (*TF*, 82). Through the juxtaposition of the two scenes there emerges, in short, a major discrepancy between the experience of environmental burdens and spectacular conceptions of natural disasters. This discrepancy haunts Davey, who 'in some humble, deeply buried part of him, believed in truth, and accuracy [... but] lived in a world that preferred entertainment' (*TF*, 83). Fittingly, this is a predicament which *The Flood* itself goes on to rehearse in its own resolution.

Resolution and Conclusions

The Flood appears to use what is effectively a tragic composition: the follies of humankind reduced to nought by a cosmic indifference; the many antagonisms that the novel develops are summarily swept away by the motiveless and amoral energy force of a 'natural' disaster in its final chapters. That is, until one notes the framing of the novel as a whole; that is, the preamble and the coda of semi-paradisiacal reunification in which these antagonisms and frustrations (which abound in the novel proper) dissolve: 'No one is mad here, no one is angry' (*TF*, 323). The tone of the novel's final passage is relentlessly (and ironically, we must assume) utopic: it is the 'place of perpetual summer' (*TF*, 322) where all the principal characters 'are as they wish. All they ever hoped to be' (*TF*, 324).[4] The irony is a delicious one, for what is this resolution but what Jameson would call (1981: 83) an 'intolerable [ideological] closure'? From the perspective of the political unconscious it stands as a conspicuous reminder that, of course, everything is *not* alright – at least in the world which we currently inhabit – a world in which the prevailing trend is one that better fits Rob Nixon's (2011: 2) description of 'slow violence' discussed above: indifference or confusion in the face of an incrementally rising intensity of environmental and social crises.

The Flood's opening is perhaps even more significant, though, than its ending. Like the final scene, the 'Before' passage which begins the novel adopts an apocalyptic perspective, speaking from the point of view of total revelation. 'I am going to tell you how it happened,' (*TF*, 7) declare the opening lines, before going on to describe the setting: a place 'which holds all times and places' (*TF*, 7). Like the end, the novel's opening appears to be the fantastical realization of a transcendental view of history, where one can see the 'whole of the road, stretching out forever, before, behind' (*TF*, 9). It is, in this sense, reminiscent of Jameson's (1981: 101) straightforward description of historical materialism as an attempt to understand 'why what happened [...] had to happen the way it did.' Like Jameson, *The Flood* (whether by design or not) cannot conceal that the attainment of such an understanding is impossible, with the simple difference that it does this indirectly via its formal resolution. For *The Flood's* apocalypse does not bring a cleansing moment, only death; and its paradisiacal coda is jarring and tellingly unconvincing in its saccharine neatness. The only reliable constant is the slow, creeping violence, as the book's title suggests, of the flood, one manifested in both the environmental and social injustices that afflict its characters.

The basis of *The Flood's* political resonance, I argue, is much like the one identified by Jameson in his analysis of Conrad; that is:

> [the] unplanned harmony between this textual dynamic and its specific historical content: the emergence of capitalism as just such an always-already-begun dynamic, as the supreme and privileged mystery of a synchronic system. (Jameson, 1981: 280)

Climate change, as I have argued, is often in danger of being perceived as an 'always-already-begun-dynamic,' received by us as a 'reified force' (Jameson, 1981: 102) we could not possibly hope to contest. In reality, climate change, much like capitalism, is a contingent phenomenon, a mere symptom of a *longue-durée* process within, and alongside, which we have sought (with increasing zeal) to extract what Marx (1894/1967: 745) calls the 'free gift of Nature to capital'. Although capital accumulation on these terms, as environmentalists have been saying for decades, has become unsustainable, it is not (lest we forget) inevitable.

The Flood does a lot to set up a fruitful engagement with anthropogenic and accretive environmental problems, invariably in complex interdependency with a comprehensive range of social antagonisms. *The Flood*'s handling of social and environmental contradiction, however, works in stark contrast to its paradisiacal resolution, one which can be read as a conspicuous attempt to repress in its aesthetic form the complexity of a historical and anthropogenic climate change. This juxtaposition is spectacular in its rehearsal of the operation of ideology within environmental discourses offering, with one hand, a stark tableau of social and environmental problems and, with the other, a sensational embodiment of environmental phenomena as 'reified force[s]' (Jameson, 1981: 102). This reading is, it must be stressed, immanent within, rather than a patent feature of, *The Flood*. As I have argued earlier, Jameson's political unconscious has functioned here as that 'indispensable instrument for revealing those logical and ideological centers a particular historical text fails to realize' (Jameson, 1981: 49). This is not to suggest that *The Flood* is worthy of opprobrium for 'failing to realise' the anthropogenic logic of climate change; instead, we might argue that enacting symbolic resolution is all narrative is capable of doing. The political unconscious is thus invoked here as 'the indispensable instrument' for helping us to comprehend the political import of *The Flood*'s particular resolution.

The search for the political unconscious is not exclusively the preserve of literary criticism. Discourse around the environment in general must be examined in similar ways for signs of history being apprehended not in its observable effects (as climate change deserves to be understood) but as a reifying and depoliticizing force. The attempt to understand, let alone retrieve, these 'submerged stories of injustice' (Nixon, 2011: 280), is (as I hope I have not understated) an extremely difficult task, not least because these are problems to which only a collective response is appropriate. Nonetheless, the germ of this response is already visible across the globe, from the most concerned of our writers to the burgeoning resistance gathering at the periphery of the capitalist world system.[5] In ever more compelling ways, our literary engagements with climate change should be directed towards alerting new generations of social actors to the co-constitutive relationship between ourselves and the environment. In doing so, we expose where possible attempts to deny our collective agency, and provide a robust theoretical grounding for collective action aimed at altering and mitigating our currently unsustainable mode of production.

Notes

1. Recent developments in Ecocriticism have reflected an effort to redress this shortfall beginning with Newman (2002) though more recently with Banerjee (2008), Mukherjee (2010), Nixon (2011), Biro (2011) and Szeman (2012).
2. See, for example, Harvey (2001), Moore (2003, 2012), and Smith (2010).
3. For example, Lefebvre (1991), Harvey (2001), Smith (2010), and Wallerstein (2011).
4. See Adam Welstead's essay in this collection for an extended discussion of *The Flood* in relation to the traditions, and contemporary manifestations, of utopian and dystopian thinking and literature.
5. Agroecological groups like La Via Campesina and the Landless Workers's Movement (Portuguese: *Movimento dos Trabalhadores Sem Terra*, or MST) have enjoyed considerable success in mobilizing many millions of millions of the world's rural poor against environmental injustices (among other things), though also of note are groups like 350.org, who via their Go Fossil Free: Divest from Fossil Fuels! campaign have successfully coordinated acts of synchronized civil disobedience in over 180 countries. Instrumental in this effort have been the various so-called 'writer-activists' – such as Bill McKibben, Rob Nixon, Vandana Shiva, Arundhati Roy, and Chris Hedges – who continue to write about and (often) directly participate in the campaigns organized by such groups.

Works Cited

Adorno, Theodor and Horkheimer, Max (1944/1987) *Dialectic of Enlightenment*, trans. John Cumming. New York: Continuum.

Banerjee, Subhabrata (2008) 'Necrocapitalism', *Organisation Studies* 29: 1541–63.

Biro, Andrew (ed.) (2011) *Critical Ecologies the Frankfurt School and Contemporary Environmental Crises*. Toronto: University of Toronto Press.

Clark, Timothy (2011) *Literature and the Environment*. Cambridge: Cambridge University Press.

Commoner, Barry (1972) *The Closing Circle*. London: Cape.

DeLoughrey, Elizabeth et al. (2005) *Caribbean Literature and the Environment*. Charlottesville: University Of Virginia Press.

Dillon, Sarah (2007) 'Imagining Apocalypse: Maggie Gee's *The Flood*', *Contemporary Literature* 48(3): 374–97.

Dolezal, Joshua A. (2008) 'Literary Activism, Social Justice, and the Future of Bioregionalism', *Ethics & the Environment* 13(1): 1–22.

Glass, Rodge (2013) 'Global Warning: The Rise of "Cli-fi"', *The Guardian*, 31 May, URL (consulted September 2014): http://www.theguardian.com/books/2013/may/31/global-warning-rise-cli-fi.

Gadamer, Hans-Georg (1960/2006) *Truth and Method*, trans. Joel Weinsheimer and Donald G. Marshall. London: Continuum.

Harvey, David (2001) *Spaces of Capital: Towards a Critical Geography*. Edinburgh: Edinburgh University Press.

Hulme, Mike (2009) *Why We Disagree About Climate Change*. Cambridge: Cambridge University Press.

Jameson, Fredric (1981) *The Political Unconscious*. Ithaca, NY: Cornell University Press.

Jameson, Fredric (2004) 'The Politics of Utopia', *New Left Review* 25: 35–54.

Johns-Putra, Adeline and Trexler, Adam (2011) 'Climate Change in Literature and Literary Criticism', *WIREs Climate Change* 2: 185–200.

Kerridge, Richard (2013) 'Ecocriticsm', *Year's Work Critical and Cultural Theory* 21(1): 345–74.

Lefebvre, Henri (1991) *The Production of Space*. Oxford: Blackwell.

MacFarlane, Robert (2005) 'The Burning Question', *Guardian*, 24 September, URL (consulted September 2014): http://www.theguardian.com/books/2005/sep/24/featuresreviews.guardianreview29.

McKibben, Bill (2003) *The End of Nature*. London: Bloomsbury.

Marx, Karl (1894/1967) *Capital: A Critique of Political Economy, Vol. III*, ed. Frederick Engels. New York: International Publishers.

Marx, Karl (1852/1972) *The Eighteenth Brumaire of Louis Bonaparte*, trans. Progress Publishers. Moscow: Progress Publishers.

Marx, Karl (1867/1990) *Capital: A Critique of Political Economy, Vol. I*, trans. Ben Fowkes. London: Penguin.

Moore, Jason W. (2003) 'Capitalism as World-Ecology: Braudel and Marx on Environmental History', *Organization & Environment* 16(4): 431–58.

Moore, Jason W. (2012) 'Cheap Food & Bad Money: Food, Frontiers, and Financialization in the Rise and Demise of Neoliberalism', *Review: A Journal of the Fernand Braudel Center* 33(2–3): 225–61.

Morton, Timothy (2007) *Ecology without Nature*. Cambridge, MA: Harvard University Press.

Mukherjee, Upamanyu Pablo (2010) *Postcolonial Environments: Nature, Culture and the Contemporary Indian Novel in English*. Basingstoke: Palgrave Macmillan.

Newman, Lance (2002) 'Marxism and Ecocriticism', *Interdisciplinary Studies in Literature and Environment* 9(2): 1–25.

Nixon, Rob (2011) *Slow Violence and the Environmentalism of the Poor*. Cambridge, MA: Harvard.

Smith, Neil (2010) *Uneven Development*. London: Verso.

Specter, Michael (2009) *Denialism*. New York: Penguin Press.

Szeman, Imre (2012) 'Crude Aesthetics: The Politics of Oil Documentaries.' *Journal of American Studies* 46(2): 423–39.

Wallerstein, Immanuel (2011) *The Modern World-system*. Berkeley: University of California Press.

7

'THE END TIMES AND AFTER'
UTOPIA, DYSTOPIA AND BEING-TOGETHER IN *THE FLOOD*

Adam Welstead

Authors of early twentieth century dystopian literature frequently imagined disconnected societies, fervent crowds, and mindless mass populations in their work. These visions developed in reaction to both a literary legacy of utopian conceptions and a volatile European context, where dangerous utopian ideals had served as a foundation for nationalist propaganda, racist violence and brutal totalitarian regimes. Seminal dystopian texts such as H. G. Wells's *The Sleeper Awakes* (1910), Aldous Huxley's *Brave New World* (1932) and George Orwell's *Nineteen Eighty Four* (1949) contribute most eminently to these radically negative illustrations. In *The Sleeper Awakes*, Graham, the Sleeper, is exposed to the ideological mechanisms behind utopian revolutionary rhetoric as Ostrog, the revolutionary tyrant, rouses the divided masses of a dystopian metropolis. Disempowered labourers are given arms to lay siege to the White Council's rule, and Graham becomes embroiled in the 'congested masses' of a 'struggling humanity' (Wells, 1910/1930: 68) within London's mass urban cityscape of the year 2100. Wells's powerful chapter 'The Battle of the Darkness' conveys an unforgettable allegory, describing a calamitous human condition to come where, in rage and impotence, human beings destroy each other only for their revolution to produce conditions that alienate and oppress them even further. Similarly, Huxley's infamous novel *Brave New World* concludes with the image of a frenzied mob consuming John the Savage in their 'orgy-porgy' (Huxley, 1932/1934: 305). Their hedonistic existence is a definitive depiction of the infantilizing culture that Darko Suvin explores in 'Theses on Dystopia 2001'. Here, Suvin (2003: 195) argues that it is late capitalism and mass culture's 'violence exercised upon the imaginary' that most significantly infantilizes and depoliticizes the individual in the twenty-first-century context. This recalls Winston Smith's London, in which the collective mind of indoctrinated party members crushes and oppresses all shreds of individualism. Orwell's *Nineteen Eighty Four* thus skilfully expresses how suppressed subjectivity becomes fleetingly fulfilled in the mob mentality of routine hate sessions. Even Winston, a secret dissident of the Party, observes how 'a hideous ecstasy of fear and vindictiveness [...] seemed to flow through the whole group of people like an electric current, turning one even against one's own will into a grimacing, screaming lunatic' (Orwell, 1949/2003: 17). *Nineteen Eighty-Four's* tale of Ingsoc's totalitarian regime has lived long in both literary and public imaginations for over half a century, representing the ultimate dystopian existence within a brutal state of suspicion, surveillance and terror.

Critiques of utopian literary experiments frequently take issue with the 'utopians' conceived in these Edenic worlds. In his essay 'The Politics of Utopia', Fredric Jameson (2004: 40) argues for the inevitability of 'desubjectification' in the utopian political process, suggesting that the 'effect of anonymity and of depersonalization is a very fundamental part of what utopia is and how it functions'. Consequently, desubjectified 'utopians' ultimately prove to be as homogeneous as their dystopian counterparts. Despite the decline of such flawed instances of utopian thought in the twenty-first century, the dystopian imagination has continued to flourish, particularly in the speculative fictions of British writers such as J. G. Ballard, Sarah Hall, Sam Taylor and Rupert Thomson. In *Kingdom Come* (2006),

Ballard portrays a Britain where a social and cultural malaise has led disempowered individuals, stirred by fear and anger, to engulf themselves in crowds. Through spectacle, intimidation and violence these masses exhibit, by night, features similar to the homogeneous masses of twentieth century dystopias. By day, many of them amble mindlessly through the Brooklands Metro-Centre, an infantilizing consumerist nirvana where they escape both the quotidian boredom of suburban life and the disconnectedness of a depoliticized British society. In *The Carhullan Army* (2007), Sarah Hall imagines a brutally-administered Britain in the wake of economic and ecological disintegration. The novel's malcontent protagonist, Sister, escapes from the regime of 'the Authority' in the hope of a better life amongst the dissident community at Carhullan. Despite the fanaticism of Carhullan's leader, Sister joins the sisterhood's revolutionary attempt to overthrow the Authority and liberate the people of Rith from their confined, monitored existence. Meanwhile, in *The Republic of Trees* (2005), Sam Taylor conceives of a utopian community formed in reaction to the 'cages' and restraints of the modern world:

> At school, you learn to obey the numbers; you learn to see the bars of your cage. Of course they may be imaginary bars – the cage may be an illusion – but that does not mean you are not imprisoned by it. It is not what exists that matters, after all. It is what you believe exists. (Taylor, 2005: 6)

Revolted by civilization's internal 'garrisons', as Freud conceives of them, Taylor's novel depicts a group of expatriate British youths who found a 'republic' in which Jean-Jacques Rousseau is their idol and *The Social Contract* their sacred text.[1] A contemporary retelling of William Golding's 1954 dystopian classic, *Lord of the Flies*, Taylor's *The Republic of Trees* similarly traces the thought that Utopia's doom has not been wholly due to flawed economic and political policies and actions, but rather to the destructive impulses and insatiable desires of a human nature that precludes such social harmony and cohesion. This idea is extended in Rupert Thomson's *Divided Kingdom* (2005), in which the British population has been split according to their divergent personality groups in a 'Civil Reorganization'. Charged with administrative responsibilities in his ministry position, Thomas Parry is one of the few who manages to see beyond the barriers of his quarter. Transcending the quartered boundaries of a divided Britain, Parry soon discovers that the homogenization of space has resulted in the thorough homogenization of society.

Each of these contemporary novels, then, seeks to challenge and interrogate our present and prospective modes of 'being-together'. Through their extrapolated futures, the texts discussed above reflect a growing preoccupation with the meaning of collectivity and community in the twenty-first-century context. Maggie Gee's *The Flood* (2004) makes a compelling contribution to this wave of dystopian writing through an elucidation of radically different modes of 'being-together' in both the pre- and post-apocalyptic settings of the novel. Being-together, in the Arendtian sense, refers to the condition of human beings mutually engaged in speech and action in a public domain. Siobhan Kattago (2013: 173) neatly summates that, for Hannah Arendt, 'being with others, the fact of human plurality, *is* the foundation of the human condition' (emphasis in original). In *The Human Condition*, Arendt (1958/1998: 23) accounts for the 'special relationship between action and being together', particularly in terms of the ways in which power functions in this 'special relationship'. Power itself is a 'potentiality in being together' for Arendt, rather than an explicit force applied or strength possessed (Arendt, 1958/1998: 201). Power can never belong to mob rule, or ochlocracy, which is a mere 'perverted form of "acting together"' (Arendt, 1958/1998: 203). This distinction between the potentiality of collective action in being-together, as opposed to the crowd's fleeting form of 'acting together', is one that underlies this chapter's negotiation of Gee's insightful representations of crowds, marginalized malcontents, and a conscious, diverse collectivity.

Mine Özyurt Kiliç (2013: 101) notes that in *The Flood*, as in her earlier novel *The Ice People* (1998), Gee 'portrays the prevailing conditions through the generic features of a near-future dystopia, which enables her to investigate the social crisis in tandem with the environmental one'. The novel's dystopian, pre-apocalyptic setting depicts a waterlogged Britain where ecological demise has further exacerbated the unequal living conditions of the poor, the frivolity of the wealthy, and contributed to a disconnected and divided society. The depoliticizing socio-cultural malaise and post-political impasse has gradually eroded hopes for social transformation in this 'drowned kingdom', and rendered radical change inconceivable (*TF*, 108). Yet, following the apocalyptic tidal waves that consume *The Flood*'s preapocalyptic world, Gee's characters are seen to exist harmoniously in London's Kew Gardens. There, the novel concludes with a quasi-utopian affirmation of the possibility of an unrealized mode of being-together, founded on virtues of heterogeneity, difference and acceptance. *The Flood* thus exhibits a '*post-traditional* utopian imaginar[y]', which Caroline Edwards (2011: 178, emphasis in original) describes as 'a mode of utopian thinking that is flexible, pluralized, heterogeneous and dialectical' as opposed to the 'programmatic blueprints' and 'static perfectionism' that characterized traditional utopian thought. Sarah Dillon (2011: 16–17) claims that Edwards's exploration of the post-traditional utopian imaginary and 'minor' utopian possibilities 'foregrounds the ways in which contemporary novelists [...] are rejuvenating speculative fiction and using emerging cosmopolitan identities to reveal the possibilities and impossibilities of utopian writing in the twenty first century'. Rejecting and transcending a mere dreamy utopian wishfulness, *The Flood* can thus be identified as engaging with urgent issues and debates of twenty-first-century Britain, grappling with questions of revolution and social change, and meaningfully interpreting the relationship between subjectivity and intersubjectivity in the contemporary socio-political climate.

1. Living in the End Times

> The global capitalist system is approaching an apocalyptic zero-point. Its 'four riders of the apocalypse' are comprised by the ecological crisis, the consequences of the biogenetic revolution, imbalances within the system itself (problems with intellectual property; forthcoming struggles over raw materials, food and water) and the expansive growth of social divisions and exclusions. (Žižek, 2011: x)

Slavoj Žižek's prophetic announcement is echoed in the notable thematic rise of apocalypticism in twenty-first century literature, philosophy and film. In *Living in the End Times* (2011), Žižek sets out his analysis of how our social consciousness reacts to the concept and threat of apocalypse by re-appropriating Kübler-Ross's five stages of grief as a critical framework. Žižek (2011: xi) argues that these stages (of denial, anger, bargaining, depression and acceptance) can be discerned in the ways that our social consciousness 'attempts to deal with the forthcoming apocalypse'. *The Flood* is most notable for its concern with the first of Žižek's 'four riders', the contemporary ecological crisis, and the potential zero-point to which it may lead. Kiliç (2013: 116) has furthermore demonstrated that *The Flood*'s 'dystopian energy' provides a means for engagement with issues of present concern such as the third and fourth riders: social division, inequality and the imbalances of late capitalism itself. While we glimpse several of Kübler-Ross's stages throughout *The Flood*'s narratives, the stage of denial in the face of impending apocalypse stands as the most prominent. As *The Flood*'s fanatical 'Last Days' sect continually reminds us, Gee's characters are living in their own end times, with a complacent population unaware of the disastrous tsunami to come. Despite the glaring evidence of impending disaster and ecological destruction throughout the novel, many of Gee's characters are unable to comprehend or accept the reality of their situation, exhibiting a condition that Žižek (2011: x–xi) describes as a *collective fetishistic disavowal*: 'we live in a state of collective fetishistic disavowal: we know very well that this [apocalypse] will happen at some point, but nevertheless cannot bring ourselves to really believe that it will'.

Following the minimal drop in the city's flood waters it is assumed by the novel's large cast of characters that the threat has subsided, and thus news of 'flood sickness', an emerging illness, can mean little to a population so desensitized to their failing ecosphere: 'it was just something new, in the bones of their heads, a new little swimmer, dim and featureless, struggling, quietly, to make some headway against their conviction that the floods were over' (*TF*, 263). This 'collective fetishistic disavowal' imaginatively conveys Jameson's claim (2009:

50) that 'it seems easier for us today to imagine the thoroughgoing deterioration of the earth and of nature than the breakdown of late capitalism'. As the prevalence of denial and the perpetuation of the respective endgames of late capitalism and neoliberalism in *The Flood* suggest, neither apocalypse nor radical social transformation can be conceived as realistic possibilities in Gee's text. Nevertheless, in the time preceding the fatal tsunami, an imaginative fascination with apocalypse emerges. The teenage friends Lola and Gracie, for example, stare 'riveted for a moment, at a computer simulation of a tidal wave [...] tiny people struggled like ants [...] something big and important at last [...] something marvellous that would sweep them away [...] something massive, sexual, final' (*TF*, 57). The cathartic effect of witnessing the disaster *as simulation* leads to a denial of the reality of the impending Event itself. Similarly, Davey Luck, a TV celebrity astronomer, reads the programme for the *End of the World Spectacular*, where 'the footage, his producer promised, would be stunning' (*TF*, 82). The sublime experience of the simulation mystifies the inherent warning of Davey's show, and the threat of apocalypse is deferred, having become abstract and unreal. In spite of the likelihood of a comet strike, which would provoke catastrophic tsunamis, precautions are not taken to safeguard lives and move people inland (*TF*, 283). The narrator informs us that '[n]o-one on the show seemed to care what was true' (*TF*, 83), and everyone – from the overexcited producers of the broadcast to government authorities in the unnamed city – remain oblivious to the real implications of the show's content, so consumed are they by the lure of the spectacular.

The staging of an extravagant Gala best expresses this prevalent condition of 'collective fetishistic disavowal' in *The Flood*. The ceremony, incidentally, marks the twenty-fifth anniversary of the founding of a 'pleasure zone' (*TF*, 149) for tourists, recalling both the Pleasure Cities of Wells's *The Sleeper Awakes* and the hedonistic leisure centres of Huxley's *Brave New World*. The memory of the riots that followed the closure of the old city dock site has been slowly stifled by the distractions of these pleasure zones and, similarly, the Gala provides a means of distraction from present crises in the novel. Reflecting Žižek's claim (2002: 7) that late capitalism's 'frantic mobilization conceals a more fundamental immobility', the Gala's bright lights, extravagant refreshments and whirring cameras all mask the underlying socio-political stasis of a dystopian existence. To adopt Darko Suvin's terminology (2003: 191), the Gala's projected utopian 'horizon' (that is, the happiness, wealth and ephemeral promise of its exotic cuisines, bright lights and glamour) veils the static 'locus' of the city's dystopian present.[2] The lavishness of the event obscures the reality that this horizon's function is precisely to ensure that the city's current situation is glossed over, as well as ignored in larger political terms. In this sense, the dystopian locus remains immobilized: in its crushing of any possible utopian hope for progressive sociopolitical change, the static 'locus' constitutes a safeguard for the failing socio-political structures of Bliss's Britain and the inequality and social abjection they have enabled. Weaving between sharp-witted perceptions of indelibly human peculiarities and an ominous foreshadowing of ecological and socio-political ruin, Gee deftly depicts the hollow frivolities of a society on the brink of collapse. As the country escalates its military conflicts elsewhere in the world, the feeling is that the war effort is 'happening a long way off; nothing to depress the mood of the Gala' (*TF*, 234). While home and foreign affairs crumble around them, chauffeured politicians arrive to the Gala in high spirits, and when all resources ought to be addressing flooding damage and dire living conditions, the Gala provides a glamorous platform for a wealthy upper class to indulge in their excesses. 'The crowd feels good; the crowd feels great' (*TF*, 250), the narrator informs us, as these affluent citizens dine from a wide choice of endangered species, engage in sexual flirtation and snort cocaine. The city's iridescent lights sell hope and happiness: 'Signs flashed, gorgeous, over Victory Square [...] selling Hesperican sugars, fats, drugs, shows, sex, hopes, holidays' (*TF*, 81). A lingering sense of hope resounds through *The Flood*, from the wealthy to the poverty-stricken dwellers of the Towers; however the Gala's crowds elect to fulfil their yearnings in the momentary euphoria of bright lights and spectacle, remaining fundamentally unhappy in a city that has 'gorged on dreams' (*TF*, 83). As Guy Debord's (1967: 22) conception of the 'lonely crowd' contends, in crowds 'spectators are linked only by a one-way relationship to the very center that maintains their isolation from one another'. *The Flood* suggests throughout that the group feeling of such crowds is symptomatic of a fundamentally disconnected society.

In a rebellion from their society, the impressionable young girls Lola and Gracie rather farcically become anti-capitalists for a fortnight. The tragic hilarity of their dissidence emerges from their thoughtless subscription to the very pop-culture, materialism and decadence that they aim to protest against at the Gala. While their misapprehensions provide a continual source of comic relief in the novel – with Lola's affirmation that school is 'just another capitalist institution' (*TF*, 98) a particular highlight – Gee's satirical skill equally suggests a subtle critique of fleeting radicalism's vogue in the present day. Underlying their pseudo-rebellion is an insecurity, and a pervasive sense that they, both presently and in the future, are incapable of making an impact on their society. Dressing up, they believe that 'if they weren't themselves, they could do anything' (*TF*, 71). Gracie's naive wishfulness is evidently connected to her lack of genuine convictions. While she resents her mother Paula's 'carping' (*TF*, 53) in the domestic sphere, Gracie adopts her opinions in Paula's absence and, as with several of *The Flood*'s central characters, this adoption of a univocal world view prevents and precludes the individual's ability to conceive and create anew. Gracie's discontents with the society around her are thus confined to ineffective dreams and desires, such as her wishful remark that capitalism does not exist amidst the starry skies (*TF*, 87). In truth, Lola and Gracie 'didn't want to worry about real things, the things they lived with every day' (*TF*, 86). Like those flocking to the Gala, they seek hope, promise and distraction away from the pre-apocalyptic devastation that lies around them. Intensifying a condition of collective fetishistic disavowal, the Gala 'will go on happening forever, a fluorescent stage where they gibber like monkeys, bare-arsed, helpless, and everyone sneers' (*TF*, 264).

2. Dystopian Being-Together

The Gala's implication accords with that of thesis twelve of Guy Debord's (1967: 15) *The Society of the Spectacle*: 'everything that appears is good; whatever is good will appear'. Characters such as Elroy and Lottie feel similarly alive and exhilarated at the centre of such surroundings, revelling in their opportunity to 'dress up and see and be seen' (*TF*, 218, 233). The Gala's sinister reproduction of the social and political conditions of *The Flood*'s Britain, its espousal of the superficial and spectacular, inevitably results in the disaffection of those who do not appear. Those who exist in the worst affected regions, dissenting populations without media resources to bring their voices to the public sphere, remain on the margins of society. Discontented individuals like Zoe protest in vain, as only 'the people who the city defines itself by' (*TF*, 235) are heard, or more importantly, *seen*. In section twenty-eight of *The Human Condition* (1958), Hannah Arendt defines the 'space of appearance' as:

> The space where I appear to others as others appear to me, where men exist not merely like other living or inanimate things but make their appearance explicitly [...] to be deprived of it means to be deprived of reality, which, humanly and politically speaking, is the same as appearance. To men the reality of the world is guaranteed by the presence of others, by its appearing to all. (Arendt, 1958/1998: 199)

Arendt (1958/1998: 199) argues that the space of appearance 'disappears not only with the dispersal of men [...] but with the disappearance or arrest of the activities themselves'. In *The Flood's* dystopian, pre-apocalyptic setting, individuals *disappear* in the Arendtian sense: thought and action, the essential guarantors of 'appearance', are consistently undermined by the homogeneity of crowds, infantilizing spectacles and a climate of fear within a depoliticized public sphere. Indeed the prevalence of homogeneity and the abolition of plurality, for Arendt (1958/1998: 220), 'is always tantamount to the abolition of the public realm itself'. *The Flood* similarly suggests that the 'presence of others' no longer provides a reassurance of reality when meaningful activity has been replaced by meaningless appearance among disconnected individuals. Desires for a mode of being-together closer to Arendt's definition emerge throughout the novel, as Gee's characters yearn for a more inclusive, active community, where the individual's freedom to conceive and create anew fulfils the unrealized hopes of the novel's pre-apocalyptic world.

In that pre-apocalyptic world, however, conditions have steadily declined for the poor. As one inhabitant of the poverty-stricken Towers, Viola, tells her sister:

> 'It's been horrible here [...] we couldn't get milk, or papers, or nothing. We, you know, bartered, some days, for food. That wasn't in the papers was it? The government did fuck all for us. And then they're surprised when there's a little bit of trouble.' (*TF*, 170)

In the midst of such inequality and neglect, Viola poses a question that resonates through Gee's depictions of a disconnected society: 'Who is this "our people" they're goin' on about?' (*TF*, 166). Her anger is directed at Bliss, whose rhetoric of 'our people', 'our history' and 'the momentous present' proliferates through radio broadcasts, newspaper headlines and televised public addresses (*TF*, 254). The *Daily Mire* discards well-researched dossiers dealing with serious cases of sabotage and corruption, instead opting for sensationalist headlines such as 'Violent Riots' and 'Towers Mob Rule' (*TF*, 285, 170). Social discontent festers and flourishes in the cramped quarters and overpopulated dwellings of the city, which lie in contrast to the open spaces afforded to the wealthy. May observes this on her trip to the Towers, noting how 'the boat moved into more open spaces as it crossed a richer part of the city' (*TF*, 188). The condition of human relations is further reflected in the architecture and infrastructure of Gee's dystopian, alternative London, where all space is expedited and little room for change exists; 'every scrap of land has a building on it' (*TF*, 16) and, as Davey remarks, 'nothing was separate anymore' (*TF*, 90). The closed spaces of society and the urban city fuel the discontent of social and religious activists, who continue to protest in spite of seeming futility. These prevailing structures seem even to draw the discontent of a 'bored' galaxy that desires 'something different, something less myopic than the city dwellers' (*TF*, 261).

As an apocalyptic tsunami descends in *The Flood*, Gee's reader is presented with an opposing set of images. Several of the novel's central characters cling to each other in their last moments, a final moment of togetherness before the end of the world. In contrast:

> The crowd on the hill pushed on upwards, struggling, now, pushing, screaming, red and contorted, insects scrambling on top of each other, a mill of ants in its final terror, but till the wave comes they will fight to survive [...] and then the wave comes; then the wave comes. (*TF*, 316)

The wave annihilates the dystopian intersubjectivity *par excellence* represented in the novel: the crowd. Crowds surround the disorder and chaos of the metropolis throughout *The Flood*, with Gee's descriptions evoking powerful literary images, from the clamouring crowds of the Wellsian and Orwellian dystopias to the faceless masses that sweep the ruined London of T. S. Eliot's *The Waste Land* (1922). Kilda's presence in the novel brings to light a compelling connection between *The Flood* and *The Waste Land*. In 'The Burial of the Dead' Eliot's clairvoyant, Madame Sosostris, summons the card of the drowned Phoenician Sailor and foresees a cataclysmic end: 'Fear death by water / I see crowds of people, walking round in a ring' (Eliot, 1925/1999: 24). Kilda similarly shares her vision of a London consumed by an apocalyptic tsunami: 'I see a big wall of water [...] I do see, like, the end of the world' (*TF*, 301). Her prophecy of apocalypse envisions a demise of *The Flood*'s pre-apocalyptic world, a haunting illustration of the twenty-first-century wasteland shaped by the contemporary sociopolitical and ecological concerns of Gee's readers. However, sharing Eliot's dark poetic imagination, images of 'death by water' are similarly seen to relieve mindless masses of a dystopian existence.

Individuals are roused to action by the collective feeling of *The Flood*'s crowds, yet their energies are simply harnessed to form an uncritical mass mind: 'The sun lit up faces, blank and identical, all turned submissively in one direction' (*TF*, 37). In the tumult of the crowd, individuals feel that they traverse the unfreedoms of those rigid horizons around them, as Elias Canetti remarks in *Crowds and Power*:

> In the crowd the individual feels that he is transcending the limits of his own person ... he has a sense of relief, for the distances are removed which used to throw him back on himself and shut him in ... with the lifting of these burdens of distance he feels free. (Canetti, 1960/1973: 19)

The unburdened individual Canetti describes bears a marked resemblance to Gee's character Dirk, who immerses himself in the mobs of the 'Last Days' sect. When Kilda, *The Flood*'s clairvoyant, suggests an alternative conception of the future from Bruno's, this greatly unsettles Dirk, who had 'never been able to imagine his future' (*TF*, 126). The Last Days sect provides him with answers: the 'One Truth' of Bruno's book relieves his anxiety concerning the indeterminacy of the future; its rigid dogmas stifle his frustrated homosexual desires; their crowd spectacles provide him with fleeting moments of closeness. The crowds of One Way protestors 'clone' themselves en masse surrounding the Gala, 'hungry for the enemy' (*TF*, 232). They thrive best here, in full sight of the superfluous display of wealth. Bruno and his zealous followers frequently set upon Victory Square. Here, his fervent, homogeneous crowds treble:

> The crowd was doing well. Gathering. Breeding. From the distance, they all looked alike, turned towards the placards with their letters of blood [...] goodness was growing. Calm spread through him as he watched the crowd, more stick figures drawn in to join the others, moving slowly together, unstoppable. It reminded him of something they had once done at school, an experiment with magnets and iron filings [...] the tiny ants shuddered and shot into line. The will of the One: the One who was All. (*TF*, 40)

While Bruno addresses the crowd and aggressively compels them to 'Awake' (*TF*, 30), in truth the inherent message sanctioned is to submissively accept the millenarian, fundamentalist doctrines that he preaches. Bruno's grasp on the crowd is firm: 'his spiritual power lay over them like a net of white ice, leaving his disciples locked, synchronized, lost in a steely perfection of grace' (*TF*, 124). Serge Moscovici (1981/1985: 122) argues in *The Age of the Crowd* that 'the secret of the leader is that he embodies the idea for the mass and the mass for the idea ... he exercises his power not by organising violence, which is always secondary, but by organising beliefs, which are primary'. As Bruno desperately seeks to demonstrate, the effective leader does not herald revolutionary violence, but instead champions a powerful utopian ideology that endures in the minds of its believers and solidifies their willingness to support the transformation (or destruction) of present sociopolitical conditions.

Central to the social unrest and consensus of disavowal in *The Flood*'s Britain is an unreliable leadership consolidating a dystopian political endgame. Bliss states that 'we must have war, or there would never be peace' (*TF*, 78), that 'peace meant war' (*TF*, 102); these are chillingly Orwellian utterances which reveal the depth of rhetoric disguising the truth behind his regime's foreign policy. Government-influenced media outlets report of 'liberated' cities far away, fabricating and distorting significant events (*TF*, 78). Bliss's fearmongering urges citizens to stay near their TVs and radios in the event of an attack, to await government instruction as they deal with the enemy (*TF*, 287). According to Arendt (1953: 321), such an unreal climate of ideology and fear 'has succeeded when people have lost contact with their fellow men as well as the reality around them; for together with these contacts, men lose the capacity of both experience and thought'. Refining a culture of fear and spectacle, Bliss's regime thus alters the individual's relationships to his/her fellow men and women, and further, the individual's relation with reality. As Arendt argues, the consequent isolation effectively precludes meaningful thought, experience and action, resulting in the thorough depoliticization of the individual. In the hope of exacerbating climates of fear and hatred, Bliss's warmongering administration announces to the public that they are 'unable to substantiate' reports of enemy sabotage (*TF*, 148). The government 'habitually denied its own rumours' (*TF*, 149), a convention that posits a warped logic where denial functions by suggesting the truth of that which is denied. Bliss reflects with disdain on how Darius Blow, a dissenting minister, has yet to become 'enlightened' (*TF*, 37). His opposing views appear untenable in a political sphere where unthinking consensus is a favoured state of affairs. As in *Nineteen Eighty-Four*'s London, Gee's dystopian pre-apocalyptic vision adopts a 'Victory Square' (*TF*, 30), where the Last Days followers gather and ferment a puritanical fervour reminiscent of Ingsoc hate sessions. Constant surveillance similarly safeguards the status quo: 'the drone of helicopters, chasing burglars, monitoring demonstrations, keeping an eye on the city's pleasures, making sure nothing gets out of hand' (*TF*, 287). Such monitoring and protection of prevailing conditions means that the 'myopic' city dwellers of Gee's dystopia, even in close proximity of crowds, remain fundamentally alienated from each other.

3. Kew Gardens: 'Utopian' Being-Together

On the stage of acceptance, Žižek (2011: xii) remarks that 'after passing through [a] zero-point, the subject no longer perceives the situation as a threat, but as the chance of a new beginning'. In *The Flood* this new beginning 'holds all time and places' (*TF*, 7), a future where human experience has been fundamentally altered following the zero-point of apocalypse. Mine Özyurt Kiliç argues that this radical alterity from present structures is embedded in the post-apocalyptic narrative structure of *The Flood*: 'In reversing the order, starting with the end and ending with a new beginning, the text defies the linearity and transgresses the conventional understanding of time, as if to suggest a new order that will shatter the present system' (Özyurt Kiliç, 2013: 122). At the core of *The Flood*'s quasi-utopian scene at Kew Gardens is a principle of possibility and difference, and a critique of social, cultural and political hegemonies that endorse homogeneity to preclude future alterity. Gee's vision eludes the pitfalls of traditional utopian construction, and shares the concerns that Ronald Bogue (2011: 81) locates in Gilles Deleuze and Félix Guattari's *What Is Philosophy?* (1991), namely that 'utopias are the antithesis of becoming, process and movement toward a future that is genuinely new and thus inherently unpredictable, defiant of any mapping'. A resistance to similarly destructive, systematizing worlds is played out in the contrast between Kilda's clairvoyance and the principles of Bruno's 'Last Days' sect. The 'One Way' – the sect's name for its dogmatic, fundamentalist narrative of life's journey – is disrupted by her premonition of a world where 'there's lots of different endings' (*TF*, 301). This realization debunks Bruno's metaphysical monism in favour of the pluralistic understanding that foregrounds the basis of the better world to come, as Kilda describes:

> It isn't, like, One Way, not at all. There are worlds that are all bright, like worlds of light, and a world of darkness, but it all, like, splits, it goes on and on, so there's lots of worlds, and pieces get shuffled ... It's doing it now. Every day, every moment. (*TF*, 302)

Kilda's description of the world connects with those of Harold Segall's long-unfinished monograph. Harold eloquently echoes Mr Ramsay of Woolf's *To the Lighthouse* (1927) in his search to find meaning and understanding through his theoretical work. Unlike Ramsay's work on metaphysics, Harold's book on time, simultaneity and connectedness finally proves to be a success and source of fulfilment for him. Despite her pessimism about the book, Lottie too is struck with a sense that 'the whole world was connected' (*TF*, 15). Rather than imposing a set of margins upon our knowledge of temporal structures, Harold's theoretical endeavours primarily seek to offer a more profound and meaningful understanding of the human being's experience of the world. Similarly, for May (a character Gee revives from her previous 2002 novel *The White Family*) 'all of life seemed to come to a point' (*TF*, 12). She appears haunted by the past and occupies a lonely, widowed present for much of the novel, recalling her lost husband and musing upon the events that ruptured relationships in her family. This recurrent sense of interconnectedness, however, is not reduced to impotent wishfulness; rather than precluding the agency of Gee's central characters, the contemplation of a connected world actually confers agency upon them: inciting Kilda's rejection of dogmatic univocity, inspiring Harold's influential theory, and prompting May's journey to reconcile with her son Dirk.

The Flood's post-apocalyptic space of the heavenly realm of Kew Gardens is depicted as an idyllic setting, far removed from the decaying urban environment of Gee's (pre-)apocalyptic, alternative London. In an earlier visit, Lottie remarks how Kew Gardens 'left her unusually thoughtful' (*TF*, 133). Its open spaces, unlike the cramped and crumbling cityscape, are thus shown to stimulate thought and reflection in the novel's characters, validating Michel Foucault's (1986: 24–5) considerations of the garden as 'heterotopia': 'The garden is the smallest parcel of the world and then it is the totality of the world [...] the garden has been a sort of happy, universalizing heterotopia since the beginnings of antiquity'. Foucault (1986: 24) defines heterotopias as 'something like counter-sites, a kind of effectively enacted utopia in which the real sites, all the other real sites that can be found within culture, are simultaneously represented, contested, and inverted'. The Kew Gardens of *The Flood* is a site of growth, flourishing and renewal, and its presence similarly invokes and challenges both its preceding dystopian society as well as the 'real sites' of present-day London. Even Moira Penny, the embittered academic and 'One Way' follower, has a final vision where the bucolic space takes on a heterotopic and transformative character. Welcoming the tidal wave's destruction of the society she despises, she takes a final look towards the horizon and sees 'something other, outside the city, something surviving, a blueness, a greenness' (*TF*, 306). While the novel's post-apocalyptic space evidences a recovery of the natural world and a blissful community within a 'happy, universalizing' garden, it resists assimilation into either utopian or religious narratives; its modest 'principle of hope' is, as Marder and Vieira (2012: x) articulate, 'a hope detached from [the] divine or messianistic roots [of utopian thinking] and placed in the hitherto unforeseen possibilities of human togetherness'. Along these lines, Dillon (2007: 375) demonstrates that while *The Flood* engages with the Judeo-Christian apocalyptic tradition, it ultimately 'breaks with this tradition in its refusal of final judgement and in its intimation that justice remains to come'. While the earthly paradise of *The Flood*'s 'After' section is suggestively Edenic, far from heralding the recovery of a lost paradise or pre-lapsarian garden, Gee's Kew Gardens is represented as a pointedly *post-lapsarian* setting. The inequalities, prejudices and failures that characterize the novel's pre-apocalyptic world provide a basis for the radical alterity of its post-apocalyptic space and thus *The Flood*, in Edwards's aforementioned terms, both resists *traditional* utopian thought (which tends towards stasis and the projection of a monolithic realization of utopia) and revitalizes the utopian impulse (understood as processual, heterogeneous and provisional) through a *post-traditional* imaginary.

Consolidating Jameson's (2004: 37) point that 'there are a variety of ways to reinvent utopia – at least in the first sense of the elimination of this or that "root of all evil"', the combination of Gee's pre-apocalyptic 'critical dystopia' and its subsequent post-apocalyptic, heterotopian space ultimately offers a minor utopian 'moment of possibility' (Edwards, 2011: 185). It presents a modest reinvention of utopian thinking through an assault on those features of contemporary society that prove the most destructive in an extrapolated near-future.[3] This interconnectedness of utopia and dystopia further supports Kiliç's (2013: 126) reading of Margaret Atwood's conception of 'ustopia' in *The Flood*.[4] Gee does not depict 'utopians' as such; even those characters who revelled in the destructive apocalyptic possibilities of an approaching ecocatasrophe endure. There is room for Bruno in *The Flood*'s earthly garden: in contrast to the inflexible religious narrative he supports, there is no 'final judgement' awaiting him in Kew Gardens, no eternal damnation or rewarded salvation. Bruno can repose in the sunlight, and while portrayed at a distance from the others (*TF*, 323), he is not alienated and can live among a heterogeneous collectivity with diverse beliefs and desires that has rejected the intolerance and fundamentalism of the 'Last Days' sect. Arguments for an eradication of the racist and homophobic undercurrents that mar contemporary society feature significantly in Maggie Gee's fictions, most centrally in *The White Family* (2002). Such a desire for pluralistic acceptance is fundamental to the hope that forms the basis of the 'here and now' utopianism of *The Flood*'s scene at Kew Gardens, as Gee (Kiliç, 2013: 126) has suggested: 'I want to return us to the real world [...] I want to say that heaven is here and now'.

4. Concluding Remarks

Darko Suvin (2003: 187) states that utopianism is 'an orientation toward a horizon of radically better forms of relationships among people'. *The Flood*'s 'utopianism', in this sense, comes to light most compellingly in the interplay between Gee's radically opposing conceptions of being-together. This 'utopianism' is not constructed on a principle of perfection; rather, an acceptance of imperfection and diversity enables the microcosm of Kew Gardens to be a setting where 'all are welcome' (*TF*, 325). The apocalypse of the novel brings about the end of a dystopian society, and in its place a redeeming post-apocalyptic world is founded upon values that form the basis of a new beginning and new modes of being-together. Kew Gardens effectively becomes a site where the discourses of utopia, dystopia and community are explored, challenged and conceived anew. It is a heterotopic space through which *The Flood* transcends dreamy utopianism and nihilistic dystopian pessimism to achieve a more fulfilling critique that can accommodate both utopian and dystopian impulses and confront the pressing sociopolitical issues of the twenty-first-century present. Moreover, Gee's illustrations of disaffected individuals and tumultuous crowds are eerily prescient of the social unrest that emerged across Britain at the beginning of the twenty-first century's second decade – most notably the London riots in 2011. *The Flood*'s attentive representations of the marginalized individuals that compose any crowd, however, further signal a shift away from what Kurt Vonnegut (1952/1969: 171) memorably referred to in his novel *Player Piano* as the 'homogenised pudding'; a vision of uniform, unthinking collectivity that animates the dystopian crowds imagined in novels such as *The Sleeper Awakes*, *Brave New World* and *Nineteen Eighty-Four*. Instead, *The Flood* rejects the unthinking consensus of *Daily Mire*-like sensationalism and provides a more insightful reading of the politics of social abjection and its disastrous consequences. Rather than a defeated depiction of an inevitable catastrophe to come, *The Flood*'s 'dystopianism' suggests, as Davey remarks, that there are 'merely two worlds: one where it happens, where everything returns to nothing, and one where all of life goes on' (*TF*, 283). The novel thus presents two worlds of the future: one in which the ecological destruction of the present continues to be deferred by a 'collective fetishistic disavowal'; the other in which such problems are addressed with an appropriate urgency, and where the depoliticizing tenets of neoliberalism and late capitalism are made obsolete.

The Flood points to the claim that more fulfilling modes of being-together can never be achieved through programmatic, 'traditional' utopian thought, and endorses Jameson's (2004: 53) suggestion that without challenging such flawed creations of 'perfected' communities, 'our visions of alternative futures and utopian transformations remain politically and existentially inoperative, mere thought experiments and mental games without any visceral commitment' (Jameson, 2004: 53). It is in this spirit that Deleuze and Guattari (1991/1994: 218) close their seminal text *What is Philosophy?* with the affirmation of a 'people to come'. As Bogue (2011: 89) explains, the concept of a people to come rebukes the conventional image of utopian populaces, mere 'aggregates that form an amorphous mass', in favour of plurality and difference. *The Flood*'s 'people to come' should therefore be understood as a heterogeneous utopian collectivity defined by divergent hopes and desires. Through this vision – which we might call the novel's 'post-traditional' utopian imaginary – Gee further contributes to a discernible preoccupation with notions of utopian and dystopian modes of being-together in twenty-first century speculative fictions. In line with Bogue's (2011: 94) claim that 'fiction promotes the thought of a people to come as something that [...] may assist us in *our* attempts to imagine, invent and enact alternative modes of existence' (emphasis in original), *The Flood*'s hopeful post-apocalyptic vision poses a challenging set of questions and possibilities that we might well identify as literature working in its most potent and transformative form.

Notes

1 As Freud argues in *Civilization and its Discontents* (1930/2004: 77): 'Civilization overcomes the dangerous aggressivity of the individual, by weakening him, disarming him and setting up an internal authority to watch over him, like a garrison in a conquered town'.

2 In Thesis 11 of his 'Theses on Dystopia 2001', Suvin (2003: 191) defines the locus as 'the place of the agent who is moving', and the horizon as 'the *Horizon* toward which that agent is moving'.

3 In *Scraps of the Untainted Sky: Science Fiction, Utopia, Dystopia*, Tom Moylan (2000: 188) describes critical dystopias as 'texts that are emancipatory, militant, open and "critical"' as opposed to 'compensatory, resigned' and anti-critical.

4 For Atwood (2011: 85), 'ustopia' suggests that utopia and dystopia do not stand as polar opposites; they exist in a 'yin and yang pattern; within each utopia a concealed dystopia; within each dystopia, a hidden utopia'.

Works Cited

Arendt, Hannah (1953) 'Ideology and Terror: A Novel Form of Government', *The Review of Politics* 15(3): 303–27.

Arendt, Hannah (1958/1998) *The Human Condition*. Chicago, IL: University of Chicago Press.

Ballard, J. G. (2006/2012) *Kingdom Come*. London: Fourth Estate.

Bogue, Ronald (2011) 'Deleuze and Guattari and the Future of Politics: Science Fiction, Protocols and the People to Come', *Deleuze Studies* 5: 77–97.

Canetti, Elias (1960/1973) *Crowds and Power*. Harmondsworth: Penguin.

Debord, Guy (1967/1995) *The Society of the Spectacle*. New York: Zone Books.

Deleuze, Gilles, and Felix Guattari (1991/1994) *What is Philosophy?* New York: Columbia University Press.

Dillon, Sarah (2007) 'Imagining Apocalypse: Maggie Gee's *The Flood*', *Contemporary Literature* 48(3): 374–97.

Dillon, Sarah (2011) 'Introducing David Mitchell's Universe: A Twenty-First Century House of Fiction' in Sarah Dillon (ed) *David Mitchell: Critical Essays*, pp. 3–23. Canterbury: Gylphi.

Edwards, Caroline (2011) 'Strange Transactions: Utopia, Transmigration and Time in *Ghostwritten* and *Cloud Atlas*' in Sarah Dillon (ed) *David Mitchell: Critical Essays*, pp. 177–200. Canterbury: Gylphi.

Eliot, T. S. (1925/1999) 'The Waste Land' in *The Waste Land and Other Poems*, pp. 21–46. London: Faber and Faber.

Foucault, Michel (1986) 'Of Other Spaces', *Diacritics* 16(1): 22–7.

Freud, Sigmund (1930/2004) *Civilization and its Discontents*. London: Penguin.

Hall, Sarah (2007) *The Carhullan Army*. London: Faber & Faber.

Huxley, Aldous (1932/1934) *Brave New World*. London: Chatto and Windus.
Jameson, Fredric (2004) 'The Politics of Utopia', *New Left Review* 25(1): 35–54.
Jameson, Fredric (2009) *The Cultural Turn: Selected Writings on the Postmodern*. London: Verso.
Kattago, Siobhan (2013). 'Why the World Matters: Hannah Arendt's Philosophy of New Beginnings', *The European Legacy: Toward New Paradigms* 18(2): 170–84.
Marder, Michael and Vieira, Patricia (2012) 'Utopia: A Political Ontology' in Michael Marder and Patricia Vieira (eds) *Existential Utopia: New Perspectives on Utopian Thought*, pp. ix–xv. London: Continuum.
Moscovici, Serge (1981/1985) *The Age of the Crowd: A Historical Treatise on Mass Psychology*. Cambridge: Cambridge University Press.
Moylan, Tom (2000) *Scraps of the Untainted Sky: Science Fiction, Utopia, Dystopia*. Boulder, Colorado: Westview Press.
Orwell, George (1949/2003) *Nineteen Eighty-Four*. London: Penguin.
Özyurt Kiliç, Mine (2013) *Maggie Gee: Writing the Condition-of-England Novel*. London: Bloomsbury Academic.
Suvin, Darko (2003) 'Theses on Dystopia 2001' in Raffaella Baccolini and Tom Moylan (eds) *Dark Horizons: Science Fiction and the Dystopian Imagination*, pp. 187–202. London: Routledge.
Taylor, Sam (2005) *The Republic of Trees*. London: Faber & Faber.
Thomson, Rupert (2005) *Divided Kingdom*. London: Bloomsbury.
Vonnegut, Kurt (1952/1969) *Player Piano*. St. Albans: Granada Publishing.
Wells, H. G. (1910/1930) *The Sleeper Wakes: and, Men Like Gods*. London: Odhams Press.
Woolf, Virginia (1927/2008) *To the Lighthouse*. Oxford: Oxford University Press.
Žižek, Slavoj (2002) *Welcome to the Desert of the Real!: Five Essays on September 11 and Related Dates*. London: Verso.
Žižek, Slavoj (2011) *Living in the End Times*. London: Verso.

8

FROM THE 'NATIVE OUTSIDE' TO THE 'FOREIGN WITHIN'
RE/NEGOTIATING URBAN SPACE IN *THE WHITE FAMILY*

Irene Pérez-Fernández

In his 1997 proposal for a workshop entitled 'Reinventing Britain' Homi Bhabha commented on the hybrid aspect of contemporary British society and how this hybridity was entailing an evident cultural transformation.[1] Three years later, the Parekh Report on *The Future of Multi-ethnic Britain* (2000) pinpointed some of the factors that had helped bestow British society with a sense of heterogeneity, as it examined the state of multi-ethnic Britain and its rich and diverse cultural heritage. The report acknowledged the need to recognize the existence of cultural differences and to respect diversity, defining Britain's status as 'both a community of citizens and a community of communities, both a liberal and a multicultural society' (Commission on the Future of Multiethnic Britain, 2000: ix). At the same time, the report did not fail to admit that respect for cultural diversity is a complex process that requires the need 'to reconcile [these communities'] sometimes conflicting requirements' (Commission on the Future of Multiethnic Britain, 2000: ix).

The last years of the twentieth century and the first years of the twenty-first have borne witness to the acclaim by readers and literary critics alike of an increasing number of literary works by first- and second-generation Black and Asian British authors.[2] Exploring the works of all these authors would go beyond the scope of this chapter, yet I shall briefly name a few of the writers who have paved the way in the passage to the present-day inclusion of Black and Asian writers into mainstream British cultural production. George Lamming and Sam Selvon are two of the earliest first-generation writers who give voice to the experience of migration and the problems of racism, dis/placement, and the drudgeries that post-Second World War immigrants had to face in Britain. George Lamming's novel *The Emigrants* (1954) and Sam Selvon's novel *The Lonely Londoners* (1956) are perhaps the most widely known instances of this trend.[3] Some of the most acclaimed first-generation male writers who continued this tradition and published their works in the late 1970s and early 1980s include Linton Kwesi Johnson, David Dabydeen, Salman Rushdie and Fred D'Aguiar.

In the 1980s, first-generation Black women writers such as Buchi Emecheta, Joan Riley, Beryl Gilroy and Amryl Johnson started publishing their works, adding a gender perspective to the experience of migration to, and settlement in, Britain.[4] In theatre, there were many critically acclaimed works such as Hanif Kureishi's *My Beautiful Launderette* (1986) and Caryl Phillips's first play *Strange Fruit* (1981). Playwrights started to portray a vision of Blacks and Asians that questioned essentialist paradigms of citizenship and mapped a more diverse Britain. In so doing they were questioning and enlarging the term 'Britishness' and were proof of the diversity that characterized Britain at the time. Since the turn of the twenty-first century, Zadie Smith's *White Teeth* (2000), Monica Ali's *Brick Lane* (2003), Andrea Levy's *Small Island* (2004), and Diana Evans's *26a* (2006) have continued addressing these issues of immigration, colonialism, and their outcomes, by focusing on Britain's multiethnic and multicultural society. More recently, John McLeod has referred to the literary works of Black British authors as 'contemporary black writing of Britain' in order, as he writes, to:

make a distinction between an older, dominant sphere of literary endeavour and an emergent one that is indebted to, but not overdetermined by, previous contexts and achievements, the political and aesthetic goals of which might be somewhat different, especially as regards writing the nation. (McLeod, 2010: 46)[5]

Contemporary British fiction therefore undeniably echoes British multiculturalism in the twenty-first century. I employ the term 'contemporary British fiction' following James English's work (2006). English (2006: 13) employs the term to refer to a moment in British fiction, from the 1980s onwards, marked by the literary works of 'the immigrant and postcolonial writers ... the Scottish and Welsh New Waves, the brash new celebrity authors who won Booker prizes and appeared in Granta magazine's "Best of the Young British Novelists" (in 1983 and 1993)'; and those novelists and literary works that embrace contemporary British fiction as 'the scene of something radically new' (English, 2006: 2).

While not included under the label 'postcolonial', British writers like Maggie Gee (included in the 1983 Granta list of the 'Best of Young British Novelists'), Rose Tremain, Chris Cleave or Amanda Craig, among others, have also participated in the process of redefining British cultural identity. Described as an 'indigenous writer' (Nasta, 2004: 5), Gee, has engaged with questions of im/migration and cross-culturalism in her recent writing, which includes the novels *My Cleaner* (2006) and *My Driver* (2010), and especially in her novel *The White Family* (2002): a socially committed piece of writing inspired by the murder of Stephen Lawrence, the black teenager who was stabbed to death by a group of young white thugs while he waited at a bus stop in Eltham, southeast London on 22 April 1993.

The death of Stephen Lawrence is a landmark event in the context of race relations in Britain, since the murder and its police investigation prompted an inquiry, headed by Sir William MacPherson, known as 'The MacPherson Report', which was published in 1999 and had significant political impact. The Report identified the challenge of 'institutional racism' and led to a series of legal changes and institutional reforms intended to eradicate overt racism. Moreover, since the *White Family* was written, the world changing events of 11 September 2001, which resulted in much anti-Muslim sentiment, and the later 7 July 2005 London transport tube and bus suicide bombings, accelerated British public discourse away from the conflicts explored in Gee's narrative to focus on Muslims and fears of Islamic extremism which has been called 'Islamophobia' (Allen, 2010a). These events are indicative of dramatic changes in the tectonic plates that now constitute British society. Since the terrorist attacks of 11 September 2001 and 7 July 2005 a new 'racism' has thus arisen which is no longer based on biological differences and biological superiority but on the idea of a cultural clash and incompatibility between different cultures (Donald and Rattansi, 1992). Predominantly directed at Asian communities, this new type of racism has brought to light the fact that there is 'cultural racism' as well as 'colour racism' (Modood, 2005). The former discursive focus on 'race' has thus been reoriented towards 'religion' as new threats to society and family are increasingly framed in the language of the religiously different; which is widely perceived to be located within Islam.[6] Meanwhile, England's urban landscape, and London in particular, continues to be ever increasingly diverse and pluralistic, meaning that there are, to rephrase the Parekh Report, conflicting requirements still to be reconciled.

In this context, Gee's depiction of contemporary British social space is an excellent example of the way in which people negotiate their sense of space and identity in a changing society. Gee's depiction of the White family functions as a trope for contemporary Britain, understood as a society that is currently still engaged in finding a redefinition of Britishness. In this chapter, I shall concentrate on analysing the relation that the characters in *The White Family* establish with the spaces in which they are located. This spatial dimension is paramount in Gee's novel. Non arbitrarily, *The White Family* is formally divided according to different spatial references – 'The Beginning' (*WF*, 9), 'The Hospital' (*WF*, 19), 'The Shop' (*WF*, 93), 'The Park' (*WF*, 195), 'The Church' (*WF*, 347) – and subdivided into chapters according to the characters's names. By means of this, Gee emphasizes each character's views and experiences of those public places. Therefore, Gee's narrative highlights a conception of space that is not fixed and static but is based on each person's understanding and experience of space(s) and that is, thus, dynamic. As Michel Foucault puts it: 'our epoch is one in which space takes for us the form of relations among sites' (Foucault, 1986: 22).

Drawing on theories of space that perceive it as relational (de Certeau, 1988; Foucault, 1986; Lefebvre, 1974/2005; Massey, 1994), I am interested in highlighting the ways in which characters in *The White Family* succeed or fail to establish connections with the urban spaces surrounding them, and how this is implicitly related to the extent to which they acknowledge the ethnic and cultural diversity that shapes London's cityscape in the early 1990s. In this respect, I shall make use of Lefebvre's terms of the 'lived space' versus the 'conceived space' to account for the feelings of unbelonging in, and disassociation from, space from which some of the characters in the novel suffer. The 'lived space' is understood by Lefebvre (1974/2005: 39) as 'space directly *lived* through its associated images and symbols, and hence the space of "inhabitants" and "users"' (emphasis in original). This space is by nature alive, 'essentially qualitative, fluid and dynamic' (Lefebvre, 1974/2005: 42). It is, therefore, malleable and changing in the same way that Hillesden proves to be a transforming location in *The White Family*. The 'conceived space', by contrast, is considered by Lefebvre (1974/2005: 38) to be an abstract 'conceptualized space', and tends to be static. This is the conception of space that, I shall argue, some characters such as May, Dirk and Alfred attempt to retain and secure – this attempt is the reason behind their inability to renegotiate the malleable space in which they are located. Finally, in the last section of this chapter, I shall read Albion Park as a heterotopic space that represents both Britain's traditional – in the above-mentioned characters' minds – and ever-changing society. Following Foucault's (1986: 24) conceptualization of the heterotopia, I will conclude that the Park becomes a heterotopia for Gee's characters in that it becomes 'a sort of simultaneously mythic or real contestation of the space in which we live'. The Park can thus be read as a relational space – connected with all the other possible spaces that exist in the novel, both in the characters' imaginaries as well as in the actual suburban space of Gee's fictional Hillesden (itself, a reimagining by Gee of a north London suburb like Willesden).

Portraying the 'Native Outside' and the 'Foreign Within'

The White Family can undoubtedly be considered a 'radically new' novel – to return to English's term – if its thematic content is taken into account. The novel can be read as Gee's attempt to understand the racist attitudes exhibited within a section of the white British population, which perceived the post-Second World War immigration and settlement of other ethnicities in Britain as initiating the loss of a traditional (white) notion of Britain.[7] As Gee has said in interview: 'I thought, I have to try and understand why white people every now and then kill black people in London, ... I felt quite naively, "I want them to know all white people aren't like that"' (Gee cited in Jaggi, 2002: 5). Most characters in *The White Family* fail to re/define Britain in multiethnic and multicultural terms, and Gee tries to explore the reasons behind their inability to acknowledge the right of these other ethnicities to be a re/defining constituent of the concept of Britishness.

Although Gee first submitted the manuscript of her novel in 1995, it was rejected and *The White Family* was not finally published until 2002. One of the reasons for the delay in publication of the novel might have been the political impact of Stephen Lawrence's murder or, as Gee herself explains in the following quotation, the fact that publishers and British society were not ready at that time to face a novel that dealt with race, racism and racial relations in Britain:

> [*The White Family* was not published] due to, I must think, at least in part the problems and anxieties aroused by writing across colour boundaries and dwelling on the still taboo subject of racism. (You may think it is no longer taboo: I think that it is. We are all supposed to be post-racist now. Yet the UK is not really post-racist, nor probably is any country in the world). (Gee, 2009: 14)

Gee's construction of national identity in *The White Family* undermines an assumed connection between Britishness and a particular ethnicity, that is, Britishness and whiteness, and offers a poignant rejoinder concerning the need to incorporate other ethnicities into the concept of Britishness. These other ethnicities provide new ways of understanding British identity and citizenship, and new modes of negotiating what it means to be British arise in the novel, which some members of the White family are incapable of recognizing. In this respect, Gee's *The White Family* portrays both what I shall refer to as 'the native outside' and 'the foreign within' and in so doing it destabilizes 'Otherness'.

Gee's narrative presents white characters such as Alfred White, the park keeper, his wife, May, and their son Dirk, all of whom are examples of the 'native outside'. I use this label to refer to subjects who display an inability to psychologically adjust, negotiate and/or identify themselves within the social environment in which they are located. These characters become 'Others', yet their 'Otherness' is not defined following traditional postcolonial theories of racial or ethnic difference (Said, 2003). Rather, it is an 'Otherness' that renders them unable to adapt to the new social reality. As a result, these white characters paradoxically occupy a similar position to Gee's black characters like Winston, Elroy or Kojo, who they continually attempt to label as 'Other', as non-British. The latter are examples of what I refer to as the 'foreign within', for they have negotiated senses of belonging within Britain. *The White Family*, therefore, advocates the need for changes to be wrought on traditional ideas of British identity in order to recognize present-day ethnic diversity and its resistance to homogenization and definition in singular terms. Thus, Gee's narrative highlights a notion of Britishness that does not rest on an essentialist idea of identity and unity, but which is conceived as a relational concept by which one is able to find one's own space within the society in which one is located, root one's identity and, at the same time, acknowledge the right of others to establish a different relation to the concept.

Even though Gee (2005) has described *The White Family* as a story of 'very strong passions in an ordinary London family', the White family is less than 'ordinary'. The novel allows Gee to symbolically represent Britain's changing society and some of the social problems affecting Britain in the last years of the second half of the twentieth century: such as racism, dis/encounters with the family and the nation, or feelings of spatial dislocation. These problems are related to the need to negotiate a different sense of identity – 'the native outside' and 'the foreign within' – and as such they belong within what Avtar Brah (1996: 194) has named a 'diaspora space'; that is, a 'multi-locationality across geographical, cultural and psychic boundaries'. Gee (2009: 18) presents these issues as affecting white and black characters alike, and therefore proposes 'a de-stabilising shift of the imaginative centre'. Although *The White Family* depicts characters that are located within two opposing positions – 'the native outside' and 'the foreign within' – these positions should be read as examples of the two extreme ends of a continuum where citizens who live in a multiethnic, diasporic space, such as London, might locate themselves. Gee acknowledges that London is a diasporic space inhabited not only by those who have migrated and their descendants but, equally, by those who are constructed and represented as 'indigenous' (Brah, 1996: 181). In this respect, Gee's novel addresses a complex topic that is still being considered in present-day Britain; that is, how to recognize and engage with the changing urban space within which one is located and, in a related sense, how to construct within this space a sense of identity both on an individual and collective level.

Re/defining Britishness: The White family as a Trope for 'Britishness in Crisis'

In the subjective imagination of the members of the White family, London as a 'representational space' (Lefebvre, 1974/2005: 39) is changing. It is becoming a location they are unable to invest with meaning and from which they feel disassociated. Members of the White family find it difficult to root themselves within their particular urban setting – the fictional suburban area of Hillesden, unmistakably a reference to the North West multiethnic suburban area of Willesden – which is losing its once traditional and homogenous cultural composition and is gradually becoming defined by singular practices, plural trajectories and different 'spatial stories' (de Certeau, 1988: 115). What Michel de Certeau (1988: 95) calls 'Concept-city' and Henri Lefebvre (1974/2005: 33) defines as the 'representation of space' – that is, the architectural and scientific view of the city as a 'field of programmed and regulated operations' (de Certeau, 1988: 95) – is continuously put into question in Gee's narrative by the novel's presentation of a conflict between the collective and the individual, between the objective and the subjective; or, to continue to use Lefebvre's terms, the 'conceived space' and the 'lived space'.[8] Alfred, Dirk and May White attempt to engage with their immediate urban space with recourse to obsolete perceptions and memories. These characters fail to understand the suburban space of Hillesden in terms of late twentieth-century modes of experiencing the city and new ways of practising and making space in London. They do not recognize the urban space in which they live to be synonymous with the modern city of London and feel uprooted and detached. This has deep implications for the way in which they negotiate their surroundings, since 'urban space is a crucial aspect of identity construction, knowledge acquisition and social action' (McDowell, 1999: 101).

Alfred and May long for the permanence of the traditional values they associate with Hillesden: 'We like it here. It was our – El Dorado. Once upon a time, it had all we needed' (WF, 121). Their son Dirk, for his part, feels threatened by present-day multicultural and multiethnic Britain and desires a single and authentic public culture which he identifies as being an exclusively white English culture, as manifested by the shop where he works: 'this is an English shop. What have they got against us?' (WF, 126). Unable to negotiate the new social reality that surrounds them, the three characters yearn for a sense of tradition that would secure the continuity they desire. As Elizabeth Wilson describes: '[t]he continual flux and change is one of the most disquieting aspects of the modern city. We expect permanence and stability from the city. Its monuments are solid stone and embody a history that goes back many generations' (Wilson, 1991/1997: 279).

This disassociation with the urban space in which Gee's characters are located is made manifest in a passage of the novel in which May walks down the main road in Hillesden and in this act of walking performs a failed 'pedestrian speech act' (de Certeau, 1988: 97). That is to say, May is unable to appropriate, act out and establish a relation with the road she is walking down; the three main functions, according to de Certeau, that are present in every pedestrian speech act (de Certeau, 1988: 98). Rather, May's act of walking does not engage with the space surrounding her but is steeped in nostalgia and reminiscence. Consequently, her act of walking almost becomes transformed into an act of running, as if she is trying to escape from an urban space she no longer recognizes:

> It was all going faster than May had realized. Almost trotting down the street, her blue coat clutched around her, she saw that more than half the shops were boarded up, or had their fronts covered with aluminium shutters, which rattled coldly in the winter winds. 'To Let', the boards said ... So the boards got battered, and looked grimy, guilty, each one a confession of failure and emptiness. *It was over, Hillesden Rise was over,* and May found the tears welling up again, and realized *she was crying for herself and Alfred and the silly young couple they had once been.* (*WF*, 121, emphasis added)

The main disassociation of the members of the White family with their surrounding environment is materialized in terms of their inability to recognize new and varied ethnic, class, religious and/or family households that are to be found in the area of Hillesden and, by extension, London. Alfred claims that: 'There weren't any coloureds when I was a kid. It was just a normal part of London. We were all the same. We were all one. No one was rich. We stuck together' (*WF*, 223). In this respect, *The White Family* emphasizes that Britishness for Alfred means, at all times, whiteness and Englishness. The use of the term 'Englishness' as a signifier of 'Britishness' shows the historical and cultural supremacy that England has had in Great Britain, with its origins in the history of imperialism. In this sense, the British state has functioned as an imperial state in a double sense: it constructed an external Empire that exploited its colonies, and also established an internal Empire in terms of England's political superiority over Wales, Scotland and Northern Ireland. Moreover, traditional conceptions of

Britishness have been grounded in an idea of ethnic homogeneity; a myth that was, nonetheless, put into question after the decline of the Empire from the 1940s until the 1990s and the migration of former colonial subjects to the metropolis.[9]

Alfred's stable and homogenous view of Britain is a fallacy since 'Britishness has never been a solid and uncontested concept. ... It has never been static and fixed, but has fluctuated in meaning as different Britons have made claims upon it' (Ward, 2004: 172). Alfred is, however, unable to identify this malleable aspect of all national constructions, for his views on the nation are imbued with a strong sense of patriotism. In a sense, Alfred's idea of Britain and his role within the nation – as a park keeper – is closely related to that displayed by Rudyard Kipling's lines from 'The Glory of the Garden', written in 1911. Kipling's text can be seen as an example of the idealized view of the nation that prevailed at the beginning of the twentieth century and was present in the minds of those soldiers who enrolled in the army to fight for the nation during the First World War. Kipling depicts the soldiers' willingness to form part of a collective agenda to work for the country in these terms:

> Our England is a garden and such gardens are not made
>
> By singing:– 'Oh, how beautiful,' and sitting in the shade
>
> ...
>
> Then seek your job with thankfulness and work till further orders,
>
> ...
>
> So when your work is finished, you can wash your hands and pray
>
> For the Glory of the Garden, that it may not pass away! (Kipling, 1934: 712)

Kipling's garden is a metaphor of the nation, which clearly manifests the connection between the idea of the nation on a symbolic, conceived level, and the physical materiality of space. Gee's novel thus depicts with poignancy the substantial changes that are taking place in received ideas of the nation in the latter half of the twentieth century – both spatially and symbolically. Gee does so by depicting the White family as a trope for the idea of Britain and, as I argue in the next section, by presenting urban public spaces – primarily the Park – as tools traditionally used by the national apparatus to enhance a sense of Britishness. In *The White Family* it is both the family itself, as well as urban public spaces, that are depicted as in the process of changing and being re/negotiated; in the same way that 'Britishness' is currently being redefined as a non-fixed, unstable category in both popular and scholarly discourse (Caunce et al., 2004; Gamble and Wright, 2009; Modood and Salt, 2011). In this sense, Gee's novel portrays a disrupted family that is breaking-up and, by so doing, represents the nation in crisis at the end of the twentieth century.

This national crisis affects traditional conceptions of Britishness which project a stable, homogenous conception of national identity that rests, as Gamble and Wright (2009: 2) explain, on 'the two enterprises that defined a large part of what Britishness meant in the twentieth century: empire and welfare'. This traditional view of the nation is rooted, therefore, in pre-Second World War ideas and propaganda as well as in post-war efforts to reconstruct the nation that find their epitome in the character of Alfred White and the values he represents. However, such ideas of the nation have to be challenged and redefined in order to recognize the diasporic, post-Second World War British national landscape, which is, undoubtedly, marked by its history of imperialism, post-imperialism, immigration and globalization.

Gee takes this idea further by symbolically embedding London's transcultural character in the White's own family household through the character of Shirley, May and Alfred's daughter, who marries Ghanaian Kojo and, after becoming his widow, British-Jamaican Elroy.[10] With such acts, she brings an ethnic diversity to the White family that ironically puts into question the 'whiteness' of its name, as it is evident in her father's disapproval:

> The White family. Dad was so proud of their name: the Whites. It was the Whites this and the Whites that. ... *'The White family sticks*

together ...' *(But we didn't, did we?)* ... And later Dad was always pushing me away because he couldn't stand Kojo or Elroy. That force of hatred like a wall. You could never break it down, you could never climb over – (*WF*, 351, emphasis added)

The White Family can thus be identified as portraying the family as a malleable urban space in which London becomes presented as a 'profoundly disruptive location, incubating new social relations and cultural forms which conflict with the advocacy of a national culture or the pursuit of a cultural nationalism' (McLeod, 2004: 18); a location that, despite Alfred's beliefs, challenges traditional ideas of the imperialist nation-state as a homogenous community.

Hillesden Public Spaces: Albion Park as a Heterotopia

In *The White Family*, the park, the hospital and the library offer spatial examples of the continuing impact felt by those great architectural narratives of the end of the nineteenth century, which became consolidated in the construction of the British Welfare State after the Second World War. As May states, 'we fought the last war for places like this. Hospitals and parks and schools' (*WF*, 24).[11] Nonetheless, these public spaces (the park in particular) are depicted at a symbolic level in the novel as simultaneously undergoing a process of change as well as maintaining traditional stability; and they are used in various different ways by the members of the White family, thus emphasizing the struggle between conceptions of space understood as both static and malleable, stable and heterogeneous.[12] This tension is connected to the conceptualization of space as a social construct – space is not only a mere canvas where things and people are located but is imbued with ideology, serves specific purposes and, therefore, can be used to regulate social relations. Urban space is constructed through myths, ideas and representations that give meaning to it in various ways. As Lefebvre points out:

> We should have to study not only the history of space, but also the history of representations, along with that of their relationships – with each other, with practice, and with ideology. History would

have to take in not only the genesis of these spaces but also, and especially, their interconnections, distortions, displacements, mutual interactions, and their links with the spatial practice of the particular society or mode or production under consideration. (Lefebvre, 1974/2005: 42)

Following Lefebvre's thesis, it is useful to analyse the characters' connections to Hillesden's public spaces in *The White Family*; that is, their 'conceived space' in relation to their changing 'lived space'. In this light, the Park functions as an urban public space in terms of the experiences it offers those characters who enter it; and in this reading I take as my starting point the idea that spaces and places, as well as our perceptions of them, are not stable or fixed but vary according to the perspective of the subject encountering them. A Lefebvrian understanding of the Park in Gee's novel thus highlights the conflict between the different meanings associated with it. Some of the characters – mainly Alfred and May – use this public space as counter space to the (apparently) disrupted social space of Hillesden and attempt to preserve obsolete traditional constructed meanings of it; whilst others – mainly Dirk and Winston – challenge such constructed meanings of this urban space with their actions.

Albion Park, described as a space 'we can all share' (*WF*, 16–7), is for Alfred and May a marvel at the heart of Hillesden: 'In dirty Hillesden, the Park seemed miraculous. Just past the notice-boards, life came back. The sky poured in through the gap in the roof-tops. Thousands of miles of cloud and sunlight, tethered to the neat square mile of grass' (*WF*, 46). The park can be read as the fictional counterpart of London's Roundwood Park, situated at the border between Harlesden and Willesden. Gee's description of the park throughout *The White Family* unquestionably matches the geography of Roundwood Park with its unusual hillock, its old bandstand at the top of the hill, and its Victorian drinking fountain. The latter elements, together with the lodge for the Park keeper, are described in the following passage as being at the centre of the Park, which symbolizes their importance:

Albion Park. It was a hundred years old, built in the spate of philanthropy that heralded the end of the nineteenth century, when the local hospital was built, and the library, both of them by the same local builder, who had a deft hand with stone and red brick and a love for details: pediments, cornices. *The drinking-fountain was a marvel*, a spired, four-sided, stone creation modelled like a miniature Gothic cathedral. *It was the focal point to which all paths led.* Not far away the Park Keeper's lodge was a solidly impressive Victorian pile, two-storey, detached, with fine large windows. (*WF*, 48, emphasis added)

As this quotation demonstrates, the aesthetics of the park, with its Victorian buildings, is undoubtedly imbued with an Imperial national identity that contributes to the process of making and forging cultural identity for Alfred and May. With its central point, the Park becomes a symbol of British colonial history since it recalls the view of London as the seat of the Empire. The building of public parks was a well-established practice by the end of the Victorian era; in fact, the majority of public parks were opened between 1885 and 1914 (Jordan, 1994). Moreover, parks were originally meant to be key places that fostered the enjoyment of the working classes and provided symbols of pride for British citizens.[13] As public spaces, such parks were designed for the people and functioned as locations that provided citizens with a common sense of ownership and the idea of belonging to, and partaking of, the urban landscape. In this sense, during the Victorian era – and I would argue that this notion still operates today – parks are clear examples of how architecture was used as a tool to enhance a sense of unity and identity. Like literature, architecture was another form of ideological intervention that created a national identity, for 'aesthetic culture reinforced the culture of the dominant political and social ideologies; and it re-presented and reconstructed the notions of national identity' (Arnold, 2004: 1).

The Park in *The White Family* thus symbolizes traditional Britain for Alfred and May, and this symbolism is highlighted by the name Gee chooses in the novel for the Park: Albion. The name unquestionably reminds the reader of the Albion of mythical Arthurian England and frames the Park's real and symbolic functions within the country's national identity: characterized not only by its mixture of myth and ancient history, but typified also by its timelessness. The latter is crucial for the reading of the park I propose, for, as Sam Smiles (2004: 164) argues, 'if the Arthur story invokes a sense of mysticism and timelessness, in an overtly de-historicized narrative, these same qualities can also be found applied to Britain itself'. This is precisely the idea of the nation that Alfred, May and Dirk attempt to retain throughout the narrative: England as an immovable, timeless nation and the Park as the physical embodiment of this national identity. This perception is connected with Rudyard Kipling's poem 'The Glory of the Garden', especially if Alfred's views on his role as the 'Park Keeper' (*WF*, 11) are taken into consideration. Alfred deeply associates the park with Britain as a glorious, invincible nation, and sees himself as the protector of this timeless and changeless public space that represents the old national values.

Alfred is first presented to the reader as 'a small brisk figure in a military greatcoat' (*WF*, 11); his military outfit favours an understanding of this character as a fighter and protector of Britain and, by extension, of British national identity. The initial title of Gee's novel was, unsurprisingly, *The Keeper of the Gate*; a title which resonates with immigration laws and discourses on racism and racial relations from the late 1960s.[14] It is no coincidence that Gee chooses to introduce Alfred's job as a park keeper to the reader by showing him trying to protect the grass from a black family who are stepping on it in order to recover their child's toy. Alfred's thoughts are narrated through an echo of the terms employed by Enoch Powell in his 'Rivers of Blood' speech – 'If everyone walked here, there'd be no grass left –' (*WF*, 12) – and continue with an insight into his orientalist prejudices concerning the allegedly savage and illiterate nature of black people, whom he identifies as responsible for changing Britain: 'they'd turn the park into a jungle. There are notices. These people can't read… They go on the grass. Always doing it. English people know not to go on the grass –' (*WF*, 14). Alfred's words are thus striking in their reaffirmation of the homogenizing, patriotic views of the white citizen, who understands himself to be a paradigm of refinement and civilization.

In Gee's novel Alfred is constructed as a soldier who protects and has protected the nation: 'Alfred White who holds the fort' (*WF*, 11). Alfred served in the army in Palestine and his physical description and the moral values he stands for – characterized by a strong sense of what is right and wrong – are depicted as anchored in the past values and ideals he received during his period of National Service. Alfred wishes to retain a specific view of what constitutes British national identity that is rooted in pre-Second World War ethics and aesthetics rather than in London's diverse post-Second World War social reality. In Alfred's imagination Albion Park suspends time in the same way that heterotopias do and, therefore, the Park could be read, following Michel Foucault's (1986: 26) theses, as a heterotopia which is 'linked to slices of time – which is to say that [it] open[s] onto what might be termed, for the sake of symmetry, heterochronies' and, thus, 'begins to function at full capacity when men arrive at a sort of absolute break with their traditional time'. Albion Park symbolizes for Alfred a break with time as he retains a fixed and static vision of this space representing a social reality characterized by white ethnic homogeneity. Moreover, the park can be read as a heterotopia since it is a real place that acts as a counter-site in which, as Foucault describes, 'the real sites, all other real sites that can be found within the culture, are simultaneously represented, contested and inverted' (Foucault, 1986: 24). The Park symbolizes for Alfred all the moments of his life together, as he explains to Thomas: 'Did you know I was born twelve yards from the Park? So it really has been my life, in a way' (*WF*, 240–1). The Park thus retains memories of his past, frames his present, and will become his future. Nonetheless, the Park is also a place that younger generations are inscribing with different meanings by establishing different spatial trajectories within its boundaries. For Winston, the young black man who is murdered, the Park is the place where he can express the homosexual identity he is compelled to repress at home as a result of his family's lack of understanding: 'At first he thought that only white men were queer ... And so his life became a net of secrets. He had to go with girls, or his family would suspect him' (*WF*, 281).

Meanwhile, Dirk and his gang of friends use the Park (and the streets of Hillesden) as subversive spaces in which to enact their acts of racist violence (*WF*, 305). In one of their 'hunts', the Park becomes a crucial location. The hunted black men find refuge in the Park and Dirk perceives their act of trespassing the Park's boundaries as a disrespectful violation of his own family, of his father's skin and his own selfhood: 'Why did they decide to climb over the wall? That was disgusting. Showed no respect. *My father's the Park Keeper, remember* ... It was a personal insult, like, to Dad' (*WF*, 304, emphasis in original). This chase culminates with the murder of Winston – who, in a tragic coincidence, was in the Park toilets at the time – at the hands of Dirk. Winston's murder transforms the Park at the end of the novel into a crucial space in which the values Alfred has tried to preserve throughout his life – defending the Park as a safe space – are completely subverted.

For Dirk, Winston is a scapegoat, the external embodiment of his inner fears towards those he perceives as 'foreign'. He murders Winston with his father's army knife in an explicit attempt to complete his father's vocation: 'I'll clean the Park' (*WF*, 343). Gee narrates Dirk's interior monologue in order to present the reader with a character who feels that he has been made a stranger in his own country, and who directs his anger to those he perceives to be the culprits: '*They come here and try and walk on our faces*' (*WF*, 342, emphasis in original). Dirk's racism reveals a desire to return to a past that he does not know, that he has not lived before. In this respect, he differs from his parents, who Gee presents as nostalgically longing for a British past that they knew in their youth: Britain before the Second World War, where the presence of other ethnicities in their neighbourhood was less visible and where they felt there was a sense of collective unity. In an attempt to root his identity and negotiate a sense of belonging, Dirk seeks to rebuild a mythical Albion and protect his father's Park but, paradoxically, in trying to do so, he destroys its values.

The novel's concluding sections reveal that Dirk not only violates the physical space of the Park with such an atrocious action, but also murders a member of his own family. Winston is Shirley's partner's brother and therefore an extension of the White family. This is the further symbolic reading that the novel conveys. By killing its own members, the White family – synonymous in symbolic terms with Britain – is mutilating itself. Gee's use of symbolism in this respect is crucial, for Winston's name is not arbitrarily chosen.[15] Winston is identified by white Britons such as Dirk as a 'foreign outside' (subverting the 'native outside'/'foreign within' dichotomy) yet his name bears the mark of ultimate patriotism as it is the first name of British Prime Minister Winston Churchill. Unlike Dirk, Winston has built up a sense of belonging within Britain and rooted his identity in the social space where he is located. He has also negotiated his (sexual) identity within the urban space of the Park:

> This Park had changed forever one day. .... he had come into the Park and sat alone on the seat near the gates. He was going to kill himself, that was clear. ... But a young white man in jeans and a black singlet came and sat beside him. They looked at each other. Then Winston got up and followed him.
> It was a kind of pattern, for the next six years. (*WF*, 283)

The murder, by symbolic extension, destroys additional members of the family, since Alfred dies shortly afterwards and Dirk is imprisoned. Ironically, and contrary to Dirk's expectations, it is his own father who hands him over to the police, an act that reinforces once again Alfred's sense of morality and duty (*WF*, 399).

Escaping from his hospital ward in order to reach the police station to inform officers of his son's responsibility for Winston's murder, Alfred encounters a group of African young men whom he initially mistakes for the enemy: 'Then he saw the enemy come out into the daylight, three or four of them, between him and his goal' (*WF*, 401). However, and in another symbolically pertinent twist, the men turn out to be his allies, as they help Alfred's exhausted body to reach his destination. Gee expresses Alfred's realization of his mistakes in the sentence he utters at the police station: '"It's my fault," he started, 'all my fault. I am the Park Keeper. I was the Park Keeper ... What I have to tell you concerns my son"' (*WF*, 403). Alfred's utterance and, in particular, the reformulation into the past tense of his role in society, underscores the way in which Gee's radically new novel conveys those 'conflicting requirements' that characterize present-day British society. Alfred seems to understand that he is to some extent responsible for the murder that has taken place in the Park and, therefore, the values that this space represented in his mind have been destroyed. Likewise, he acknowledges that he has instilled hatred, disdain and fear for other ethnicities in his son and that Winston's murder is the terrible outcome of this upbringing.

The White Family's last chapter is entitled 'No ending' (*WF*, 411), for Gee's novel cannot give answers to what is impossible to reduce to essentialist terms – racist hatred and violence – or what is still being negotiated: what the nation is, what it means to be British, and who is included or excluded within that definition. However, the tragic ending Gee gives in *The White Family* offers a denouement that can be read as presenting a hint of optimism for the future.[16] In an explicitly symbolic gesture, Gee suggests that Winston's and Alfred's bodies will rest in the same space in the cemetery, thus sharing a common space in this British soil. The cemetery, we should recall, is the ultimate Foucauldian heterotopic space since its link to all other possible spaces in a city is represented by the fact that people who inhabit the city bear a close connection to it through the relatives that rest there. Moreover, in another explicitly symbolic gesture, Gee presents both Winston's and Alfred's funerals as taking place on the same day, 'side by side, a triumph of mismanagement' (*WF*, 412), emphasizing another way that unites them further as members of the same family.

Conclusion

The White Family not only narrates the death of these protagonists, but also suggests that their deaths are linked to new beginnings through the character of Shirley, the one member of the White family who exemplifies a positive embodiment of ethnic diversity in contemporary British culture and identity. Shirley gives birth to twin boys who, in another twist of the narrative, the reader knows might have been fathered either by Elroy, a black man, or Thomas, a white man. In addition, the previously scattered family is reunited again when Shirley finds the daughter she gave up for adoption when she was a teenager. With this ending Gee suggests that the White family becomes whole after the novel's tragic events and presents a more tolerant, ethnically diverse family to her readership. When Sophie, Shirley's sister-in-law, quotes from the psalm of David following Winston's and Alfred's funerals: *'the night will shine like the day. And darkness will be as light... He has created both darkness and light...'* (WF, 414, emphasis in original) she is highlighting one of Gee's main literary aims, that is, to represent Britain as a shared society and shared community. This is something that the Parekh Report (Commission on the Future of Multiethnic Britain, 2000: ix) expresses very effectively: the fact that families – and societies by extension – should 'be cohesive as well as respectful of diversity, and must find ways of nurturing diversity while fostering a common sense of belonging and a shared identity among its members'.

Through their inability to adapt to a socially changing cityscape, *The White Family* thus presents characters who function as foreigners in their own country of birth, and, thus, as the title of the chapter suggests, become 'natives outside' – Alfred, Dirk and May – together with those who are seen by those natives as foreign – Elroy, Kojo, Winston and even Shirley – the latter group of whom, however, are able to root a sense of identity and relate to the changing nation in ways that native characters fail to establish.[17] In fact, these 'foreign outsiders' successfully become the best example of the new 'native within'; a native within that has managed to acknowledge the dynamic nature of the space in which they are located and accordingly displays a fluid and adaptive sense of identity.

The White Family thus recognizes diverse ways of being and becoming British within the continuum 'native/foreign within/ outside' regardless of ethnic, racial or national differences and emphasizes how 'being British is not a matter of sharing certain individually possessed contingent attributes but rather a form of relationship, a way of relating to the country and its people and seeing it as one's country and them as one's fellow members' (Parekh, 2009: 33). As such, Gee's novel offers an abidingly relevant narrative of how different people negotiate – or fail to negotiate – their sense of space and identity in a changing society. For this reason alone, her work will stand the test of time.

Notes

1 For further reference on this proposal see Bhabha's (1999) Manifesto in *Wasafiri*.

2 Proof of such recognition is the number of Black British and Asian British authors who have been awarded renowned literary prizes and/or have been included in the Granta list of the Best of Young British Novelists since 1983. Regarding the former, and to name just a few, Hanif Kureishi's *The Buddha of Suburbia* (1990) won the Whitbread First Novel Award, Monica Ali's *Brick Lane* (2003) was shortlisted for the Man Booker Prize, Andrea Levy's *Small Island* (2004) won the Orange Prize for Fiction, the Whitbread Novel Award, the Whitbread Book of the Year, the Commonwealth Writer's Prize Best Book and the Orange Prize 'Best of the Best' award. Levy's lastest novel *The Long Song* (2010) was shortlisted for the Man Booker Prize. Likewise, Kureishi and Ali were included in the Granta list in 1993 and 2003 respectively, and so have been Salman Rushdie, Caryl Phillips and Zadie Smith in 1983, 1993 and 2013 respectively.

3 A later work such as Andrea Levy's *Small Island* (2004) resembles these first literary works in a number of respects: concentration on life in post-First World War London, racial discrimination faced by Jamaican immigrants in the hands of a part of the British population, difficulties of finding a job or the process of being déclassé through immigration are some points of similarity. However, Levy presents a wider view of the social problems affecting that period of time by acknowledging that the coming of immigrants to Britain was a two-way process that had an effect on both the newcomers and the white British population. Moreover, unlike in Selvon's *The Lonely Londoners*, Levy also gives voice to an element of the immigrant population that had frequently been silenced in earlier literary works: the women.

4 The emerging interest in Black and Asian women writers' works brought about the publication of anthologies of women's writing and non-fictional studies such as Stella Dadzie, Beverley Bryan and Suzanne Scafe's *The Heart of the Race: Black Women's Lives in Britain* (1985) and Margaret Prescod-Roberts's *Black Women: Bringing It All Back Home*

(1980). Some of the best known anthologies include Sneja Gunew's *Displacements: Migrant Storytellers* (1982), followed by *Displacements II: Multicultural Storytellers* (1987), Centreprise Trust's *Breaking the Silence* (1984), Barbara Burford's *A Dangerous Knowing: Four Black Women Poets* (1985), Rhonda Cobham and Merle Collins's *Watchers and Seekers: Creative Writing by Black Women in Britain* (1987), Lauretta Ngcobo's *Let It be Told* (1987), and Shabhnam Grewal, Jackie Kay et al's *Charting the Journey: Writings by Black and Third World Women* (1988). In 1978, Amrit Wilson's 'voicing' of the almost until then unheard experience of Asian women immigrants in Britain, *Finding a Voice: Asian Women in Britain,* also saw the light.

5 The main difference, in very broad terms, between the first and second generation is the fact that first generation writers tend to focus on denouncing the drudgeries, difficulties and racial discrimination faced in Britain while they retain an idea of home which is not located in Britain but abroad. The second generation, by contrast, are trying to negotiate and assert a sense of identity that is rooted in Britain (as it is the only 'location' they know) and they are asserting their hybrid identity. They do not focus as much on denouncing racial discrimination.

6 The Sociologist Chris Allen (2010a,b,c) has analysed this matter highlighting how this particular discourse practice was in part sanctioned by a lack of legislative protection which 'failed to afford protection to multi-religious groups such as Muslim ... It therefore became unlawful to discriminate against Blacks, Asians, Pakistanis, Bangladeshis, and so on, as well as Jews and Sikhs, but perfectly within the law to discriminate against someone on the basis of their being Muslim: a loophole that was exploited by the far-right political groups following the attacks of 9/11' (Allen, 2010b: 17). Another critic who studies this issue is Kalim Siddiqui (1990).

7 Gee's first collection of short stories, *The Blue* (2006), continues exploring this issue as it is also set against the backdrop of a multicultural and multiethnic Britain. The collection presents thirteen short stories that focus on individual conflicts to depict universal topics related to fears and anxieties arising out of encounters taking place among people of different social, cultural and ethnic backgrounds. Gee explores immigration and the problematics of coming to terms with a changing social space in stories such as 'The Artist', 'Righteousness' and 'What is Important'.

8 In Lefebvre's (1974/2005: 38) terms, the representation of space is scientific because, as he goes on to describe, the representations of space is 'conceptualized space, the space of scientists, planners, urbanists, technocratic subdividers and social engineers, as of a certain type of artist with a scientific bent'.

9 For further discussion on the ways in which Britishness has been defined as a fixed category see Linda Colley (1992) and Richard Weight (2002).

10 London is a city where different cultures coexist, a city 'becoming more and more global (or transnational) and less and less traditionally – that is, ethnically, racially, or even nationally – English or British' (Ball, 2004: 4–5).

11 What May fails to acknowledge is that subjects of the former British Empire also fought in the war alongside British citizens.

12 It is important not to forget that the novel started to be written in 1995, considerably earlier than other novels that have been appraised for presenting London as a multicultural location, such as Zadie Smith's *White Teeth* (2000), were published.

13 For further reference on the meaning and social implications of urban public parks see Taylor (1995).

14 The clearest exponent of such discourse is to be found in the famous Enoch Powell speech 'Rivers of Blood', which he delivered in Birmingham in April 1968 and where he stated that 'permitting the annual flow of some 50,000 dependants, who are for the most part the material of the future growth of the immigrant-descended population ... was like watching a nation busily engaged in heaping up its own funeral pyre' (Powell, 1968/2007).

15 The symbolic use of names is a constant in the novel. Note, for example, the fact that Dirk is named after the actor Dirk Bogarde and, like the latter, there are hints in the novel towards Dirk's possible homosexuality, for 'Dirk hated women. They hated him and he hated them. And foreigners' (*WF*, 300). Alfred's name recalls the Anglo-Saxon king Alfred the Great (871–99) who fought against Viking raids.

16 A refusal of the apocalypticism of endings and a persistence in hope is a feature of Gee's work, from the '... Against Ending' final chapter of her second novel, *The Burning Book* (1983) to the 'After' final chapter of *The Flood* (2004).

17 There are numerous references throughout the novel to Alfred's and Dirk's constant regard of non-white people as outsiders and foreigners and attempts to deny their Britishness. One clear example is the argument that takes place between Shirley and Alfred at the hospital, regarding Elroy: "'Elroy is English', said Shirley. "Well – British. Elroy is as British as me or you." "Oh yes?," said Alfred. ... "He's about as British as bananas, is Elroy'" (*WF*, 63). Shirley, on her part, is made an outsider by her father and brother when she chooses as partners two black men, as Dirk explicitly says: "'You ... nigger-lover ... Dirty slag ... Can't believe you're my sister ... Dad made a stand about things like that'" (*WF*, 298).

Works Cited

Ali, Monica (2003) *Brick Lane*. London: Black Swam Allen, Chris (2010a) *Islamophobia*. London: Ashgate.

Allen, Chris (2010b) 'Islamophobia and Anti-Muslim Hatred: Causes and Remedies', *Arches* 4(7): 14–22.

Allen, Chris (2010c) 'Fear and loathing: the political discourse in relation to Muslims and Islam in the British contemporary setting', *Politics & Religion* 2(4): 221–35.

Arnold, Dana (ed.) (2004) *Cultural Identities and the Aesthetics of Britishness*. Manchester: Manchester University Press.

Ball, John Clement (2004) *Imagining London: Postcolonial Fiction and the Transnational Metropolis*. Toronto: Toronto University Press.

Bhabha, Homi (1999) 'Reinventing Britain: A Forum: The Manifesto', *Wasafiri* 29: 37–8.

Brah, Avtar (1996) *Cartographies of Diaspora: Contesting Identities*. London: Routledge.

Burford, Barbara (ed.) (1985) *A Dangerous Knowing: Four Black Women Poets*. London: Sheba Feminist Publishers.

Caunce, Stephen, Mazierska, Ewa, Sydney-Smith Susan and Walton, John K. (2004) *Relocating Britishness*. Manchester: Manchester University Press.

Centreprise Trust (1984) *Breaking the Silence: Writing by Asian Women*. London: Centreprise Trust.

Cobham, Rhonda and Collins, Merle (1987) *Watchers and Seekers: Creative Writing by Black Women in Britain*. London: Women's Press.

Colley, Linda (1992) *Britons: Forging the Nation 1707-1837*. Yale: Yale University Press.

Commission on the Future of Multiethnic Britain (2000) *The Future of Multiethnic Britain: The Parekh Report*. London: Profile Books.

Dadzie, Stella, Bryan, Beverley and Scafe, Suzanne (1985) *The Heart of the Race: Black Women's Lives in Britain*. London: Virago.

de Certeau, Michel (1988) *The Practice of Everyday Life*, trans. Steven Rendall. Berkeley: University of California Press.

Donald, James and Rattansi, Ali (eds) (1992) *'Race', Culture and Difference*. London: Sage.

English, James F. (ed.) (2006) *A Concise Companion to Contemporary British Fiction*. Oxford: Blackwell.

Evans, Diana (2006) *26a*. London: Vintage.

Foucault, Michel (1986) 'Of Other Spaces', trans. Jay Miskowiec, *Diacritics* 16(1): 22–7.

Gamble, Andrew and Wright, Tony (eds) (2009) *Britishness: Perspectives on the British Question*. Oxford: The Political Quarterly Publishing Company.

Gee, Maggie (2005) *Meet the Author: The White Family*, 29 Jun 2005, URL (consulted December 2009): http://www.meettheauthor.co.uk/bookbites/733.html

Gee, Maggie (2009) 'Imagining Difference: Girl Writes Boy, White Writes Black' in Marian Amengual, Maria Juan and Joana Salazar Noguera (eds) *New Perspectives on English Studies*, pp. 12–18. Palma de Mallorca: Servei Publicacions UIB.

Grewal, Shabnam, Kay, Jackie, Landor, Liliane, Lewis, Gail and Parmar, Pratibha (eds) (1988) *Charting the Journey: Writings by Black and Third World Women*. London: Sheba Feminist Publishers.

Gunew, Sneja Marina (1982) *Displacements: Migrant Storytellers*. Victoria: Deakin P.

Gunew, Sneja Marina (1987) *Displacements II: Multicultural Storytellers*. Victoria: Deakin P.

Jaggi, Maya (2002) 'Maya Jaggi in Conversation with Maggie Gee: *The White Family*', *Wasafiri* 17(36): 5–10.

Jordan, Harriet (1994) 'Public Parks, 1885–1914', *Garden History* 22(1): 85–113.

Kipling, Rudyard (1934) 'The Glory of the Garden' in *Rudyard Kipling's Verse: Inclusive Edition 1885–1932*, 4th edn. London: Hodder and Stoughton.

Kureishi, Hanif (1990) *The Buddha of Suburbia*. London: Faber

Kureishi, Hanif (1986) *My Beautiful Launderette*. London: Faber

Lamming, George (1954) *The Emigrants*. New York: McGrawHill.

Lefevbre, Henri (1974/2005) *The Production of Space*, trans. Donald Nicholson-Smith. Oxford: Basil Blackwell.

Levy, Andrea (2004) *Small Island*. London: Review.
Levy, Andrea (2010) *The Long Song*. London: Headline Review.
Massey, Doreen (1994) *Space, Place and Gender*. Minnesota: University of Minnesota Press.
McDowell, Linda (1999) *Gender, Identity and Place*. Oxford: Polity Press.
McLeod, John (2004) *Postcolonial London: Rewriting the Metropolis*. London: Routledge.
McLeod, John (2010) 'Extra Dimensions, New Routines', *Wasafiri* 25(4): 45–52.
Modood, Tariq (2005) *Multicultural Politics: Racism, Ethnicity and Muslims in Britain*. London Edinburgh: Edinburgh University Press.
Modood, Tariq and Salt, John (eds) (2011) *Global Migration, Ethnicity and Britishness*. Hampshire: Palgrave Macmillan.
Nasta, Shusheila (2004) *Writing Across Worlds: Contemporary Writers Talk*. London: Routledge.
Ngcobo, Lauretta (1987) *Let It be Told: Essays by Black Women in Britain*. London: Pluto.
Parekh, Bhikhu (2009) 'Being British' in Andrew Gamble and Tony Wright (eds) *Britishness: Perspectives on the British Question*, pp. 32–40. Oxford: The Political Quarterly Publishing Company.
Phillips, Caryl (1981) *Strange Fruit*. Charlbury: Amber Lane Press.
Powell, Enoch (1968/2007) '"Rivers of Blood" Speech', *The Telegraph*, 6 Nov 2007, URL (consulted March 2011): http://www.telegraph.co.uk/comment/3643826/Enoch-Powells-Rivers-of-Blood-speech.html
Prescod-Roberts, Margaret (1980) *Black Women: Bringing It All Back Home*. Bristol: Falling Wall Press.
Said, Edward (2003) *Orientalism*. London: Penguin.
Selvon, Sam (1956) *The Lonely Londoners*. London: Macmillan
Siddiqui, Kalim (1990) *The Muslim Manifesto: A Strategy for Survival*. London: The Muslim Institute.
Smiles, Sam (2004) 'Albion's legacy – Myth, History and "the Matter of Britain"' in Dana Arnold (ed.) *Cultural Identities and the Aesthetics of Britishness*, pp. 164–81. Manchester: Manchester University Press.
Smith, Zadie (2000) *White Teeth*. London: Penguin
Taylor, Hilary A. (1995) 'Urban Public Parks, 1840–1900: Design and Meaning', *Garden History* 23(2): 201–21.
Ward, Paul (2004) *Britishness since 1870*. London: Routledge.
Weight, Richard (2002) *Patriots: National Identity in Britain 1940-2000*. Basingstoke: Macmillan.

Wilson, Amrit (1978) *Finding a Voice: Asian Women in Britain*. London: Virago.

Wilson, Elizabeth (1991/1997) 'Into the Labyrinth', in Linda McDowell and Joanne Sharp (eds) *Space, Gender, Knowledge: Feminist Readings*, pp. 277–84. London: Arnold.

9

FAITH AND GRACE
MAGGIE GEE'S SPIRITUAL POLITICS

Susan Alice Fischer

Titling this essay 'Faith and Grace' seems an odd thing to do for a person neither raised nor trained in Christian traditions, or for one who has always placed much more trust in political and social analyses than on those relying on the non-material realm. Nonetheless, it seems to me that Maggie Gee's political vision is intertwined with an eclectic spirituality that is partly Christian, as she herself has suggested in her recent memoir, *My Animal Life* (2010). Or perhaps it would be more accurate to write that Gee's work, which is clearly political – addressing as it does such issues as nuclear disaster, war, domestic violence, racism and so on – has a strong spiritual dimension. With the terms 'political' and 'spiritual' I am not suggesting anything particularly esoteric. By politics, I mean an analysis and solution having to do with the access to, and distribution of, power and resources among diverse groups of people in the material world, as well as with how we act individually and collectively in that world. With the term 'spiritual', I mean a mode of understanding beyond the material, and indeed human, realm. Yet even these divisions become artificial and arbitrary in Gee's creative world. Instead, what I shall look at are the ways that Gee's fiction engages with some of the most compelling issues of contemporary life through what I shall call a 'spiritual politics', which intertwines both dimensions, and I shall also suggest that it is her preoccupation with the natural world that enables this interconnection to take place. This emerges in Gee's early fiction, and is also evident in her more recent work, which I shall focus on in the second part of this chapter.

I. 'Spiritual Politics'

The title for this chapter, 'Faith and Grace', was suggested by two of the characters in Gee's 1988 novel, *Grace*, though the terms appear elsewhere in her work as well. In this book, Grace is an 85-year-old woman who, towards the end of the novel, assists a young chambermaid named Faith in giving birth. Like so much of Gee's work, *Grace* can be read on a political level. In addition to the more general backdrop of Thatcherism and its concomitant privatization and other nefarious doings, Gee draws upon several very specific events. *Grace* refers to the Chernobyl disaster of 1986 and the environmental concerns it provoked, the transport of nuclear waste materials in Britain, and the 1984 murder of the anti-nuclear activist Hilda Murrell, upon whom the character Grace is based. The role of the State is apparent in *Grace*, where it operates not only through the official channels of the Thatcher government, but also as a sort of shadow state with covert operations carried out at various levels, including using small-time thugs such as the character Bruno.

Another political aspect of *Grace* is that it is a state-of-the-nation novel. In *Grace*, the ramshackle hotel that Arthur Fraenkel works in is called the Albion, while Grace stays in the Empire. That the Albion is frequented by clients down on their luck and run by displaced workers with nowhere else to go suggests Gee's view of Thatcher's Britain, as does the owner's decision at the end of the novel to follow his young Thatcherite upstart son's advice to sell the Albion. However, at the Empire, while an old man dies, a baby is born, suggesting hope and continuity. Feminist politics also undergird much of Gee's writing and are present in *Grace*. A character from an earlier generation of feminist pioneers, with shades of Virginia Woolf and *To the Lighthouse* (1927), Grace is a woman who has had the courage to break the rules and to attempt to carve out a space for her own creativity as a writer, and although she becomes swallowed up in the creativity of her painter-lover, she ultimately does not agree to have his child. Thus with *Grace*, Gee raises important political questions about the environment and the bullyboy tactics of the British secret service to present both a political and a broader ethical vision about the value of nature and of love.

Yet, for all its political implications, *Grace* – and Gee's other work – also demands to be read in a spiritual light. Certainly there is recourse to religious imagery with the names Faith and Grace, and the words 'faith' and 'grace' – and related ideas of hope, compassion, love, luck and miracles – crop up elsewhere in Gee's work. However, I shall suggest it goes further than that. Christianity refers to faith as 'the substance of things hoped for, the conviction of things not seen' (Hebrews 11.1); it also means belief in Christ and the resurrection. Faith can mean 'belief' or 'hope' – and the latter definition seems particularly apt for Gee's work. The character Faith has hope in a better life that will be realized with her child. In *My Animal Life*, Gee writes about her own relation to spirituality and defines faith, not in strictly Christian terms, but as part of a '[r]espect for other living things – the respect that should always be there, but which fails us – [that] might be easier to maintain if we granted every other being a soul' (*MAL*, 227).

Grace, on the other hand, can refer to 'profound mystery'; it can also be called '"compassion," "kindness," and "love"' (Campbell 1993/2004). According to Edward Campbell, the Bible generally '*portrays* grace rather than naming it' – something that can be seen in Gee's work as well (Campbell, 1993/2004, emphasis added). In the novel, Grace shows love to Faith, whom she had previously seen as a rather annoying housekeeper, by helping to deliver her baby; in the end she enters a state of grace herself in which she is able to let go of the past and see her connection to the life cycle as she is miraculously saved, perhaps just long enough to learn that her niece, Paula, is pregnant. Thus the concept of grace 'concerns the interaction between gracious person and graced recipient, involving the wills of both' (Campbell, 1993/2004). As such it involves '[t]he motives of the grace giver [which can be human or divine]; [... and] the life-renewing impact of the gift [...]. A gracious one reaches out to the poor, the needy, the oppressed, the forsaken – a movement intrinsic to God and to righteous humans' (Campbell, 1993/2004). This definition of grace seems to permeate Gee's work, though at times she calls it other things, such as 'miracle' or 'luck'. For instance, in *Light Years*, Lottie Lucas – whose name sounds like a lot of luck – only encounters a state of grace once she has become gracious herself. During her first attempt at charity, she foists a wad of cash at a drunken, homeless man in Camden. But she has acted in this moment from insincere motives – a desire to be *seen* to be doing good – and ends up kicking him and wanting to hammer him with her handbag. Only when she is truly gracious, giving money to feed the Tamarins at the zoo without expectation of return, does she open herself up to receiving grace. That is, as suggested by Galatians 5.6, Lottie has demonstrated faith by working in love, and thus attains a form of grace. This concept resonates in other spiritual traditions as well, and Gee seems to draw upon the idea of karma for her 'spiritual politics' as well as on the Buddhist idea of compassion and of giving without the expectation of receiving.

Indeed, in *My Animal Life*, while Gee states that her influences growing up were Christian, she references 'the Buddhist Goddess of Compassion, Kuan Yin, who is described as "an incarnation of Mary", whose person embodies loving kindness', and she recognizes that different belief systems 'have aspects of the same beauty' and 'value compassion, love, forgiveness, charity' and speak of 'the compassion in the universe' (*MAL*, 225–6). She also refers to Matthew Fox, whose '(r)evolutionary Creation Spirituality movement' recognizes the vulnerable – 'the *anawin*, the humble and excluded' – as those who can show the way (*Matthew Fox: Friends of Creation Spirituality*; *MAL*, 225). These intertwined spiritual traditions offer Gee '[a] mirror reversal of the world we know, quietly radical, the gentlest miracle. An image, an otherworld that hangs there beckoning, beyond the hills of hurt and worry' (*MAL*, 225). These ideas of the *anawim*, a 'mirror reversal' of our world and an 'otherworld' urging us towards a better life reverberate throughout Gee's fiction, particularly in *My Cleaner* and *My Driver*, as I shall show below.

In this recognition of the vulnerable, Gee's work suggests seeing politics in a more spiritual light, which moves it away from the mundane aspects of power play and into a more cosmic sphere, which includes not only humans, but all living beings. It is in the preoccupation with nature and with motherhood in *Grace*, and elsewhere in Gee's fiction, that the slippage between a clear-cut distinction between politics and spirituality occurs. It is not only that humans destroy nature with nuclear energy, but that nature itself is unpredictable, and the hurricane of October 1987 appears in *Grace* to represent this sense of the ineffable, as does the timing, which allows Arthur to arrive while Grace is still alive and thus represents fate or what elsewhere Gee refers to as a 'miracle' or 'animal luck'.

The connection of nature and motherhood with politics and spirituality in Gee's world derives, I would suggest, from her interest in the intersection between art and science and specifically in the scientific notion of Gaia. As Mary Midgley (2007: 6) explains, the concept of Gaia represents the Earth as a living force, with love as a central power of attraction and where 'nature' is seen neither as mechanistic nor as 'dead matter', but as 'nurturing mother'. In her article 'Imagining Gaia: Art Living Lightly With Science', which comes out of a Gaia Network collection edited by Midgley, Gee (2007: 96) discusses Gaia theory, the name born of 'conversations between the scientist James Lovelock and the novelist William Golding in 1967'. As a metaphor, Gee writes, Gaia helps to explain 'Lovelock's complex idea of a self-regulating planet' to a lay audience because it draws on the idea of 'Earth, a single mythic figure, the Greek goddess, first to be born after Chaos, mother of all that lives' (Gee, 2007: 96). According to Midgley (2007: 3), Gaia theory understands 'Earth and the life on it as an active self-maintaining whole', which she argues is an important notion for science and spirituality and their interconnectedness. They are different ways of attempting to understand the patterns in the world. These patterns, Midgley (2007: 4) maintains, are not just those of 'measurable' 'mechanisms'. Rather other sorts of patterns are needed 'to give sense and meaning to our lives' by looking at 'various kinds of forces and fields and in webs of connection, rather than in separate items to be connected' (Midgley, 2007: 4). This resonates with what I am calling Gee's 'spiritual politics', which draws upon multiple modes of understanding – artistic, scientific, spiritual and political – to recognize the interconnectedness of all life forms. This conception underpins the ethical vision of Gee's work.

In her article on Gaia, Gee (2007: 97) recounts how friends she met as a young woman at Oxford – 'the ecologist C. S. Elton and the poet E. J. Scovell' – made her understand 'the interrelationship of species' and see '[t]hat science and art were two sides of the same observant curiosity' to make sense out of the seemingly 'random and chaotic' (Gee, 2007: 98). Charles Elton advanced a 'sombrely apocalyptic view of the damage that excessive human numbers would do to the planetary ecosystem' (Gee, 2007: 99), which made quite an impression on Gee. She dealt with the fear this engendered by 'telli[ing] apocalyptic stories; but also [by] imagin[ing] redemptive endings, ways of surviving. My fascination with science helps to contain both hope and fear within a continuum of rationality' (Gee, 2007: 99). Recognizing the interconnection between species becomes, for Gee, a mode of survival and redemption. She writes about regularly visiting a family of orang-utans at the zoo with her husband in the early 1980s: 'And [we] saw ourselves. [...] My mind and body connected in a way it never quite had before [...]. We understood we were primates. And we saw what human beings were doing to this particular small family of captive primates' (Gee, 2007: 100). This image recurs in her fiction. In *Light Years*, Lottie – ironically the daughter of a fur merchant – finally recognizes herself when visiting the animals at the London Zoo, which is also where she and her husband Harold connect with one another. Similarly, in a key scene in *My Driver*, Vanessa perceives the connection across species with the gorillas in Uganda. Gee concludes her article in Midgley's collection on Gaia, *Earthy Realism*, by saying: 'To live more lightly on this planet, *our mother*, to try to look with her eyes, to learn from science and to teach through art: this might be a way of loving Gaia and ourselves while there is still time' (Gee, 207: 101, emphasis added).

This understanding of Gaia, which is both scientific and spiritual, and which has political implications as well, resonates throughout Gee's work. It has to do with her notion of her 'animal luck' and the interconnectedness of 'three hundred generations of couples, linked in the dance, in the heat of the bed, all of whom were lucky, who begat children. Link after golden link: my luck' (*MAL*, 231). But it is also her connection to all life forms, and her belief in the 'soul' which is, she says, '"an unwavering band of light", invisible but real, shining at the centre of us all' (*MAL*, 227). That is, it is part of the interconnectedness of life, and part of our ability to see each other.

The capacity to see the other manifests itself in Gee's work by finding a way to fight the forces of destruction – *Thanatos* – in opposition to the counter-posing life force of *Eros*. At the same time, Gee's empathic vision also enables us to see the humanity of even the most destructive among us – the racists, the misogynists, the murderers – by exploring the damaging home relations and larger societal issues that produce their psycho-sexual drive to hate and to destroy. Hence the importance of such characters as Bruno in *Grace*, Dirk in *The White Family* (2002), Guy in *The Burning Book* (1983), and to a lesser degree, perhaps, Smeggy in *Light Years*. Paradoxically, such characters also show the possibility of reclaiming even the worst among us by demonstrating that if only they had not been belittled and humiliated at home and in the larger world – if only they had received the love that is at the centre of Gee's vision – they could not possibly act as they do, and the world would be a better place.

In 'Why Writers Can't Be Told They Have Responsibilities' (2004), Gee has said, 'I do try to write compassionately because I think that one of the great things about fiction is that it helps us to imagine each other.' The need to see the other recalls Cynthia Ozick's wonderful essay, 'Metaphor and Memory' (originally published in 1986 as 'Moral Necessity of Metaphor'), in which she writes:

> Through metaphor [...] [t]hose who have no pain can imagine those who suffer. Those at the center can imagine what it is to be outside.

> The strong can imagine what it is to be weak. Illuminated lives can imagine the dark. Poets in their twilight can imagine the borders of stellar fire. We strangers can imagine the familiar hearts of strangers. (Ozick, 1986/1996: 328–9)

Like compassion, love is central to Gee's vision: *'L'amore, che muove il sole e l'altre stelle'* ('Love, which moves the sun and the [other] stars'), as Dante writes in *Paradiso* (3: XXXIII, line 145), a line Gee uses as one of the epigraphs to *Light Years*. Gee's vision focuses on how the lives we lead as interconnected individuals and societies – and the questions we ask – generate the larger world we inhabit. To explore Gee's spiritual politics further, I shall now turn to how these ideas manifest themselves in *My Cleaner* and *My Driver*.

II. 'Spiritual Politics' and 'Race'

Among the issues that Gee's fiction addresses through what I am calling a 'spiritual politics' are racism and the residual force of colonialism, but they are rarely seen in her work as solely political. Taking on this subject as a white author has not smoothed Gee's path to publication, as the author has discussed with Maya Jaggi and in *My Animal Life*. This is especially true of *The White Family*, written in the 1990s in response to the 1993 Stephen Lawrence murder in London, though not published until 2002 (see Jaggi, 2002: 6). Gee's work has defied expectations that white writers cannot write about black subjects, thus resisting what Susie Thomas (2005: 309) has termed 'literary apartheid', which has as much to do with the choices writers make as with the difficulties that the publishing industry creates by attempting to pigeon-hole writers and readers into 'racial' categories.

While *The White Family* is a state-of-the nation novel that looks at race relations and national identity, *My Cleaner* and *My Driver* move beyond national borders, looking at postcolonial relations between Britain and its former protectorate, Uganda, mostly through the eyes of – and interactions between – two forceful, yet flawed female characters. *My Cleaner* (2005) is the first half of a diptych, followed by *My Driver* (2009). Indeed, the relation between the two novels is stronger than a sequel, as one novel is in many ways a 'mirror image' of the other, as van Bleijswijk also notes (n.d.: 2). While each novel can stand on its own, the two are best seen together as one work. Textual evidence in *My Cleaner*, the first of the two novels, suggests that the books were planned this way.[1]

In describing the relation between these two novels, I have deliberately used the word diptych, which the *Oxford English Dictionary* defines as '[a]n altar-piece or other painting composed of two leaves which close like a book' ('Diptych, n.'). Usually the two panels bear a striking resemblance and communicate with one another, forming one larger composition, two parts of one story. The 'spiritual politics' of these novels is bolstered by the use of the literary equivalent of a diptych. That is, each novel presents a mirror image of the other and offers two perspectives of a similar story that focuses on the necessity of seeing the other – 'the familiar hearts of strangers', in Ozick's (1986/1996: 329) iteration. I would take the metaphor further and suggest that this diptych is indeed an altarpiece of sorts, as it asks us to contemplate not only the political imperatives of seeing the other, but also larger spiritual ideas that connect us to a life force much greater than ourselves which should be revered in all its forms, human and otherwise.

In *My Cleaner*, Vanessa Henman, a white, English, middle-aged, middle-class author and creative writing lecturer, pleads with her former domestic worker, Mary Tendo from Uganda, to return to London to help her young adult son, Justin, who is in the throes of depression. Mary sees this as an opportunity to earn a considerable amount of money that will enable her to make a long overdue return to her village to bring her relatives the resources they need. Despite a complicated history of exploitation with Vanessa, Mary agrees to come, but now at the distance of 11 years is able to negotiate her own terms. Mary refuses to be a 'cleaner' when in fact she has been hired to take care of Justin. While Vanessa finds that the house 'had got filthy' (*MC*, 92), Mary maintains the upper hand in the power struggle between them, and Vanessa is in denial about her own responsibilities. Mary will manage to get Justin out of his deep funk and also set in motion – we learn later in *My Driver* – his marriage to Zakira, the Anglo-Moroccan woman whom he loves and who is pregnant by him. Just as Vanessa has sought Mary's help, Mary will enlist Vanessa's ex-husband Trevor's plumbing services to build a well in her village in Uganda, something that is alluded to in the first novel, but unfolds in the second.

My Driver opens a couple of years after Mary has returned from London to Uganda, where she is now married to Charles, with whom she has a baby daughter, Theodora. She has secured the prestigious job of Executive Housekeeper at the local Sheraton, and she continues to nurture her desire to write. Her deepest pain is that her son, Jamil, from her first marriage remains lost. She has nonetheless decided to go home to her village after an absence of many years where she will help her family and community with their well, with the help of Trevor. Meantime, unbeknownst to either of them, Vanessa is winging her way to Kampala to participate in a British Council literary event to which she seems to have been invited as an after-thought, and she will later visit the Gorilla Forest Camp in western Uganda. Many paths cross, so that just as Mary saves Justin at the end of *My Cleaner*, so Vanessa, through an act of compassion, brings Mary her long-lost son at the end of *My Driver*.

Both *My Cleaner* and *My Driver* are told from different perspectives: in the first novel, Mary and Vanessa narrate in first person, so that each woman's voice emerges, and there is also third-person omniscient narrator, which takes over in the second novel, though the two perspectives remain through shifting points of view. On a political level, these novels use satire to highlight the misbegotten ways that black and white, Western and African, people often see each other, and indeed themselves. For instance, Vanessa is famously in denial, often 'forgetting' what she has said to Mary when it is something particularly appalling (*MC*, 94), while Mary cannot believe that the spoilt Vanessa could possibly have any problems not of her own making. The first novel thus focuses on the 'polite' racism of white, middle-class life and the exploitation of immigrant domestic workers, whilst the second lays out the current political situation in Uganda and its deeper roots in British colonialism.

At first it seems that Vanessa and Mary have little in common, and certainly they see each other as very different. However, both have escaped humble origins in villages to be educated in the city. In *My Cleaner*, Mary states: 'I am in the city, and it is in me' (*MC*, 23). Similarly, 'Vanessa is proud to be a Londoner, a sophisticate, a creature of the city' (*MC*, 12). Both have struggled to be wives, mothers and professionals. Like Vanessa, who is now branching off into life writing, Mary wishes to tell her story. In *My Driver*, Mary still wants to get her work noticed after Vanessa's agent singled it out as promising, and Vanessa struggles with her own sense of importance in the vicious hierarchy of the literary world.

One of the themes in both novels involves the failure to see oneself accurately or to acknowledge the other. Both women are convinced of their own inherent superiority, though Vanessa, in her hypocrisy, would not put it like that. As a former cleaner, Mary feels that: 'I was never equal to the people I cleaned for. I knew all about them, all their dirtiness, the secret habits that no one else knew [...]. And so, I was superior' (*MC*, 32). For her part, Mary 'has hated' Vanessa (*MC*, 57), whom she often refers to as 'the Henman'; she also believes that 'English people are like children. The Henman still has a toy bear on her bed' (*MC*, 67), although Mary recognizes that the English say the same about Africans. When she is not merely selfish, Vanessa's intentions are decent, but she has a hard time seeing Mary as an individual and not as solely black or African. She thinks that she is so different from Mary by having 'chosen' a single-parent family, which makes her 'modern' unlike African women (*MC*, 32). Vanessa believes that since she has spent a brief time in Kampala, she now understands everything about the country. But she does not recognize her bigoted ways of looking at people and the world. For instance, she refers to her ex-husband Trevor's new girlfriend, as 'some kind of Indian who doesn't speak English' (*MC*, 27). Referring to Mary, Vanessa says, 'she'd look at me blankly, in that African way' (*MC*, 42). Vanessa relies on stereotypes as she negotiates a price for Mary's labour: 'Naturally there would be a deal to be done. In any case, this was the African way. When they dealt with white people, they bargained upwards, just as they beat people down in the markets. I understood things better now

I'd been to Africa' (*MC*, 43). Vanessa thinks in terms of 'they' rather than 'she': '*they*'re unpredictable. Even though I have known Mary for years. You never really know what *they*'re thinking' (*MC*, 91, my emphasis). Although relying on Mary to help her son, she also resents Justin's closeness to Mary. Vanessa's inability to recognize Mary as a unique, individual subject manifests itself, for instance, in Vanessa's inability to decipher the very familiar sound of typing emanating from Mary's room simply because she cannot conceive of her as a writer, as Özatabak-Avci (2012) has similarly noted. To Vanessa, Mary is merely 'my cleaner'.

Despite her tenacity and perspicacity – and the repeated references to sight and detection in the novel – Mary also fails to see Vanessa clearly. This is most evident when she drives with Vanessa to visit the village from which Vanessa – like Mary from her village – has been away a very long time, as she has moved into middle-class life. This visit represents a turning point in the novel as it challenges Mary's view that she and Vanessa have virtually nothing in common. She originally assumes that everything in life has been easy for Vanessa and that she is merely selfish, dirty and a useless mother. While Mary can find Vanessa insufferable – and she still occasionally fears Vanessa's power over her as her employer – by the end of the trip, she sees Vanessa in a very different light. Symbolically, this is shown by the fact that the glasses she thought she had left at home somehow appear in her pocket, and she drives back to London seeing more clearly. Thus vision returns after Mary has seen Vanessa's family home, described as not much more than the meagre dwelling that Mary's family has in her village. As van Bleijswijk (n.d.: 4) has noted, this clearer vision begins when they literally see themselves reflected together in a mirror on the road, reflecting 'two small living things on an enormous planet' who 'merge together into the same bright dot' (*MC*, 242).

Throughout the novel Mary insists that she is not a cleaner. Indeed, this is part of the political point in that she refuses to bend to Vanessa's construction of her as a domestic worker who is there to clean up after a well-off, white Westerner, and she turns the tables by insisting that Vanessa hire a white, Austrian immigrant cleaner.

But from a spiritual point of view, Mary does *cleanse*. She recognizes that Justin 'is sick in his soul' (*MC*, 72), something she addresses by cleaning out the family's intestines with high-fiber meals and getting Vanessa to clear out the clutter of her Western middle-class life. This connection between nature, spirit and body is represented by the way that Mary literally nourishes Justin back to health by feeding him real, rather than processed, food. Mary transforms the kitchen: 'The earth has spilled roots out on to its lap, great brown and red tubers, white in cross-section where Mary has sawed some off for the pot' (*MC*, 81). Vanessa is 'uneasy at this vegetable flood, this weird invasion of living things into her kitchen' (*MC*, 81), but she eats the lunch Mary prepares, even though she goes into work 'feeling as if she has swallowed a farm' (*MC*, 81). Vanessa views the beauty of natural abundance of multi-coloured vegetables 'all sitting like *grace* on the plate' (*MC*, 28, emphasis added). Here the natural world is constructed as a cure for the sickness of the soul that has clogged up the Henmans's lives. Indeed, the metaphor of unblocking is further reflected in the need to call Vanessa's former husband Trevor, who is a plumber, to unblock the toilets that have themselves been obstructed by the no-longer constipated family.

Mary saves Justin as she cleanses his body and soul. As her first name suggests, she is a Marian figure. (In Latin, her family name *Tendo* means 'stretch out' or 'extend', and she does extend herself to Justin.) A religious person, Mary thanks Jesus, *'for bringing [her] back'* to London where she believes 'God will make Justin well again' (*MC*, 55, emphasis in original). When Mary first arrives, Vanessa thinks '[s]he looks like someone who can – save the day. *Mary, Mary. Stay here and save me*' (*MC*, 63). Justin has faith that she will 'save me, Mary' (*MC*, 72). When she buys a new mobile phone, Mary tries out different ring tones while on the bus: 'Amazing Grace', 'Ave Maria' and 'When the saints'. A drunkard comments that the last thing he needs is 'Amazing grace' and grabs the phone from her until she threatens him with an umbrella, which leads him to exclaim, 'Mother of Jesus' (*MC*, 87–8). Like her namesake, Mary feels compassion and love for Justin when as a little boy he misbehaved to draw his mother's attention: 'I saw he needed her to look at him. At the same moment, I started to love him' (*MC*, 32). However, this earthly Mary is not perfect, as she will need to learn to have compassion for Vanessa, something she fails at spectacularly when Vanessa is attacked by a student and Mary worries only about whether he may have stolen her hard-earned savings.

This understanding of Mary as a spiritual mother figure is important, not only to recognize the compassion that enables her to save Justin, but also because it may clarify the intention of one of the more troubling images in the novel. On the day that Mary arrives, Vanessa cooks a chicken and offers Justin some '[l]ovely white breast' (*MC*, 64), which he refuses. Instead, he wants Mary's breast, and she suckles this grown man whom she had breastfed as a child and still thinks of as her 'baby' (*MC*, 106). While this seems to cast her in the role of 'black mammy', it is perhaps meant to be read more symbolically as a Virgin mother and child. The image of Mary cradling the waning young man suggests a *pietà*. Even though Justin is not dead, Vanessa has just voiced her fear that he might die (*MC*, 63), and Mary ultimately helps to resurrect him, as she '*dream[s] that in heaven it will be made right*' (*MC*, 106, emphasis in original), not only for Justin, but also for her own son, Jamil, whom she fears dead. Another interpretation of this image of Mary is that she represents 'Mother Africa', especially since in *My Driver*, there are references to the Rift Valley, the source of human life. Even so, this remains a curious image.

By the time we next meet her in Kampala in *My Driver*, Mary has herself suffered a loss of faith because her own son, Jamil, is still missing. In many respects her life is going well – she likes her job, and she is happy with Charles, with whom she has a young daughter. She has also arranged for Trevor to come to build a well in her village, to which she will make her first return in years. But her wavering faith manifests itself as an inability to show her love fully to her daughter and as a long absence from church, to which she does ultimately return. Here she hears the story of 'The Prodigal Son', foreshadowing the return of her own son, who will also require forgiveness.

Vanessa's journey to Uganda takes her on a path towards a greater connection to nature that will lead her to become more compassionate. When she first arrives in the Gorilla Forest Camp in western Uganda, she is at her worst. She humiliates 'her' driver Isaac – the sacrificial son – in a way that he will remember all the days of his life. However, her encounter with nature changes her, particularly because of a fleeting, yet profound, connection with a female gorilla, whose 'eyes meet Vanessa's, who's laid aside her camera: shadows pass over them, sun and shadows; *part of it all*; they look at each other; *alive like me; alive like her* –' (*MD*, 287–8, emphasis in original). This is a moment of spiritual transformation for Vanessa, who thinks 'I believe she saw me. […] And I saw her. I think we wondered about each other' (*MD*, 290). The experience leads her to see the other, and also to wonder at other connections within the natural world, and to realize that 'I understand nothing, I saw the gorillas but there's so much else', after which she 'dreams of kinds of life she has never known, planets where humans have never been, stars shining like a million dancing midges' (*MD*, 290). This recognition of her connection to nature – to Gaia, mother earth – opens Vanessa to a spirituality which enables her to act compassionately when she and Trevor are driving back to Kampala in a storm, and she recognizes the humanity in a war-ravaged Jamil, who smells of death. Not knowing who he is, but seeing his need, she offers him a lift, thus bringing him to Mary. The grace – or karma – she experiences brings a return of love between her and Trevor: 'The wordless miracle of the body, the living body of the person who loves you' (*MD*, 336).

Fate, the miraculous, or 'luck' plays a large part in this literary diptych. While in *My Cleaner* Mary thinks of Vanessa's offer to come to England as 'chance, or fate', wondering whether 'perhaps God wants me to leave my country' (*MC*, 37), and feels she has 'thrown her fate in with them' (*MC*, 59), the role of fate is even more important in the second novel. In his review of *My Driver* for the *Guardian*, Patrick Ness (2009) points out that Gee's plot relies heavily on coincidence: 'four or five key characters keep bumping into each other in a country of 30 million'. He rightly notes that 'Gee treats coincidence less as a literary convenience than as an inevitable stirring of fate', adding that she is 'after bigger and more interesting game here' (Ness, 2009). In the hands of a less able writer, the coincidences in this novel would not work so well, but they feel right here because there is some sort of connection to a purpose which is almost cosmic, miraculous and thus inexplicable – part of what Gee has called 'animal luck' (*MAL*, 7). When Vanessa delivers Jamil to Mary, Mary and Vanessa see one another for the first time: 'Through their thin clothes, they feel the hearts thudding. Through tears and tiredness and the limits of skin. *Mary: Vanessa. Vanessa: Mary*' (*MD*, 355, emphasis in original). In this mirror-image reiteration of their names, separated each time by a colon, the two panels of the diptych become one whole composition. Each woman's story mirrors the other woman's. And the altarpiece celebrates not only the 'miracle' of the return of the prodigal son, but also the promise of salvation.

My Driver alludes to at least two biblical stories: the Good Samaritan and the Prodigal Son. When Vanessa is mugged as she wanders into the back streets of Kampala, a Good Samaritan intervenes and saves her. Coincidentally, this turns out to be Charles, who later says that God put him in her path. This echoes Trevor's act of generosity when he not only helps to build the well for Mary's village, but also spontaneously decides to pay for a water tank that will enable the schoolchildren to have water throughout the day without a long walk to the well. The most important act of compassion, which recalls the story of the Good Samaritan, is Vanessa's decision to stop at the road-side to pick up a young man in the storm, who turns out to be Mary's long-lost son, Jamil, who has been kidnapped by Kony's Lord's Resistance Army and forced to witness and enact atrocities. But this itself was preceded by other acts of compassion: a woman by a stream giving him something to eat, which reawakens a desire in him not to commit further acts of violence. He leaves her unharmed and also decides not to rob and kill another woman, who turns out to be Vanessa. The story of the Prodigal Son is about both compassion and forgiveness. As is often the case in Gee's work, accessing compassion follows recognizing one's connection with nature, Gaia and the life force that is in us all.

This brings me to the title of the novel: *My Driver*. While it is quite clear that the 'cleaner' in the title of the first novel is meant to be Mary (and the 'My' is, on the face of it, a statement of Vanessa's proprietary attitude towards her), it is not immediately clear who the 'driver' is in the second novel. At first glance, it seems to be Isaac, the driver who takes Vanessa to the Gorilla Forest Camp and who refuses to see her equality as a woman and whom she, in turn, treats without compassion. Certainly, he plays an important role in bringing Vanessa to the edge of the forest where her transformation will take place. However, he seems too minor to be the title character, even though Gee's use of 'my' again underscores postcolonial relations between the West and Africa, foregrounded in their exchange. Nonetheless the metaphor of driving is central to the spiritual vision of the novel, and indeed to the diptych as a whole. Mary drives Trevor to her village, Trevor drives to find Vanessa, Jamil drives them back to Kampala. And there are other references to cars and driving. Charles buys Mary a car, which suggests he respects her independence and autonomy. Back in London, when Vanessa's son Justin needs to take his gravely ill young son Abdul Trevor to hospital and his car is not working, his friend Davey Lucas – who first appeared in *Light Years* – drives them both. At the end of both novels, there are mirror driving scenes with Mary or Vanessa and the other's son in a car in a storm. At the end of *My Cleaner*, Mary forces Justin to drive alone, which symbolizes his rebirth – on Christmas day – and thus his readiness to take charge of his life. At the end of *My Driver*, Vanessa hands the wheel over to Jamil, who leads them out of the storm to safety. Just as Mary delivered Vanessa's son, so Vanessa delivers Mary's.

So, who is the driver in *My Driver* and who is the referent in the pronoun? Driving seems to be a metaphor for taking care of others. To paraphrase, we are our brother's *driver*. Thus, the 'my' in the two titles of the diptych shifts meaning – along the lines of *my* saviour, *my* keeper. While driving may suggest a sense of control, in Gee's world, humans are never fully in control of their lives, as other forces – political or natural – can intervene at any moment. However, they can act in faith, love and compassion, and it seems, if they are very lucky, attain a state of grace. The happy outcomes of the novel suggest the miraculous. By making some connection across the vast chasms that separate us because of geopolitics and greed, humans can find grace.

In the course of this diptych, the two women, who at first seem worlds apart with nothing to bind them but need and an economic contract, come to realize that they are indeed each other's cleaner and driver, each other's saviour and keeper. They begin to cleanse themselves of their illusions and save themselves and each other by seeing that they are not driving their lives, but that they are part of a larger pattern. Through acts of faith, love and compassion, they attain a state of grace that transcends their difference and that allows them to recognize each other's worth and generosity. In the end, they have managed to save their sons, Justin and Jamil, whose names represent truth and beauty, and to love Mary's daughter, Theodora, whose name means gift from god.

Note

1 My discussion of the two novels shows in detail how they mirror each other. However, it is also worth noting that in *My Cleaner* there is already a reference to the second novel, *My Driver*. Mary reflects that Westerners 'go on safari with polite black drivers. Without the drivers they would be too frightened (yet they think they own them: they always say "my driver", "Could you go and see if my driver is waiting?"' (*MC*, 90).

Works Cited

Campbell, Edward F. (1993/2004) 'Grace' in Bruce M. Metzger and Michael D. Coogan (eds) *The Oxford Companion to the Bible*, unpaginated. Oxford: Oxford University Press. *Oxford Reference Online*, accessed 1 September 2013, http://www.oxfordreference.com/view/10.1093/acref/9780195046458.001.0001/acref-9780195046458-e-0298

Gee, Maggie (2004) 'Why Writers Can't Be Told They Have Responsibilities', The Dawson-Scott Memorial Lecture English PEN's International Writers' Day, 29 May 2004, Regent Hall, Salvation Army, Oxford St. London, URL (consulted 6 August 2012): http://www.englishpen.org/legacy/downloads/Events/maggiegee_why_writers_cant_be_told.pdf

Gee, Maggie (2007) 'Imagining Gaia: Art Living Lightly With Science', in Mary Midgley (ed.) *Earthy Realism: The Meaning of Gaia*, pp. 96–101. Exeter: Societas.

Jaggi, Maya (2002) 'Maya Jaggi in Conversation with Maggie Gee: *The White Family*', *Wasafiri* 17(36): 5–10.

Matthew Fox: Friends of Creation Spirituality website, URL (consulted 10 September 2014): http://www.matthewfox.org/

Midgley, Mary (2007) 'Introduction: The Not-So-Simple Earth', in Mary Midgley (ed.) *Earthy Realism: The Meaning of Gaia*, pp. 3–39. Exeter: Societas.

Ness, Patrick (2009) 'Out of Struggle', *Guardian*, URL (consulted 29 July 2012): http://www.guardian.co.uk/books/2009/mar/28/my-driver

Oxford English Dictionary Online (June 2013), URL (consulted 1 September 2013): http://www.oed.com.

Özatabak-Avci, Elif (2012) 'Reconfiguring "Home": An Analysis of Maggie Gee's *My Cleaner*', Maggie Gee Conference, School of English, University of St Andrews, 30 August 2012. Conference paper.

Ozick, Cynthia (1986/1996) 'Memory and Metaphor', in *Portrait of the Artist as a Bad Character and Other Essays on Writing*, pp. 311-29. London: Pimlico.

Thomas, Susie (2005) 'Literary Apartheid in The Post-War London Novel: Finding The Middle Ground', *Changing English: Studies in Culture and Education* 12(2): 309–325.

van Bleijswijk, Corneeltje (n.d.) 'Imagining Difference in Maggie Gee's *My Cleaner* and *My Driver*', URL (consulted 25 August 2012): http://193.147.33.53/selicup/images/stories/actas4/comunicaciones/minorias/VAN_BLEIJSWIJK.pdf

10

THE RESURRECTION OF THE AUTHOR
ON *VIRGINIA WOOLF IN MANHATTAN*

E. H. Wright

'[t]he twentieth-century appearance of the author in his work is in fact a reappearance [...]'

(Gee, 1981: 10, emphasis in original)

In her 1981 PhD thesis Maggie Gee argues that the 'reappearance' of the author is not the reappearance of an 'authoritarian patriarch', but of a writer who enters into 'a cooperative relationship with his reader' (Gee, 1981: 93, 94). In stating this she rejects Roland Barthes's 1967 postmodern literary manifesto 'The Death of the Author' in which he claims: 'literature is that neutral, composite, oblique space where our subject slips away, the negative where all identity is lost, starting with the very identity of the body writing' (Barthes, 1967/1977: 142). Barthes's claim is untenable because authors must inevitably write from their own experiences, desires and feelings and these must leave a mark upon the text whether the reader chooses to read them into it or not. Imagination is clearly based on the platform of personal experience and a specifically personal reality. Writers like Gee and critics such as Laura E. Savu have rejected authorial death and explored the presence of the author in the text in two ways, either as a latent self-consciousness or as an actual physical presence. For Gee, writing fourteen years after Barthes's essay was published, the twentieth century increasingly appears to be 'a selfconscious century [sic]' (Gee, 1981: 15). Gee argues that this self-consciousness will lead us inevitably towards writing as individuals and from thence towards a metafictional self-referencing that constantly draws attention to the presence of the individual as author. Therefore, the death of the author is impossible for there must be 'a living centre' (Gee, 1981: 62). What Gee calls 'the selfconscious novel [sic]' is a type of writing 'which tends to remind us with insistent force of the individual author ordering the words we are reading' and therefore reveals how Barthes 'miscast[s]' the 'individual author as reactionary villain' oppressing the reader (Gee, 1981: 97). The author in self-conscious fiction works with the reader to construct the novel and its multiple meanings. Moreover, the author has the *right* to construct their own world into which the reader is invited; writing is a form of individual rebellion with which the reader is asked to collude. As the twentieth century drew to its close it appeared that 'postmodernism [was] not the abolishment of the author but a relocation and reconsideration of his (its) function' (Fokkema, 1999: 39).

In Gee's thesis, the author is clearly accepted as a presence behind the text and she moves on to show how Virginia Woolf, Vladimir Nabokov and Samuel Beckett are self-conscious writers who maintain a palpable presence in their work. However, self-conscious novelists of the late twentieth century such as Robin Chapman, Peter Ackroyd, Robert Nye and A. S. Byatt take authorial presence and actualize it by resurrecting past authors and re-creating them as characters on the page.[1] Taking her own place in this tradition, Gee's *Virginia Woolf in Manhattan* (2014) moves the critical arguments of her 1981 PhD thesis into her fictional practice by quite literally bringing the figure of Virginia Woolf back to life.[2] In this novel Woolf appears in the New York Public Library's Berg Collection, pulled out of darkness – 'bedraggled' (*VW*, 19), and smelling of 'mud and roots' (*VW*, 28). Perhaps the Woolf of *Virginia Woolf in Manhattan* is a reflection of Gee herself, who remains the real author behind the text. As Franssen and Hoenselaars (1999: 20) note of such author fiction, 'some degree of self-projection on the part of the modern author seems inevitable'. After all, as Gee states in her interview for *The Scottish Herald*, in the novel Woolf is 'very much my construction' (Gee cited in McGlone, 2014). This is arguably the ultimate in self-conscious authorship, the definitive response by Gee to Barthes.

Defining a New Genre: Author Fiction

This type of fiction has been given a variety of different names including biofiction, *biographie romancée*, author fiction (Fokkema, 1999), biografiction (Saunders, 2004), 'psycho-historical novels' (Dee, 1999), 'nonfiction novels' (Ryan, 1997), 'life-texts' (Epstein, 1991), 'psychobiographies' and 'fiction biographies' (Jacobs, 1990). These fictions differ significantly in where they place their emphasis: some are flights of fancy, impossible to believe, such as the *biographie romancée*; others lean so far towards biography that they are more factual than fictional; while psycho-biography and psycho-historical novels are more concerned with building the inner reality of their subjects within the factual framework offered by biography proper. Author fiction, on the other hand, mixes fact, imagination and psychological speculation together adding dashes of the *biographie romancée* when a total blank in the writer's life appears. As Gee's Woolf is taken out of her own historical time (she was born in 1882 and died in 1941) and given a new life on two different continents, the terms biofiction, biografiction and fictional biography do not sit well as categorizations to describe this novel and this version of Virginia Woolf. Indeed, the context pushes the novel towards *biographie romancée* as Woolf is not reliving the events of her real life in London and Sussex in Gee's novel – her past is represented in a biographically accurate manner, but her present and her future are quite obviously not. In some ways it is a psycho-historical novel or a psychobiography, but again time and place problematize the historical and biographical elements of these terms and so it begins to meet what the French symbolist author Marcel Schwob called '*Vies imaginaires*', or imaginary lives, in his 1896 book of the same name. Author fiction, which Fokkema (1999: 39) uses to describe novels that include an author as a character, is the most flexible and capacious label. It is a term that allows the biographical, psychological and purely imaginative to sit side-by-side, and it seems particularly apt to describe Gee's novel, in which all three protagonists are authors. One of the authors is a real figure taken from history (Virginia Woolf) and there are two imagined authors who are drawn from Gee's vital fictional world – Angela, who first appeared as a baby in *The Burning Book* (1983), and her daughter Gerda, an aspiring teenage novelist who the reader first met as a younger child, along with her mother again, in *The Flood* (2004). The novel is structured by their three consciousnesses, which are frequently laid out in script form, a device that gives the reader direct access to the workings of the writers' minds. The term 'author fiction' is broad enough to indicate that Gee is taking the figure of the author and creating a fiction around Woolf, while in no way attempting a fictionalized biography charting real incidents from her life. The events of *Virginia Woolf in Manhattan* could not possibly happen or have happened, but by removing Woolf from her historical context Gee is able to comment on contemporary issues such as the affect of technology, attitudes to sex and sexuality and contemporary prejudices surrounding race, class and gender which become more obvious when set in contrast with the past as symbolized by Woolf.

Why write author fiction? Why write Woolf?

Why, then, have we seen what Jonathan Dee (1999: 77) disparagingly calls a 'veritable epidemic' of biofiction and author fiction since Gee's 1981 thesis? A wide variety of critics (including Laura E. Savu [2009], Jonathan Dee [1999], Naomi Jacobs [1990], Paul Franssen and Ton Hoenselaars [1999]) have offered reasons for this particular spate of fictions featuring author protagonists. Some have seen it as a way to comment on our own late twentieth and early twenty-first century cultural moment without direct confrontation of sensitive issues. The differences in circumstance between the contemporary author (writer-as-author) and their writer characters (writer-as-subject) thus allows contemporary writers the requisite space in which to reflect upon historical and literary contrasts – between their own 'when and where' and the 'when and where' of their writer–subjects. Biofiction is therefore 'not characterized by a retrogressive but by a decidedly progressive movement to explain and interpret the present' (Middeke, 1999: 18). Savu narrows this same idea down to author fiction in particular as a form that allows contemporary writers to:

> 'remember' the makers of these texts in order to show how their representations bear on and catalyze the 'evolving imagination of the present' (Moraru, 2005: 24–5). [...] The biographies and works of earlier authors appeal to postmodern readers and writers because they tell them who they are and how they have come to be who they are. (Savu, 2009: 30)

In particular, writing fiction about well-known authors who have preceded them helps later writers to understand where they have come from creatively; and their own retelling of the lives of such author-subjects is connected with the work of these precursors, whether that be through 'appropriation or confrontation' (Franssen and Hoenselaars, 1999: 24). These writers of author fiction thus adopt the character of other writers partly because impersonation assists understanding of the author and their work and partly because it helps them to use or experiment with another writing voice.

In his influential study of the authority that literary predecessors exert on their progenitors, *The Anxiety of Influence* (1973), Harold Bloom describes this kind of stylistic impersonation in its most successful form as 'apophrades' ('the return of the dead' [Bloom, 1973: 139]). When employed successfully, this literary technique of appropriation enables a writer to resurrect their author–precursor without sacrificing their own creative voice and, in so doing, confers authority upon them through such connection to 'illustrious predecessors' (Savu, 2009: 243). Embodied as a character, the presence of an author–subject within a text (which exerts a subtle influence on the characterization, style and structure of the novel), does not overshadow the more successful practitioners of author fiction because the writer's own creative impetus is strong enough to bear comparison with their author–subject's. To master the master is possibly the attraction of writing this form of novel and, in achieving this, canonical figures as overwhelming as Virginia Woolf are cut down to size. Indeed, Gee suggests as much in a recent discussion of *Virginia Woolf in Manhattan*: 'I feel great admiration and love for [Woolf] but there's also something anti-authoritarian in me. I needed to cheek her' (Gee cited in McGlone, 2014).

However, it is also possible to read author fictions not as a re-conjuring of a historical author, but rather as a reflection of the writer him- or herself – the 'other' author becoming the alter ego of the writer via a process that Edmund Husserl described in his phenomenological account of experience as *Einfühlen* (often referred to as empathy). More specifically, Ina Schabert translates *Einfühlen* as 'feeling aspects of myself into the other' (Schabert, 1990: 10).[3] Therefore, author fiction allows writers to 'incorporate new, original, and personal elements, such as their own experiences' (Latham, 2012: 368), which they explore through the subject–author's consciousness and experiences.[4] Or conversely, this type of fiction may also offer the chance to write about 'the other' instead of themselves, and the form is, in Naomi Jacobs' words, an 'escape from the prison of self-hood' (Jacobs, 1990: 31). The factual framework of author fiction arguably takes the pressure off writers who draw heavily on themselves for inspiration. In *Virginia Woolf in Manhattan* Gee strikes a balance between escaping into the 'other' and Woolf's world, and keeping a sense of self in relation to the 'other' by placing Woolf out of her time and space. In doing this, Gee allows herself to explore Woolf's mind and writing, but at the same time asserts her difference and her Self in the totally fictional world that she conjures around her literary mother. Gee's relationship with Woolf in this novel is complicated by Angela Lamb, the fictional author who accompanies Woolf in her twenty-first-century jaunt. In many ways Angela personifies the feelings of subsequent female authors who have had to struggle with Woolf's preeminence. Angela feels intimidated by and inferior to Woolf, she quite literally experiences the 'anxiety of influence' because she tries to gain Woolf's approval rather than accepting and embracing her difference as Gee does. Perhaps the free-spirited Gerda is really Woolf's literary heir in this novel because she is able to think about Woolf with admiration and respect rather than seeing her as a threat.

However, there are more material considerations for the writer choosing this genre, for a number of author fictions are also clearly written as a marketing ploy, attracting increased sales by relying on the reader's familiarity with the author–subject. Prior to *Virginia Woolf in Manhattan*, Gee was uncomfortably aware of this and noted in an interview that Tracy Chevalier's historical novel *Girl with a Pearl Earring* (1999), which presents a fictionalized account of Johannes Vermeer's life at the time of painting the eponymous Delft masterpiece, was successful:

> partly because she linked herself to a very prominent meme, and the meme was Vermeer's "Girl with a Pearl Earing". [...] It always happens when people re-invent the lives and times of famous historical characters: they gain instant recognition, and interest among readers. I think I used to slightly sneer at this, once I deduced it, but now I will have to stop sneering because I am about to write about Virginia Woolf, reincarnated in the present. [...] I used to feel that if I tried to write about one of my heroes [...] wouldn't that be stealing [...]? (Gee cited in Kiliç, 2013: 160–1).

This concern is echoed by Jonathan Dee who has 'a nagging sense, even in the most sophisticated of these books, of a lowering of the literary bar' (Dee, 1999: 83–4). Dee also warns that 'stealing' writers from history and their cachet not only improve sales, but promotes the contemporary author's own reputation. He argues that by 'impersonating geniuses – ostensibly as an act of homage, but also, not coincidentally, as a way of grabbing up the genuine cachet those geniuses still deliver' the writer 'enhance[s] the value of [their] own work' (Dee, 1999: 82).

Certainly author fictions are partly attractive because they offer the writer a ready-made framework in the shape of the biographemès's real life events. Phyllis Rose (1982: 119) claims that '[t]he enabling part' of basing a novel on a real person 'is that [the writer] need not be quite so inventive [...] they do not have to generate material from imagination' – an observation that echoes Gee's and Dee's concerns. Yet, the plain facts of a life-story are an incomplete version of an individual's existence. Biography is full of empty spaces where the exact events and chronology are not known, but the most important, and exciting, gaps in the narrative concern the subject's inner-life (an area of the 'other' that is never truly knowable). The writer of author fiction is creatively enabled by these omissions – they must pour their speculations into those spaces, wonder at the subject's feelings and thoughts, and expand on the possibilities proffered by the absences. Here the imagination of the writer is allowed to range freely because 'the past cannot be known at all' so 'all versions are equally valid' (Good, 2005: 287). Therefore, author fictions of the twentieth and twenty-first century are not necessarily 'ominous', they do not herald the end of originality, offering texts cramped and chained to fact with no 'legitimate claim to greatness' as Dee, Cohn and Ryan claim (Dee, 1999: 77, 84). Instead they offer 'a sign of cultural renewal' by 'shedding light on the multiple dimensions of the authorial craft, by probing the mystery of creation and the hidden complexities of the artist's mind' (Savu, 2009: 242, 48). By examining the lives and personalities of their precursors and by conjuring them anew, the writer and their readers re-examine their canonical predecessors from fresh and often surprising perspectives.

Woolf has been a particularly popular literary figure to recreate. She has appeared as herself in: *The Shadow of the Moth: A Novel of Espionage with Virginia Woolf* (1983) by Ellen Hawkes and Peter Manso; *The Hours* (1998) by Michael Cunningham; *Mitz: The Marmoset of Bloomsbury* (1998) by Sigrid Nunez; *But Nobody Lives in Bloomsbury* (2006) by Gillian Freeman; *Vanessa and Virginia* (2008) by Susan Sellers; *The White Garden: A Novel of Virginia Woolf* (2009) by Stephanie Barron; and *A Book for All and None* (2011) by Clare Morgan.[5] Hermione Lee suggests that Woolf – like Plath, Shelley and Austen – is so frequently 're-versioned' because she has been so 'variously and passionately idealized, vilified, fictionalized, and mythologized' (Lee, 2005: 39) since her death, that the only defence is to write her out in novel form. Woolf (1927/1994a: 465) herself was aware of this process of idealization and fictionalization;

as she pointed out in her 1927 review of Walter Edwin Peck's *Shelley: His Life And Work* (1927) there are 'some stories which have to be retold by each generation'. Whether biographical or biofictional, we re-read these stories, Woolf argues, because we need to get the historical figure 'more sharply outlined against the shifting image of ourselves' (Woolf, 1927/1994a: 465). This statement presciently anticipates those critical responses to author fiction cited above by Savu, Middeke and Bloom, who argue that author fiction helps us to make sense of our present and ourselves, as much as recreating and explaining the past through the pleasure of appropriating the voice of a literary predecessor. Reincarnating Woolf has thus allowed authors in the past three decades to contrast their own writing with one of the greatest twentieth-century modernists.[6] However, a number of critics take issue with these recent versions of Woolf arguing that the reader is offered 'only a simplified figure of the complex author ("Virginia Woolf lite" [Rubenstein, 2003: 3]) as well as watered-down versions of her novels.' (Latham, 2012: 369).

In summary, Woolf is resurrected as a character, not always successfully, for many different (sometimes even contradictory) reasons and purposes, some of which are perceived as positive, some negative. These include helping writers to: examine their own cultural and socio-political context; bask in Woolf's reflected glory in order to garner her readership as well as their usual readership; examine the blanks in her biographical narrative and thus come to a better understanding of her and her work; pay homage to a great writer and to defuse her power over their own work.

Gee's Woolf

Maggie Gee's *Virginia Woolf in Manhattan* responds to many of the reasons for writing author fiction highlighted earlier. The novel is structured by the consciousness of three characters: Virginia Woolf, Angela Lamb (an egocentric fictional author), and her adventurous daughter Gerda, whom Angela has sent away to boarding school. When Angela is asked to give a plenary speech at a Virginia Woolf conference in Istanbul she travels to New York to see Woolf's papers and gather inspiration. While in the New York Public Library's Berg Collection, where Woolf's manuscripts are housed, she suddenly finds Virginia Woolf herself brought back to life. The two authors, followed by the intrepid Gerda, embark on a peculiar relationship fraught with artistic and historical differences, which sees them visiting the Statue of Liberty and selling signed versions of Woolf's first editions while trying to engage with a wide range of cultural and chronological differences. When Angela flies over to Istanbul for her lecture the famously chaste Woolf accompanies her and finds out about the joy of sex with a Turkish man and woman (much to Angela's disgust and the reader's amusement). The novel culminates in Angela's speech, which makes Woolf's legacy relevant to the twenty-first century, while mocking the academic establishment as fatuous. What the novel does not make absolutely clear is whether any of the story is real, or whether Angela herself has imagined this relationship with a revivified Woolf. The turbulent flight to New York suggests that Angela 'falls through space-time' (*VW*, 12) which allows her to meet Woolf and concludes with a similarly turbulent flight in which the plane becomes insubstantial and the three protagonists sit 'side by side in another world' causing Angela to ask: 'If time had split, which fork were we on?' and to speculate that 'Maybe we never die entirely. [...] We live in others. We live in words' (*VW*, 472). Whether Woolf is real or not will be taken up later in this chapter, but what is immediately interesting is why Gee has decided to resurrect her literary mother at all.

Each writer (whether novelist, biographer or critic) has their own version of Woolf to portray and their own reason for doing so. There is certainly a peculiar possessiveness surrounding Woolf in particular, which is due to her reputation as a great *female* modernist writer and seminal feminist critic. In *Virginia Woolf in Manhattan*, Woolf is quite rightly described as having been 'fetishise[d]' (*VW*, 16) while the best-selling author Angela Lamb reflects on this penchant for dissecting Woolf's life: 'I knew too much, we knew too much' (*VW*, 85). Woolf has become an icon, her private life exposed and picked over by critics to the point where she has become dehumanized, abstracted, not herself, owned by others.[7] In *Virginia Woolf in Manhattan* this sense of ownership reaches its apotheosis in the screaming diatribe of Moira Penny (also brought back from the dead) at the academic conference in Istanbul (*VW*, 462–3). Gee reminds us that reading about the facts of someone's life does not mean that we know them, let alone 'own' them or the memory of them. Gee's Woolf is clear that she 'would not be robbed' nor 'stolen' (*VW*, 419) by 'heavy-footed critics' (*VW*, 420). Woolf's reaction to Angela's over-familiar use of her and her husband's Christian names (*VW*, 15, 56) is a case in point. Following this Angela wisely suppresses her knowledge of their pet names, which would appal Woolf who is mistakenly sure that Leonard has destroyed her private papers (in fact he kept them and published some).

It seems at times that Woolf is indeed a figment of Angela Lamb's imagination conjured by the ambiguous words: 'Virginia, I'll take you home' (*VW*, 58). It is Angela's version of Woolf that appears in the keynote lecture and it is her extempore speech about Woolf's applicability to the twenty-first century with which the novel ends. If Angela's words conjure Woolf up from her grave then perhaps she 'belongs' to Angela because she is specifically Angela's impression of her predecessor. If we reconsider Gee's discussion of Woolf in 1997 with the benefit of hindsight, it appears that Gee alluded to this 2014 version of Virginia Woolf as a character who is 'tangible enough' and yet who causes 'the author [to] cas[t] doubt on the status of his own representation by various means' (Gee cited in McKay, 1997: 23). This Virginia Woolf, apparently brought back from the dead by Angela, is certainly insubstantial enough to suggest doubt as to her physical reality: her image cannot be captured in photographs (*VW*, 74, 345); she cannot quite be physically grasped (*VW*, 59, 169) or properly seen (*VW*, 446, 453); and, most importantly, she cannot write (*VW*, 110), a fact which makes her wonder whether 'without writing, does one really exist?' (*VW*, 372). Woolf is clearly aware of her frailty in this twenty-first century reality when she asks: 'Can I survive, mute, diminished?' (*VW*, 184). If this is Angela's version of her literary heroine, her jealousy of Woolf's writing and reputation, by which she feels threatened (*VW*, 156), might mean that Angela's

Woolf cannot write because Angela does not *want* her to be able to write. Or, perhaps Woolf cannot write because this is not *her* time and writers should reflect their times, as Gee does in her other novels. Woolf thinks: '*Maybe the past can never write the present.* [...] I had had my vision. [...] I had my vision in my own century' (*VW*, 210, emphasis in original).[8] Perhaps in her second chance at life Angela's Woolf does not want to watch it passing by, but prefers to live it, as she claims in Istanbul: 'I do not want to write about it. I want to be here. Here in the moment' (*VW*, 305). Or simply, if Woolf is purely a figment of Angela's imagination, writing is obviously impossible. After all, the supposedly physical 'tussle' between Angela and Woolf in a New York hotel room (*VW*, 73), can also be read as a metaphorical one between past and present, between *ephebe* (the Greek term for a young man that Harold Bloom uses to refer to a young poet) and precursor.[9]

Why, then, does Gee specifically select Virginia Woolf to resurrect? In some ways Gee's relationship with Woolf echoes that of the protagonist Angela Lamb who claims that Woolf 'mean[t] so much to [her] back when [she] started. Yes, she was a talisman' (*VW*, 14). Woolf is someone Angela 'never learned to say "No" to' and Woolf reflects that 'Wherever she [Angela] goes, I must go' (*VW*, 49, 135). In fact, both the real Maggie Gee and the fictional author Angela Lamb seem to carry Woolf with them – Gee as a precursor whom she respects, Lamb as an embodied reality whom she finds creatively threatening. When Gee wrote her 1981 thesis on Woolf (among others) she openly admired Woolf's skill as a writer because for Woolf, like Gee, 'the language of authorship [...] is a distinctly literary language that pays little attention to the practical usages to which words might be put in ordinary life' (DiBattista, 2009: 66). In an interview for *Studia Neophilologica*, Gee speculated that:

> It may be that since my Ph.D. was on Beckett, Nabokov and Woolf, and having read those three novelists extensively, their cadences and their tricks and their tropes are in my writing more than I know. I can sometimes see it and sometimes I just think they must be. If you read

them for five years intensively then I think that just happens. (Gee cited in McKay, 1997: 217–8)

In *Virginia Woolf in Manhattan*, the presence of Virginia Woolf might be read as giving Gee permission to use a mixture of direct quotation from, and allusion to, Woolf's work. For Woolf's speaking and thinking voice Gee necessarily borrows Woolf's personal idioms including her synaesthetic language (such as her links between words, painting and music),[10] syntactical and grammatical archaisms (such as her use of the ampersand, 'one', rejection of contractions and her subjunctives [*VW*, 61–2, 74, 116, 126]), the sound of her 'hooting' laughter and her upper-middle class accent with its long vowels (*VW*, 70), all of which help to signal that she belongs to another time. However, *Virginia Woolf in Manhattan* not only conjures Woolf's character using her private texts, but also builds her presence via her fictional work.

A number of other authors have done this successfully, including Michael Cunningham in *The Hours*, Susan Sellers in *Vanessa and Virginia*, and Sigrid Nunez in *Mitz the Marmoset of Bloomsbury*.[11] In Nunez's mock-biography of the Woolf's pet monkey, a re-versioning of Woolf's *Flush*, Nunez takes quotations directly from letters and diaries which she sets in inverted commas, thus marking 'the frontier between "the two masters," reality and imagination' (Latham, 2012: 363). In Gee's *Virginia Woolf in Manhattan* some references are direct quotations delimited by punctuation such as Angela's memory of a quotation from *The Waves* (*VW*, 33), while some are quotations but not signalled as such, for example the words lifted from Woolf's suicide note which appears in italicized fragments (*VW*, 36, 41–2). Some references are half quotations such as Woolf's claim 'I am not a snob' and her comment that Angela has found her 'a room of my own' (*VW*, 114); alluding to Woolf's ironic essay "Am I a Snob?" (1936) and her feminist tract *A Room of One's Own* (1929). However, other references are more abstract. Images and ideas, clearly Woolf's, are used by all the central characters and are altered to fit the strange situation. There are too many references and allusions to chart here in full, but frequent examples include the repeated image of water and of a 'fin passing far out' (Woolf, 1980: 113) that Woolf noted in her diary in 1926 and which reappears in Gee's novel (*VW*, 165, 194). *To the Lighthouse* (1927) provides Lily Briscoe's vision which appears as Woolf's own in *Virginia Woolf in Manhattan* (*VW*, 210); the same image of loss when Mrs Ramsay dies in parentheses as Angela feels when her daughter Gerda goes to boarding school (*VW*, 236); and the 'Time Passes' section, in which the empty house stands as cypher for the slowly evolving lives of the characters, reappears to show the difference in the speed of time between Woolf's era and ours (*VW*, 159–60). Angela wonders: 'Could there be a twenty-first-century "Time Passes"?' (*VW*, 160) and it seems that Gee responds when Part Two of the novel is called 'Time Passes: London – New York – Istanbul' (*VW*, 217). Even the book *Life on Earth* that Angela is reading on the plane echoes Lucy Swithin's *An Outline of History* in Woolf's final novel *Between the Acts* (1941). Angela and Lucy both wonder what the landscape would have looked like before New York and London existed. Angela reflects that 'they have built over the past. Once Manhattan must have had fields' (*VW*, 30), while Lucy has 'spent the hours between three and five thinking of rhododendron forests in Piccadilly [...] populated [...] by barking monsters; the iguanodon, the mammoth, and the mastodon' (Woolf, 1941/2008: 8). Even Gee's narrative structure at times brings to mind the stream of consciousness soliloquies found in *The Waves* or the scripts mixed with poetry of *Between the Acts* (see, for example, *VW*, 198–200). When it comes to writing more generally, both Gee and Woolf describe writing to a rhythm or pattern. Compare, for instance, Woolf's 'I am writing *The Waves* to a rhythm not to a plot' (Woolf, 1980a: 316) with Gee's 'I do endless drafts, because of the rhythm. I like to get the rhythm of the sentences right' (McKay, 1997: 219).

It is also possible to make thematic links between Gee and Woolf, particularly their approach to time and its fluctuations. Stephen Connor has noted this recurring trait in Gee's work in his discussion of *The Burning Book* (1983), which he claims 'recalls and replicates the modernist ambition, as evidenced especially in the novels of Virginia Woolf, of remaining true to the complex unpredictability of time while yet being able to perceive the gathering design of the whole' (Connor, 1996: 238).[12] Both authors balance time's state of flux with a pattern that holds their novels together and gives some sort of coherence to the characters' lives. As Gee states: 'Like the modernists, I love pattern, and try to give each book an overall controlling form' (*MAL* 175). This is a sentiment that is not dissimilar to Woolf's statement in a letter to her brother-in-law Clive Bell that she aimed to represent life in her novels as 'a sort of pattern' which would 'be somehow controlled' (Woolf, 1976: 82). Gee and Woolf also tend to write about their respective present times, or at the very least the times through which they have both lived – in Woolf's case this stretches from 1882 to 1941 and, in Gee's, from 1949 to the present. In 1997 Gee wondered if she 'could write about the past, which I've never done. [...] But I think why I haven't done that is because I feel at home in the present' (Gee cited in McKay, 1997: 221). Meanwhile, Woolf rarely wrote about the time before her birth in her fiction except in a comic parodic manner in *Orlando: A Biography* (1928) and *Flush: A Biography* (1933).[13] In *Virginia Woolf in Manhattan*, Gee takes Woolf and turns her into a comic Orlando-esque figure, able to transcend the passage of linear time by springing back to life in present day New York.[14] Woolf's life-before-death is akin to the 'beautiful caves' (Woolf, 1978: 263) that Woolf 'tunnel[ed]' (Woolf, 1978: 272) out behind her characters in *Mrs Dalloway* (1925) in order to give them 'humanity, humour, depth' (Woolf, 1978: 263), but her presence in 2010 brings her out of darkness and into glaring lights. Time becomes an actual space in Woolf and Gee's novels, it is a stage on which the action is played, a 'platform to stand upon' (Woolf, 1985: 75) and a cave into which Woolf retreats in order to build character. This sense of time as a physical space is used by Gee in her novel when Woolf states at the point of her resurrection: 'Suddenly there's time again; & I'm in it' (*VW*, 13).

Endings, usually the stasis of time and space, are left tantalizingly open by both authors, thus suggesting the circularity of narratives. Gee's *Dying, in Other Words* (1981) keeps the dead writer Moira Penny alive through her writing, even after her plunge onto the pavement; and Moira is resurrected in Gee's later apocalyptic novel *The Flood* (2004);[15] *The White Family* (2002) ends with a chapter entitled 'No Ending'; while *The Burning Book* (1983) refuses an ending by stating that 'words beat on against death. Our bright lives beat against ending … Always beginning again, beginning against ending' (*BB*, 304). Indeed, the final page of *The Burning Book* bears marked similarities to Woolf's *The Waves* (1931) which closes with the wordsmith Bernard's final cry: 'Against you I will fling myself, unvanquished and unyielding, O Death!' (Woolf, 1931/2008: 248). In *The Flood*, Gee's characters continue their existence after a tsunami strikes, in a heaven at Kew Gardens (perhaps a nod to Woolf's story of the same name).[16] Like Gee's *The Burning Book* and *The Flood*, Woolf also considers an apparent apocalyptic event in her final novel, *Between the Acts* (Woolf's vision is of the Second World War, while Gee's respective apocalyptic depictions are informed by nuclear holocaust and rising sea levels). The threat of world war hovers ominously behind *Between the Acts* in the form of the planes flying over the Pointz Hall pageant and images of Europe 'bristling with guns' like a 'hedgehog', with Bolney Minster smashed into 'smithereens' (Woolf, 1941/2008: 49). The war gave Woolf the sense of 'writing in a vacuum – no-one will read it. I feel the audience has gone' but, as she added, '[s]till, so oddly is one made, I find I must spin my brain even in a vacuum' (Woolf, 1980b: 430). In response to this desire to continue her story even in the face of annihilation Woolf, like Gee, refuses total destruction in her last sentences of *Between the Acts*: 'Then the curtain rose. They spoke' (Woolf, 1941/2008: 197). In *Virginia Woolf in Manhattan*, Woolf-as-subject similarly reflects on her final novel: 'My last page ends with the actors starting to play their part in this bigger pageant. From their act of love, new life will be born' (*VW*, 124). As Sarah Dillon has observed, Gee (and Woolf) thus 'performatively guarantee […] the continuance of humankind and the survival of literature' (Dillon, 2007: 384); their endings 'renounce […] the final judgment' (Dillon, 2007: 392). For both, words are a promise of continuance in the face of destruction; they resurrect, keeping characters alive even when their bodies have expired. As her literary successor, Gee thus breathes life back into Woolf through her appropriation of Woolf's own words and narrative style, just as she has done to many of her other fictional characters.[17] In *Virginia Woolf in Manhattan*, the whole novel, not just the ending of it, cheats death through resurrection.

The Problematic Academic

With these references, rhythms and resonances Gee forms a hermeneutic code or 'intertextual quest' (Nüning, 1999: 27). There are obviously some issues with this type of metafictional detective hunt, most notably that the reader cannot 'successfully receive and acclaim these biofictions' unless they have 'prior cultural, literary and aesthetic knowledge of the subject's life and work' (Latham, 2012: 356). Yet conversely it is this privileging of knowledge over entertainment with which Gee takes issue: 'I never wanted to used literary allusions because I don't like that club thing where if you pick up the references you're all right but if you don't you miss a lot' (Gee cited in McKay, 1997: 214). Gee clearly respects the formal experiments that Woolf conducted in her novels as well as her tests and trials with language itself – there are certainly echoes of Woolf's 'cadences', 'tricks' and 'tropes' in much of Gee's work (Gee in McKay, 1997: 217-8). But appreciation of Gee's novels – of their comedy and their tensions – does not depend on charting these references, not even in reading *Virginia Woolf in Manhattan*. It does, however, unavoidably affect the reading of the text if the reader is familiar with Woolf's life and work.

Gee uses *Virginia Woolf in Manhattan* to explore, critique and ridicule the scholarly community who interpret and reinterpret Woolf and Gee and their work in books, conference papers and scholarly articles. The international academic conference with which Gee's novel closes suggests a continuance of Woolf not only in body and readership, but also in academic words; and yet neither author sets much store by the type of academic criticism that tries to define and concretize the meaning of creative texts. Woolf argued against the teaching of English at university, which she contended was simply a way to 'herd books into groups', reduces literature to 'ABC; one, two, three' and results in 'los[ing] all sense of what it's about' (Woolf, 1979: 450). Of criticism, she wrote to William Rothenstein, 'I always feel apologetic about publishing my own criticism, because I dont [sic] know that there is much excuse for adding to books about other books' (Woolf, 1979: 116). To Ethel Smyth she lamented that the articles of *The Common Readers* (published in 1925 and 1932), 'bore me to a kind of dancing agony at the futility of all criticism' (Woolf, 1979: 40).[18] Gee is similarly ambivalent about academia and the literary critical community which she describes as 'intimidating', a 'court of critical jurisdiction', and a 'piranha-shoal' (Gee, 1981: 89, 92). For Gee, Barthes's call for the reader 'to cover [the text] as completely as possible with one's own language' (Barthes, 1964/1972: 650) is dangerous as it leaves the text open to 'the jargons and patterns of criticism in all their well-paid and published comfort finally covering over that slim and precarious thing which once gave them birth, the creative text' (Gee, 1981: 96). Criticism for Gee and Woolf poses a 'threat' to the novelist – who places a 'very high value upon self-signature' (Gee, 1981: 89, 92) – not only because it evaluates, but also because it tries to form patterns and rules to which creativity is resistant.

In *Virginia Woolf in Manhattan*, Gee takes the opportunity to satirize the critical community, just as Woolf satirizes the figure of the critic in *Orlando* through the character of Nick Greene who becomes 'the most influential critic of the Victorian age' (Woolf, 1928/2008: 264). Gerda and Woolf both find the concept of Barthes's 'death of the author' vaguely ridiculous. Gerda asks simply: 'Wouldn't it be helpful to have the actual writer telling all the academics and people like my mother where they are going wrong?' (*VW*, 145), while Gee's Woolf argues: 'That doesn't make sense. We are the one who wrote it. [...] It's obviously ridiculous [...] I'm the living embodiment of that. I'm a dead author' (*VW*, 317). Gerda's question and Woolf's outrage are partly amusing because, if we accept the right of the author to some power over their own work, it would call into question at least one of the purposes of the critic and the academic community which is to find and secure meaning. The 'intentional fallacy' as Angela puts it, means that the author does not 'know everything about [their] work' (*VW*, 317) and thus the critics are allowed their say. However, the reader is guided towards the writer's side by Woolf who asks 'how can the critics know their own intentions? Maybe, unconsciously, they want to kill us. Yes, of course. Then they have the power' (*VW*, 318).

Reading Past and Present

The parallels to be made between Woolf and Gee as writers and thinkers far outstrip the limits of this chapter, but what *is* clear is the 'respect' (not 'reverence')[19] that Gee feels for Woolf's writing and ideology. However, 'the search for identification', as Franssen and Hoenselaars (1999: 20) argue, 'has to be balanced with the urge to establish difference and, perhaps, originality'. In *Virginia Woolf in Manhattan* Gee wisely steers clear of obvious pastiche or any complete borrowing of Woolf's style and structure – as exemplified, for instance, in Robin Lippincott's *Mr Dalloway* (1999) and Michael Cunningham's *The Hours*. Gee clearly enjoys and admires the work of her predecessor, but she also cultivates and celebrates the differences between them, not only the differences in their technological moments which are brought out wittily in this novel (see for example Woolf trying to fathom laptops and the Internet [*VW*, 80–1, 106], traffic jams [*VW*, 30], mobile phones [*VW*, 36] and modern fashions [*VW*, 86], the demise of bookshops [*VW*, 170–1] and the liberal use of profanities [*VW*, 174]), but also Gee's ability to write freely about the body and all of those things that cause 'the English to fall silent, I would say **sex, the emotions, class, race, money, success, failure, excretion** of course, **illness, age** and death.' (Gee 1996: 1, emphasis in original).

Gee takes up the 'challenge' (Gee, 1996: 4) left by Woolf of 'telling the truth about [her] experiences as a body' which Woolf, speaking in 1931 to The Women's Service League, did not feel 'that any woman ha[d] solved' (Woolf, 1942/2011: 483).[20] Gee, by contrast, feels that 'sexual experience is a part of life, and novelists should be able to write about all of life' (Gee, 1996: 4) and so *her* Woolf discovers the joy of sex in Istanbul, something which eluded the real Woolf in her marriage to Leonard, but which she found, albeit briefly, in her relationship with Vita Sackville-West. Thus, Woolf sleeps, not only with Muhsin, but also, Gee hints with the Turkish maid, Angela, suffering from an inferiority complex, prefers the popular legend of the 'chaste, traumatised' Woolf (*VW*, 381) and feels that in having sex Virginia has 'let me down [...] She was not the great writer I expected her to be' (*VW*, 408). Angela's reaction towards Woolf's sexuality shows how little attitudes have changed towards the thinking woman. Instead of allowing Woolf to try new things in a new century, Angela wants her to live up (or down) to the image of the isolated, insane genius and in doing so highlights the remaining double-standard: that women cannot have both a brilliant creative mind and sexual experience, with its consequence of motherhood. In addition to this feminist point, Gee also makes a feminist statement in selecting Woolf as the author–subject of *Virginia Woolf in Manhattan*; thus redressing the imbalance that Savu (2009: 209) highlights when she discusses the dearth of author fictions that deal with women writers, compared with 'the plethora of novels about canonical male writers'.

Author fiction, as established in the introduction to this chapter, enables comment on the contemporary by focusing on it through the lens of the past as symbolized by the figure of Woolf. Gee is thus able to confront modern attitudes towards class and money, race and religion. In fact, it is the lack of disparity between Woolf and Angela's attitudes, which are actually worryingly similar, that highlights the smug self-righteousness of a contemporary woman who thinks herself and her time above prejudice. The only real difference in their racism and class-consciousness is that Woolf's is 'correct' for her and her time and she thinks and voices these prejudices openly, almost naively; whereas Angela's issues with race, class and wealth are covert, often thought, but not spoken. Woolf reflects that 'the Africans' laughing in the street are 'the servants, out with the masters' (*VW*, 209), while on the flight to Istanbul seated with a party of Hasidic Jews, Woolf exclaims 'Jews. That is not what one expected! This whole plane is alive with Jews', to which Angela thinks 'I have to teach her not to talk like that. All the same, she is factually correct' (*VW*, 224). Gee demonstrates that the need to suppress comment on difference or the rebranding of it does not get rid of prejudice. Renaming does not stop intolerance and calling the people on the plane Jews or 'Jewish people', or altering the term African, does not stop Angela from thinking in unpleasant generalizations. When Woolf tries to strike up a conversation with a Turkish waiter Angela tells her that they 'aren't people, in that sense' to which Woolf responds: 'I was the one who was supposed to be snobbish! I was the one who made generalisations! "That's another generalization," I said.' (*VW*, 324). Angela also warns Woolf that the Turks 'will try to exploit' her (*VW*, 323) by selling her things or by flirting with her, yet when Woolf points out that the men in the lobby of the American hotel did exactly the same, Angela simply says: 'It's different here' (*VW*, 323). In fact, in many ways, Gee's Woolf celebrates difference by openly examining it rather than hushing it up. Angela's own racism is arguably more insidious than Woolf's because it is not honest and the framework of the novel, which sets the author (Woolf) outside her own time, allows Gee to make this comment.

Thanks to Woolf being shaken out of her own time and space, Angela's claim that 'Everyone is free. *Everyone*' (*VW*, 209, emphasis in original) is clearly not true. Her vision of an America in which everyone can be, say, or do anything and that this leads to happiness, is proven continually false, not least by the anti-capitalist protestors among whom they become caught with their bag of money from the sale of Woolf's first editions (*VW*, 131–3) and the religious protestors who they pass on the way to the airport (*VW*, 219–20). However, other cultures are similarly trapped, the Jewish mother/playwright seated beside Woolf on the plane to Istanbul is no more free than her own Victorian mother was and Woolf observes this woman's 'drive to write was chained to duty' (*VW*, 227). In Istanbul the religious protestors 'are crazy' according to a Turkish waiter and want to 'stop everything' (*VW*, 377). In fact, Woolf, because she is taken out of her time, can see the issues with the extremes of the twenty-first century, which she perceives as motivated by the desire for belonging in a lonely world. Through her depiction of Woolf-as-subject, Gee thus shows contemporary extremism as an almost Nietzschean desire to search in the past for cohesion and sense in the present.

Woolf's presence also opens up questions about class, wealth and privilege. Angela is jealous of Woolf's sense of entitlement, which is accurate for her time and upbringing. Indeed, it is an aspect of Woolf with which many contemporary authors struggle (Angela highlights this in her speech at the academic conference). In an earlier Woolfian author fiction, *Mitz: T1he Marmoset of Bloomsbury*, Sigrid Nunez

(1998: 18) feels the need to excuse Woolf's reliance on servants: 'if they had had to do their own shopping and cooking and tidying, how much time would have been left for reading and writing and publishing?' – an observation that is paralleled by Gee's Woolf (*VW*, 249). Angela despises Woolf's reliance on servants, her dictatorial air, her 'posh' accent. It is a dislike motivated by her own upbringing in what Woolf calls the 'lower orders' (*VW*, 245). Angela is frequently insulted by Woolf's superiority and her expectation that Angela will perform the part of chaperone, and tries to suggest that Woolf's age is dead and gone. However, Woolf cleverly points out that little has changed. The hotel staff still serve 'groaning faintly, on creaking knees because how else, pray, could you clean under beds?' (*VW*, 249), as do the flight attendants (*VW*, 269). Woolf asks of the maid 'who was to say if this African woman might have been a great poet, had she but had the chance?' (*VW*, 249). This observation rehearses Shakespeare's Sister from *A Room of One's Own* (1929) all over again.

Concluding Remarks: Gee's Author Fiction

Gee's author fiction responds to English silences about sex, money, race and class and fulfills the precepts of this emerging genre, as established by Savu and Middeke. By taking a historical author and then setting her in our contemporary, twenty-first-century context, *Virginia Woolf in Manhattan* thus succeeds in throwing our own time into sharp relief. Transported into a modern world, Woolf is able to question contemporary obsessions with consumerism, speed, technology, constant accessibility enabled by social media, racism, class, wealth, sexuality and sexual availability and all of the perks and problems associated with these things.

In *Virginia Woolf in Manhattan*, Woolf becomes what we might call half and half: half real historical figure who has lived the life she really lived, and half fictional figure experiencing a second life in the wrong century. Martin Middeke allows for this version of Virginia Woolf – 'correct' in personality but not in context – by arguing that the writer of an author fiction 'may play with [the historical material], may even invert it, if necessary, and still arrive at a heuristically impressive and plausible interpretation of that life'. And, though I doubt that he quite meant for an author to fall out of their own time and into the present day as Gee's Woolf does in her resurrection into modern-day Manhattan and Istanbul, he does allow that the contemporary writer 'may incorporate and reflect upon epistemological uncertainties caused by the aporias of time and language, without obliterating historical consciousness' (Middeke, 1999: 3). In other words, that gaps and changes in time, space, cultural context and language, do not inevitably lead to historical inaccuracy. Gee's Woolf lives up to Jacobs's view of authors in author fictions who are 'unknown, unknowable, and yet tantalizingly real; other, odd, and yet disturbingly familiar; dead, gone, yet still here and lively' (Jacobs, 1990: 44). The temporal and spatial changes wrought upon Woolf-as-subject by Gee's fiction should not therefore be read as destroying an accurate representation of the real Woolf but, rather, as helping to understand Woolf's personality by setting her against an unfamiliar and impossible backdrop.[21] Within the context of the novel, Gee's Woolf is 'real' (at least to Angela) and 'not the dead Virginia she [or we] knew from [her] writing' (*VW*, 134). Recreations of Virginia Woolf in fiction are strangely akin to Barthes's description of the photographs of his dead mother, none of which really captures who she was, even though he knew her personally. He recognizes her 'in fragments' as 'not she, and yet [...] no one else' and therefore finds himself 'struggling among images partially true, and therefore totally false' (Barthes, 1980/1981: 65-6). Recreating Virginia Woolf is similarly perplexing: Gee writes a version of her that is 'partially true' and at the same time 'totally false'. This is all that author fiction can ever do.

One wonders what Woolf would have felt about this type of literary resurrection when it comes to her life and work. Certainly she met academic critiques of herself and her life with disgust:

> I'm threatened with 3 more books upon me: Holtby has induced another publisher to print her follies: Richardson is producing another; and a man from America a third. All this means to me a kind

of fuss and falsity and talking about my husband, mother, father, and dog which I loathe. (Woolf, 1979: 97)

Would she have stood by her claim in 'The New Biography' that by attempting to mix real life with fiction 'they destroy each other' (Woolf 1927/1994b: 477)? Of course Woolf pioneered this form when she published *Orlando* (1928) which was not quite a fictional biography of Vita Sackville-West, but a magic realist parodic mock-biography partly inspired by her antipathy for hagiographic Victorian biography (the dry facts proffered as 'lives' by her father's *Dictionary of National Biography* and Sidney Lee's *Principles of Biography*).[22] Her interest in this fusion was also provoked by the experiments of her friends and acquaintances, most notably Lytton Strachey's *Eminent Victorians* (1918), *Queen Victoria* (1921), *Books and Characters* (1922), *Elizabeth and Essex: A Tragic History* (1928) and Harold Nicolson's *Some People* (1927). Her biofictional biography of Elizabeth Barrett Browning's cocker spaniel, *Flush* (1933), straddled the gap between *Orlando* and her pure biography of Roger Fry published in 1940. Gee points out that by playing with the biofictional form Woolf obliquely criticized:

> the reverence for amassed facts and catalogued detail which she disliked and distrusted in the previous generation of male novelists [and biographers]. She felt that too much respect for appearances and apparent truths allowed the real truth to escape entirely. (Gee, 1981: 138)

Indeed in 'The New Biography' Woolf argued that 'the life which is increasingly real to us is the fictitious life; it dwells in the personality rather than in the act' (Woolf, 1927/1994a: 478). Here Woolf, perhaps inadvertently, allows for the fictionalization of the self, even *herself*. For if personality rather than 'the act' is 'the life which is increasingly real' this offers fiction writers the chance to pour their imagination into the 'absences, gaps, missing evidence, knowledge or information' (Lee, 2005: 5) that comprise the personalities of other people. As Woolf made clear in *Jacob's Room* (1922), 'a profound, impartial and absolutely just opinion of our fellow-creatures is utterly unknown': 'It is no use trying to sum people up. One must follow hints, not exactly what is said, nor yet entirely what is done' (Woolf, 1922/2008: 37, 96). Perhaps in saying this Woolf has given tacit permission to writers like Gee who wish to explore the personality of their literary foremother as well as the (f)acts of her life. By resurrecting Woolf, Gee also takes the opportunity to pass the literary baton from Woolf via Angela and presumably on to Gerda. 'Write' says Woolf in the last moments of the novel, 'Your turn now ... I shall write no more' (*VW*, 470). Is Gee perhaps laying her own ghost of Woolf to rest? After all, with this novel she has paid homage to Woolf in fictional form and arguably taken control of her influence. Yet, Gee's *Virginia Woolf in Manhattan* is more than an exploration of a writer's life and personality – and a personal struggle with the power of a great female precursor – it is an exploration of how we deal with our predecessors more generally and how they can help us to examine our own time.

Notes

1 In *Christoferus or Tom Kyd's Revenge* (1993) Robin Chapman revives Kyd and his relationship with Marlowe; A. S. Byatt uses Tennyson as a character in her novella 'The Conjugial Angel' (1992); Peter Ackroyd's *Chatterton* (1987) brings the ill-fated Romantic poet back to life; while in *The Late Mr Shakespeare* (2000) Robert Nye views Shakespeare through the eyes of an unreliable, drunken protagonist called Pickleherring.

2 It is important to note that this is not a type of fiction invented by contemporary novelists as Franssen and Hoenselaars (1999: 11–28) and Schabert (1990: 42–4) highlight and as William Amos's *The Originals: An A-Z of Fiction's Real Life Characters* (1985) proves more systematically. Writers from Aristophanes – who put the philosopher Socrates on stage in *The Clouds*, to Dante – who places Virgil as character in his *Inferno*, have frequently resurrected authors on stage and in poetry.

3 See Schabert's (1990: 9–11) discussion of the other as alter ego.

4 Latham goes on to explore how Susan Sellers in her biofictional first novel *Vanessa and Virginia* (2008) represents her own relationship with her sisters as much as it explores Vanessa Bell's relationship with Woolf. Latham (2012: 368) suggests that: 'Woolf's life as portrayed by Sellers resembles both the writer-biographer's and the biographized's, thus

creating a strong affiliation between Sellers and Woolf (or between Sellers and Bell, who provides the novel's narrative voice)'.

5 Numerous writers imitate or reflect more obliquely aspects of her style, narrative voice, structure, characters and themes, for example, Michael Cunningham's *The Hours* (1998), Monica Ali's *Brick Lane* (2003) and Ian McEwan's *Atonement* (2001) and *Saturday* (2005), all engage with *Mrs Dalloway* (1925). Pat Barker and Ali Smith claim Woolf as an important antecedent and as Agata Woźniak (2014: 68) suggests 'it is difficult not to see the influence of *The Waves* (1931) on [Smith's] lyrical *Hotel World* (2001)', while Barker's *Toby's Room* (2012) is clearly a rewrite of Woolf's *Jacob's Room* (1922). Woźniak goes on to argue that '[t]he title of the high priestess of this Woolfian "renaissance" nevertheless belongs to Jeanette Winterson, whose work has consistently reworked Woolfian themes and engaged not only with such novels as *Orlando* (1928) and *To the Lighthouse* (1927), but also with Woolf's essays' (Woźniak, 2014: 68–9).

6 In 'Tradition and the Individual Talent' (1945), T. S. Eliot argued that the work of contemporary authors cannot be valued in isolation. Eliot suggested that modern writers must be 'set [...] for contrast and comparison, among the dead' (1945: 49) in order for them to be received into the canon. Author fiction, including Gee's *Virginia Woolf in Manhattan*, does this quite literally by resurrecting the dead writer whose life and work interacts directly with the life and work of the younger writer (including Angela, Gerda and Gee herself).

7 See Silver (1999) in which she examines and problematizes the stereotypes and images of Woolf that have built her into an icon.

8 Angela also feels that Woolf should not write the contemporary: 'Writing about our world was, well my job' (*VW*, 156).

9 Harold Bloom discusses in greater depth the various relationships between the later writer and his/her literary forefathers/mothers in *The Anxiety of Influence* (1973) and in his most recent discussion, *The Anatomy of Influence* (2011).

10 Woolf's description of *Between the Acts* in *Virginia Woolf in Manhattan* is a good example of how Gee takes Woolf's language in order to mimic the type of language that she really used to describe her work: 'I loved that book when it was just an essence, a wisp of pale silk, frost on the downs [...] I wanted to stipple it like Seurat, make it short & musical, & the world could be distilled in the gaps, aerations between the bright points of the brush strokes' (*VW*, 61–2).

11 For a more detailed discussion of these novels see Latham 2012. Of Susan Sellers's *Vanessa and Virginia* Latham points to the:

> Similarities to Woolf's own prose style – the rhythm of her lyrical prose, the use of arresting, overworked images, the intensity of syntactically complex sentences, the attention conferred to details, magnifying close-ups on minute objects and trivial events that have a significant impact on the subject's consciousness, motifs and refrains that resonate at precise moments throughout the narration, and so forth – are immediately detectable in this biofiction (Latham, 2012: 367).

12 Connor (1996: 239) also notices that in *The Burning Book*, Gee 'borrows the device used by Virginia Woolf in *To the Lighthouse* (1927) of introducing the death of the major characters in parenthesis'. He goes on to show how Gee then subverts the message of Woolf's parenthesis which demonstrate the 'unimportance' of these deaths 'against the power of memory to restore and sustain significance' and uses them instead to bracket the death of humanity altogether after the nuclear explosion (Connor, 1996: 239).

13 *The Years* (1937) begins two years before Woolf's birth.

14 In many ways the comic tone of *Virginia Woolf in Manhattan* also echoes Woolf's fantastical mock-biography. The strange situation of both protagonists, Woolf in Gee's novel and Orlando in Woolf's, invites humour as both characters try to come to terms with their peculiar situations.

15 J. M. Blom (1981: 436) links this plot device to Septimus Warren Smith's suicide in *Mrs Dalloway*. Indeed there are several references to this text in Gee's first novel: from the Swiss maid crying for home (*D*, 10) to Moira's scribblings which, like her death, link her to Septimus Warren Smith.

16 See also Steven Connor's (1996: 238–9) claim of the links between Woolf's 'Kew Gardens' and Gee's *The Burning Book*.

17 Dillon (2007: 380) goes through the various incarnations and reincarnations of Gee's characters in 'Imagining Apocalypse: Maggie Gee's *The Flood*'.

18 See Wright (2010: 31–6) for a fuller discussion of Woolf's vision of the role of the critic.

19 Gee is careful in an interview to draw a distinction between respect and reverence: 'I didn't want to violate her voice, but at the same time

I wanted to create my own 21st-century version of her. Reverence isn't good for a writer. Respect is important, and careful reading, but reverence doesn't help anyone' (Gee cited in O'Keeffe, 2014).

20 Angela refers to this part of Woolf's lecture which became the essay 'Professions for Women' when Woolf tries to explain her sexual stirrings (*VW*, 381).

21 Interestingly Sigrid Nunez also ponders what Woolf would have thought about her modern reputation. In *Mitz*, Nunez (1998: 46) mentions Woolf's canonization by Harold Bloom and even wonders what she would have thought about 'her picture on the side of a bus driving down Manhattan's Fifth Avenue'. 'What would Virginia have thought of this?' she wonders (Nunez, 1998: 46).

22 Lee succeeded Stephen as editor of the Dictionary of National Biography and delivered this publication as The Leslie Stephen Lecture at Cambridge on 13 May 1911.

Works Cited

Amos, William (1985) *The Originals: An A–Z of Fiction's Real Life Characters*, Boston: Little, Brown & Co.

Barthes, Roland (1964/1972) 'Criticism as Language', in David Lodge (ed.) *Twentieth Century Literary Criticism: A Reader*, pp. 647–51. Harlow, Essex: Pearson Education.

Barthes, Roland (1967/1977) 'The Death of the Author', in *Image Music Text*, trans. Richard Howard, pp. 142–8. London: Fontana Press.

Barthes, Roland (1980/1981) *Camera Lucida: Reflections on Photography*, trans. Richard Howard. New York: Hill and Wang.

Blom, J. M. and Leavis, L. R. (1982) 'Current Literature 1981', *English Studies* 63(5): 430–45.

Bloom, Harold (1973) *The Anxiety of Influence*. Oxford: Oxford University Press.

Cohn, Dorrit (1999) *The Distinction of Fiction*. Baltimore: John Hopkins University Press.

Connor, Steven (1996) 'Endings and Living On' in *The English Novel in History, 1950–1995*, pp. 199–245. New York: Routledge.

Dee, Jonathan (1999) 'The Reanimators: On the Art of Literary Graverobbing', *Harpers Magazine*, June: 76–84.

DiBattista, Maria (2009) *Imagining Virginia Woolf: An Experiment in Critical Biography*. Woodstock: Princeton University Press.

Dillon, Sarah (2007) 'Imagining Apocalypse: Maggie Gee's *The Flood*', *Contemporary Literature*, 48(3): 374–97.

Eliot, T. S. (1945) 'Tradition and the Individual Talent' in *The Sacred Wood*, 5th edn., pp. 47–59. London: Methuen and Co.

Epstein, William H. (ed.) (1991) *Contesting the Subject: Essays in the Postmodern Theory and Practice of Biography and Biographical Criticism.* West Lafayette, IN: Purdue University Press.

Fokkema, Aleid (1999) 'The Author: Postmodernism's Stock Character', in Paul Franssen and Ton Hoenselaars (eds) *The Author as Character: Representing Historical Writers in Western Literature*, pp. 39–51. London: Associated University Press.

Franssen Paul and Ton Hoenselaars (1999) 'Introduction: The Author as Character, Defining a Genre', in Paul Franssen and Ton Hoenselaars (eds) *The Author as Character: Representing Historical Writers in Western Literature*, pp. 11–35. London: Associated University Press.

Gee, Maggie (1981) *A Study of Portraits of The Artist In Contemporary Fiction: Critical Selfconsciousness as a Characterising Feature of Twentieth-Century Writing*, unpublished PhD Thesis, Wolverhampton Polytechnic.

Gee, Maggie (1996) *How May I Speak in My Own Voice? Language and the Forbidden*. The William Matthews Lecture. London: Birkbeck College.

Good, Graham (2005) 'Presentism: Postmodernism, Poststructuralism, Postcolonialism', in Daphne Patai and Will H. Corral (eds) *Theory's Empire: An Anthology of Dissent*, pp. 287–96. New York: Columbia University Press.

Jacobs, Naomi (1990) *The Character of Truth: Historical Figures in Contemporary Fiction.* Carbondale: Southern Illinois University Press.

Kiliç, Mine Özyurt (2013) *Maggie Gee: Writing the Condition-of-England Novel*. London: Bloomsbury.

Latham, Monica (2012) '"Serv[ing] under two masters": Virginia Woolf's afterlives in Contemporary Biofictions', *Auto/Biography Studies* 27(2): 354–73.

Lee, Hermione (2005) *Virginia Woolf's Nose: Essays on Biography*. Princeton and Oxford: Princeton University Press.

McGlone, Jackie (2014) 'Maggie Gee takes Virginia Woolf Out for a Bite in the Big Apple', *The Scottish Herald*, 24 May, URL (consulted 28 August 2014): http://www.heraldscotland.com/books-poetry/interviews/maggie-gee-takes-victoria-woolf-out-for-a-bite-in-the-big-apple.24269109.

McKay, M. (1997) 'An Interview with Maggie Gee', *Studia Neophilologica* 69(2): 213–22.

Middeke, Martin (1999) 'Introduction' in Martin Middeke and Werner Huber (eds) *Biofictions: The Retelling of Romantic Lives in Contemporary Fiction and Drama*, pp. 1–26. Rochester, NY: Camden House.

Moraru, Christian (2005) *Memorious Discourse: Reprise and Representation in Postmodernism*. Madison, NJ: Fairleigh Dickinson University Press.

Nunez, Sigrid (1998) *Mitz the Marmoset of Bloomsbury*. Brooklyn: Soft Skull Press.

Nüning, Ansgar (1999) 'An Intertextual Quest for Thomas Chatterton: The Deconstruction of the Romantic Cult of Originality and the Paradoxes of Life-Writing in Peter Ackroyd's Fictional Metabiography *Chatterton*', in Marton Middeke and Werner Huber (eds) *Biofictions: The Retelling of Romantic Lives in Contemporary Fiction and Drama*, pp. 27–49. Rochester, NY: Camden House.

O'Keeffe, Alice (2014) 'Maggie Gee Interview: "Writing novels is a ghastly profession"', *Guardian*, 15 June, URL (consulted 28 August 2014): http://www.theguardian.com/books/2014/jun/15/maggie-gee-interview-writing-novels-ghastly-profession-virginia-woolf.

Ozick, C. (1996) 'Metaphor and Memory' in *Portrait of the Artist as a Bad Character and Other Essays on Writing*, pp. 311–29. London: Pimlico.

Rose, Phyllis (1982) 'Biography as Fiction', *TriQuarterly* 55: 111–24.

Ryan, Marie-Laure (1997) 'Postmodernism and the Doctrine of Panfictionality', *Narrative* 5(2): 165–87.

Saunders, Max (2004) 'Biography and Autobiography', in Laura Marcus and Peter Nicholls (eds) *The Cambridge History of Twentieth-Century English Literature*, pp. 286–303. Cambridge: Cambridge University Press.

Savu, Laura E. (2009) *Postmortem Postmodernists: The Afterlife of the Author in Recent Narrative*. Madison, Teaneck: Fairleigh Dickinson University Press.

Schabert, Ina (1990) *In Quest of the Other Person: Fiction as Biography*. Tübingen: Francke Verlag.

Schwob, Marcel (1896) *Vies imaginaires*. Paris: Bibliothèque-Charpentier.

Silver, Brenda (1999) *Virginia Woolf Icon*. Chicago, IL: University of Chicago Press.

Woolf, Virginia (1976) *The Letters of Virginia Woolf: 1912–1922, Vol. 2*, ed. Nigel Nicolson and Joanne Trautmann. London: Hogarth Press.

Woolf, Virginia (1978) *The Diary of Virginia Woolf: 1920–1924, Vol. 2*, ed. Anne Olivier Bell. New York: Harcourt Brace & Co.

Woolf, Virginia (1979) *The Letters of Virginia Woolf: 1932–1935, Vol. 5*, ed. Nigel Nicolson and Joanne Trautmann. London: Hogarth Press.

Woolf, Virginia (1980a) *The Diary of Virginia Woolf: 1925–1930, Vol. 3*, ed. Anne Olivier Bell. New York: Harcourt Brace Jovanovich.
Woolf, Virginia (1980b) *The Letters of Virginia Woolf: 1936–1941, Vol. 6*, ed. Nigel Nicolson and Joanne Trautmann. London: Hogarth Press.
Woolf, Virginia (1985) *Moments of Being*, ed. Jeanne Schulkind. San Diego: Harvest/Harcourt Brace Jovanovich.
Woolf, Virginia (1922/2008) *Jacob's Room*. Oxford: Oxford University Press.
Woolf, Virginia (1925/2009) *Mrs Dalloway*. Oxford: Oxford University Press.
Woolf, Virginia (1927/1994a) 'Not One of Us', in Andrew McNeille (ed.) *The Essays of Virginia Woolf: 1925–1928, Vol. 4*, pp. 465–72. London: Hogarth Press.
Woolf, Virginia (1927/1994b) 'The New Biography', in Andrew McNeille (ed.) *The Essays of Virginia Woolf: 1925–1928, Vol. 4*, pp. 473–80. London: Hogarth Press.
Woolf, Virginia (1928/2008) *Orlando*. Oxford: Oxford University Press.
Woolf, Virginia (1931/2008) *The Waves*. Oxford: Oxford University Press.
Woolf, Virginia (1939/2011) 'The Art of Biography', in Andrew McNeille (ed.) *The Essays of Virginia Woolf: 1933–1941, Vol. 6*, pp. 181–9. London: Hogarth Press.
Woolf, Virginia (1941/2008) *Between the Acts*. Oxford: Oxford University Press.
Woolf, Virginia (1942/2011) 'Professions for Women', in Stuart N. Clarke (ed.) *The Essays of Virginia Woolf: 1933–1941, Vol. 6*, pp. 479–84. London: Hogarth Press.
Woźniak, Agata (2014) 'A Reflection of My Own – Jeanette Winterson, Virginia Woolf and the Narcissism of *Hommage*', in E. H. Wright (ed.) *Bloomsbury Influences*, pp. 68–87. Newcastle: Cambridge Scholars Publishing.
Wright, E. H. (2009) 'Woolf, The Common Readers and The Common Reader', *The Virginia Woolf Bulletin* 32: 31–6.

11

How May I Speak in My Own Voice?
Language and the Forbidden

Maggie Gee

There are silences forced on all of us, children and adults, women and men. Some begin when we are children, but continue when we are adults; other silences forced upon us in childhood make us speak unstoppably when we are adult. I want to look at the labyrinth of baffles and blind turnings in which our voices get lost, and I'll try to say how for me fiction, which of course means lying, has been the thread that leads to the lost authentic self. That self, of course, is plural. In fiction, lost selves can be found, and new selves constantly created; in fiction, the unsayable can be said.

For most of us in everyday life there are moments when the tongue will not move and the pen will not fly. Many people acquiesce in such silences; as Wittgenstein famously said, 'Whereof one cannot speak, thereof one must remain silent'. But I suppose for all writers, each silence is a challenge. The small internal voice asks, what is the silence saying? Enforced silence is an affront writers are almost honour-bound to redress.

The English, of course, are known as much by our silences as by our speech. There is a characteristically English pattern of silence, referred to in Clare McIntyre's 1996 play, *The Thickness of Skin*. 'Nobody's saying *anything*', a character complains in total frustration, when an English middle-class family is suddenly left alone and silent after a horrendous emotional scene with an outsider. Other artists have made the same point in different ways. When large disturbing forces come into our lives, the English quite often don't say anything – anything about what matters, that is.

If you asked me precisely what causes British people to fall silent, I would say sex, the emotions, class, race, money, success, failure, excretion of course, illness, age and death.

Some of these silences are international, relating as they do to the most powerful motors of our life as a species. But because I was born and brought up in Britain, I shall look at British patterns of silence, and how they find a voice in fiction. First, a small digression about academic life.

Silence was a key part of the mainstream Anglo-American academic tradition in the sixties, when I began to work in it. Written academic language tended to suppress the 'I' in favour of a more authoritative, public voice full of passive, collective or impersonal constructions. A typical sentence from my Oxford BLitt[1] thesis on English Surrealism seems to me now, decades later, comically Latinate and over-confident. I quote: 'It is indicative that a study of English Surrealism in itself cannot hope to do justice to the unified and formidable intellectual force which Surrealism unquestionably constituted in France.' I think this noisy sentence really means something small and quiet: 'I fear my study of English Surrealism will not tell you enough about the impact of Surrealist philosophy in France.' Over-confidence betrays lack of confidence. The more words there are, the more one hears silences.

I wrote two academic theses, one of sixty thousand words on English Surrealism, and a doctoral thesis of a hundred and forty thousand words on the self-conscious novel.[2] I emerged from the process, not surprisingly, implacably opposed to the idea of writing theses. And the problem was not really that seven years of my life had gone into the acquisition of two sets of initials. The problem for me was that the language I had been taught to use was so far from my own voice. I felt like a camel, awkwardly humping a huge top-heavy burden of words across the desert. At every step, something more truthful, wilder, simpler or more ambivalent was trodden into the sand. My own voice was left far behind. And there was no turning back, once set on the doctoral trail, without disgrace. Many of you must be familiar with this experience. (And why, after all, must theses be so long? Twenty thousand words is quite enough to show you have learned the official language, learned what not to say. But there is a sense that quantity will somehow make you safe; that no-one can dispute the worth of a qualification established over such a stretch of pages.)

Validation has been a very real worry for English studies. The academic study of literature in English is still not much more than a hundred-years old. It wasn't easy for the first would-be teachers of English at university level to convince the academic establishment that vernacular (as opposed Latin or Greek) literature was a respectable object of study. The ghost of that original fight for respect still haunts academic English literature. It produced initially an anxious overreaction against the chatty, opinionated, leisurely, intimate language of the amateur man-of-letters. And it's not hard to see why people reacted against that voice. This is W. M. Praed, writing about Shelley in 1821: 'Shall I turn to Shelley? – Yes! – No! – Yes! –... when I consider his powers of mind, I am proud that he was an Etonian: when I remember their perversion, I wish he had never been one'. Clearly English studies had to be more than this or they could never be taught or examined.

When T. S. Eliot suggested an aesthetic of 'impersonality' in poetry and criticism in essays like 'Tradition and the Individual Talent' (1919) and 'The Function of Criticism' (1923), it was immediately attractive to I. A. Richards, teaching at Cambridge. But a kind of scientism has stalked the corridors of literary studies ever since, policing us for vagueness, weakness and subjectivity, exhorting us to be rigorous and professional. The result, as in some structuralist and post-structuralist work, has sometimes been a literary–critical language horribly far removed from the natural speech rhythms that fiction, poetry and plays all draw upon. A valuable gain in rigour meant a loss in individuality, accessibility and pleasure, and the 'I' for a while virtually disappeared.

Students in any case always suffered more from linguistic restrictions than their academic elders, because they had less confidence in their work and more to lose if it was not acceptable. Children must obey the rules that parents can break with impunity. And the muffling of the 'I' coincided with the post-1960 rise of the doctoral thesis as a prerequisite for young people who wanted academic employment.

Of course the use of 'I' is not an absolute good. Virginia Woolf in *A Room of One's Own* associated the overuse of the 'straight dark bar' of the 'I' with an oppressive maleness. And yet, as her own practice shows, in critical writing there are places where only 'I' will do. It could be justified scientifically at a pinch by saying that the observer steps forward briefly to remind us that his or her presence affects the outcome of the experiment. Aesthetically speaking, an 'I' in the right place adds a breath of air and a welcome degree of flexibility to formal language. *The Times Literary Supplement*, which until 1974 chastened the ego in a different way by its tradition of anonymous reviewing, has on occasion changed 'I' into 'this reviewer'. The two forms are very different, aren't they? 'This reviewer' is one of an implied battalion of professionals, bearing the authority of the reviewer's function; whereas an 'I' can bring with it doubts, imperfections and passions. Yet more recently, I reviewed a collection of Janice Galloway's short stories for the TLS and,[3] anticipating the sub-editor, meekly put 'this reviewer' where the context really needed an 'I'. Imagine my pleasure when I read the proof of my review and found that the editorial pencil had cut 'this reviewer' and restored my 'I' to life. My feeling is that in general on the literary pages of newspapers a free-er and more various kind of writing is returning, perhaps in a last ditch attempt to encourage non-specialist readers to read.[4]

Meanwhile some academic literary critics like Gillian Beer or David Lodge or Isobel Armstrong are using a supple, comprehensible, living voice for close literary criticism, as a few older critics like Barbara Hardy always have done. It's interesting that of those names David Lodge is a novelist, and Isobel Armstrong a poet. Perhaps the answer is that the two languages of literature and criticism should never move impossibly far apart. But I am left wondering whether there is a similar relaxation of taboos for the foot soldiers of academic life, the students and thesis-writers. I hope so.

I shall take as my starting point for the main body of this lecture what Virginia Woolf had to say about the forbidden, nearly a century ago. That applies, in the first instance, to women, but also involves men. Sex was the silence Virginia Woolf wrote about so powerfully in her lecture 'Professions for Women', delivered in London in 1931. Woolf asks us to imagine the state of immersion in the subconscious, near dreaming, freely swimming, where she herself wrote most happily. She goes into 'the depths, the dark places, where the largest fish slumber'. But then, she tells us, she suddenly strikes against a rock. 'There was a smash; ... the most acute and difficult distress'. And the rock she strikes against is sex: 'something about the body, about the passions, which it was unfitting for her as a woman to say. Men, her reason told her, would be shocked. The consciousness of what men will say of a woman who speaks freely about her passions had roused her from her state of unconsciousness. She could write no more'. She guesses that this experience is a universal one. For any woman who writes, there is an inability to 'tell [...] the truth about [her] experiences as a body. I doubt that any woman has solved it yet'.

She leaves that statement behind as a challenge. It's certainly a challenge I have wanted to take up, because sexual experience is part of life, and novelists should be able to write about all of life. However, sex is no longer an actual silence in British life. Since the criminal prosecution of *Lady Chatterley's Lover* for obscenity in 1960, which failed, and the similar failed prosecution of Hubert Selby Jr's *Last Exit to Brooklyn* seven years later, there has been no effective legal sanction against sexual writing in Britain. Indeed the novelist Susan Hill, judging submissions from women writers for the Orange Prize, complained that she had 'never read more sexual descriptions and four-letter words dragged in willy-nilly. It's gratuitous and it's boring'.

Interesting choice of adverb there, and one may question whether descriptions of sexual acts are ever simply and straightforwardly boring, but she is making a real point about the sheer quantity of sexual writing available now. Picking headlines from the current covers of women's magazines at random, I found 'My Lover Left Me for My Brother' and 'Straight Women Pay for Lesbian Sex'. It was never like this for Vita and Virginia. But it was probably never like this for anyone; overcoloured journalism brings us no closer to authentic writing about sex.

Woolf's challenge, in fact, is still with us. The real problem is to tell the truth, as she said, about our experiences as a body, to tell the real, living, various, tender, lustful, fleshly truth about sex, and to find literary language in which to do so well. English does not have a richly varied literary vocabulary for sexual parts and actions, like French; the writer in English must fall back upon demotic slang, work through the consciousness of the characters, and hope readers will not find private language offensive or excluding. In my novel *Where Are the Snows* (1991) I did my best. Literary novelists as different as Alasdair Gray, Pat Barker, Andrew Davies and Jenny Diski have all written about sex in ways that would have been inconceivable in Virginia Woolf's day.

Is it still true that writing about sex is more difficult if you are female? I would answer that in several different ways. First, by remarking that I don't feel female as I write. My own experience of the act of writing seems to me the nearest I ever come in life to being without gender. Or rather, with every shade and variety of gender. For a brief period I can be male or female as the whim takes me, imaginatively able to enter the minds and bodies of men and women equally. I know some people feel that to say such a thing is in some way reneging on my gender, refusing to acknowledge my bodily self, but I can only say, that's the way it feels. For me it's part of what I mean when l say that in fiction, I can truly speak in my own voice, because my own voice is plural. I'll return to that point later.

Woolf said many different things on the topic of writing and gender; on the one hand she thought, like the poet Coleridge and like me, that 'a great mind is androgynous', and warned that too much consciousness of gender caused 'distortion' and 'weakness' in women's writing; on the other, she took seriously Dorothy Richardson's idea of 'psychological sentence of the feminine gender', and she claimed that 'no-one ... can possibly mistake a novel written by a woman for a novel written by a man'. I myself would separate my writing practice, which feels androgynous or polymorphous, from my sense of my writing as it enters the world, my writing as an object of critical scrutiny. My writing enters the world with a gender, because a woman's name is on the book jacket.

Let's return to the question that started my digression: 'Is it more difficult to write about sex as a woman?' Although I enjoy the experience of writing about sex very much – it feels transgressive, unpredictable, exciting – I suspect sexual love is still a problematic topic for a woman's novel entering the English literary-critic arena. *Where Are the Snows* did receive some long and favourable reviews, but it was also ignored by certain journals where I had been well reviewed previously, and received some reviews I can only call 'jeering' in tone.[5] I noticed how one male critic at least did the same thing to Pat Barker's Booker-Prize-winning novel *The Ghost Road*, fastening in a prurient fashion upon the variety of sexual experience Barker describes ('Few women can have imagined their way into the male sex organ more thoroughly than Miss Barker', etc.) and neglecting the complex connections and antitheses she was drawing between sex and death in battle. However, at least Barker's trilogy was firmly set in the First World War, and dealt with respected male literary figures like Wilfred Owen and Siegfried Sassoon. After seven novels, I have begun to realize that the novels I write that have what might crudely be called 'male' topics – war, espionage, murder, politics – have always been better and more seriously reviewed than those I have written with superficially 'female' central themes, such as children, the family, or that most dangerous one of all, sexual and romantic love. So my first answer to the question, is it still harder to write truthfully about sex as a woman? Is – 'No, but it may be harder to be taken seriously if you do'. Perhaps this is a small price to pay when you consider that we seem to have at any rate won a real freedom, to be able to write what in Woolf's day was unwritable in Britain.

It would be dishonest to pretend that the problems of writing about sex as a woman are purely to do with literary criticism. Woolf talked about her 'consciousness of what men will say of a woman who speaks freely about her passions'. As a feminist I once would have crossly denied that I could possibly be affected by any fear of shocking, or on the other hand unduly exciting, men. However, I have become uneasily aware that when I read in public I am censoring sexual passages in my own work. I'm afraid something like Woolf's sensitivity to male disapproval or male prurience lies behind it. I don't worry in the same way about men *reading* me, though. I think the explanation is that the act of reading aloud in a public place rejoins my work to my personal body, and therefore in the minds of the audience to my personal sexual identity and history. There is a difference between reading words presented on the page in private, and being confronted with the same words in public by a human voice from a gendered human body.

In any case, it really isn't surprising that sex, with its primal place in our life as a species, deciding, as heterosexual sex potentially always can, how our genes will go forward through time into the future, still weighs down our tongues with silences and difficulties.

– And at the very same instant, it makes us long to speak.

Freedom and danger come hand in hand. Writing creatively is a risky activity. You are not writing about something that was there already, like historians or biographers or writers of textbooks; whatever is in a novel, a play, a poem is your fault. But I do not complain, for with that sense of risk comes equally a little surge of bliss. Imaginary space, the space of invention and creation, is the place where we can re-create ourselves, play with the patterns into which our lives have fallen, explore the paths which have been forbidden to us. It's where we can find what Virginia Woolf called in her last novel *Between the Acts* our 'unacted parts', our unrealized secret selves. When I first read *Between*

the Acts I recognized that description of art with delight. In all our imaginations there co-exist heterosexual and homosexual, active and passive, introvert and extrovert; the real social world narrows things down by making us choose certain roles and acts, and preferring us to choose consistently. But all our other possible choices and possible selves can be kept alive through writing and reading.

Writing in private for those who will read in private, the writer enters a weightless zone where both partners, writer and reader, are freed from the personal gendered body with its particular history, its particular constraints. Those personal bodies, of course, are never entirely lost; they are there to be stirred by what we read or write, to connect us to the page through memory and desire; but they no longer limit us. We live instead through the many imagined bodies on the page. We can be re-embodied as children or the very old; as men if we are women, black if we are white; white if we are black; as people far more generous or perceptive than ourselves, or as cruel parents, fascist thugs or murderers – the world of fiction is not a world of sweetness and light.

As a novelist I do love all my characters, even homicidal Bruno in *Grace*, even the fascist boy Guy in *The Burning Book*. Through finding language for characters like that I suspect I am in the first place finding and releasing violent parts of myself, searching for the sorrow that underlies the violence, and finally containing them in the formal and moral framework of the novel. That final act of placing is important to me, but it's no good censoring yourself too soon, when you're writing fiction. Having been 'a good girl' for too many years of my life, I've decided not to worry about being a 'nice novelist'. Whatever horror is in others is probably in me in some form; what is in me I can make real for my readers. If it is in me, I want to express and understand it, otherwise I can never make sense of what I am, or of what it is to be human. In any case, wickedness is a great energizer of language, though innocent members of your extended family do tend to look at you anxiously after reading the book and ask 'How did you make up that horrible X, Y or Z?' The truthful answer, 'Oh, he's part of me,' is not generally a great success in these circumstances.

Of course writers mustn't write to please their families. In the privileged space of the novel, we must first try to be truly ourselves, otherwise we can never hope to represent other people. Once again Woolf was there before me, saying in her lecture 'Professions for Women' that 'the young woman had only to be herself', or advising in *A Room of One's Own*, 'write what you wish to write, that is all that matters'. I am sure the original, underlying question that drove me to write was indeed that 'How may I speak in my own voice?' I couldn't speak in my own voice at home, where I had to be well-behaved and quiet; I couldn't speak in my own voice at school or university, where I had to be clever and obedient; I couldn't speak in my own voice with boyfriends, where I had to charm and collude. But here, here, I could have my desire: to exist fully, to be known for what I was.

Any kind of spontaneous writing – diaries, letters, notebooks – can free the silenced voice. On the written page we no longer have to please or flatter or defer to the prejudices of particular individuals. This is perhaps particularly important for women, who are taught as infants to be sensitive, often too sensitive, to others' needs and wishes, while ignoring or suppressing their own. Writing fiction offers an additional kind of freedom because it comes, in effect, with a disclaimer. The novelist is usually very aware that his or her novel is, in a deep sense, true. And yet there is an escape clause, because everyone knows (though they sometimes forget) that fiction is not literally copied from life. The husband is not your husband; the father is not your father. Perhaps women are especially attracted to novels for another reason, too: because it gives them a chance, maybe a rare chance, to talk at length without being interrupted.

All this was true of me, growing up as I did in a house with two brothers and a dominant father. I am going to move now from the first item on my list of taboo subjects, sex, to the last, death, because it will illustrate the relationship between language and the forbidden in my own work.

Death is an area where in some ways Britain is now less advanced than it was in Virginia Woolf's day. Death for the Victorians was a public process. The dying, as we know from Victorian narrative paintings of deathbed scenes, lay and died among their family; mourning was long, elaborate and made manifest by mourning dress. The last vestiges of mourning dress in England were the black crepe armbands I remember as a child forty years ago in the 1950s.

I remember seeing them – but not in my family. I think the repressions about death in my own birth family were a central fact in my early life as a writer. Death and illness were never spoken about, at home. I never went to a funeral until I was adult, and my father refused to consider himself mortal until he actually began to die. He would not take out life insurance, and he didn't arrange for his pension to continue for my mother after his death, not out of callousness but because, I think, death wasn't something he could think about rationally. Certainly not something we could talk about. He wouldn't even tolerate conversations that implied the passage of time; if we tried to look forward to things in the future, he would say 'Don't wish time away'; if we reminisced about the past, he would say 'I don't want to dwell on it. You can't live in the past'. This left us isolated in a rather narrow band of the present. Photograph albums of our childhood were banished to deep cupboards and only very reluctantly unearthed. Time was a very dangerous element, and I can only think that this was because time implied transience, and transience implied death.

I have always been very attracted to the psychoanalytic concept of 'the return of the repressed', because it seems to me eminently true of my own life. The forbidden glows like an enormous ruby in the darkness to which it has been banished, its red light growing brighter and more seductive the further it is pushed into the distance.

When I wrote my first published novel, I decided to call it *Dying In Other Words*. Oddly enough, I was completely unaware of violating a family taboo. I told myself I was challenging a social taboo. Probably because when you are twenty-five-years old, as I was when I wrote that book, you can't see clearly how your family has affected you. You refuse to see it, in fact, because you so much want to be yourself.

The title is really a subtitle. *Dying In Other Words* really means *Living: Dying, In Other Words*. I was saying in that title that living implies dying, that they are implicitly connected. Of course this is obvious enough, but not in my family. Not in my country, either.

There really was a general social taboo on talking about death in Britain when I was a child. It still exists today, though over the last fifteen years there has been a deep and intelligent movement towards overcoming it from within the religious, philosophical and, at last, medical communities. But even ten years ago, and I suspect in a few places still today, doctors found it almost impossible to speak the truth to dying patients or their families.

Death, ageing and illness, which I listed separately in my pantechnicon of taboos, are of course connected. In 1960s Britain, the beginnings of the cult of youth changed the way we looked at age. London was suddenly the youth capital of the world; everything was possible. 'All you need is love' – everything was possible, that is, if you were young. The underside of all that bright life, the pay-off for all that wonderful inflorescence of colour and music and sexuality, was probably that death, ageing and illness were pushed further back into the shadows. 'I hope I die before I get old', sang the pop singer Pete Townshend of *The Who*. In actual fact, with increased life expectancy, more and more people were dying much older than before, but out of sight and out of mind.

In Virginia Woolf's day, people died at home, attended by friends and family. In the last decades of the same century in the same country, the majority of deaths take place in hospital, the care of the dying is professionalized, and so death has become separated from our everyday experience. Modern expressions of mourning are similarly muted. Clenched brave smiles and a lot of talk about the flowers and the weather afterwards – that's the English at a funeral.[6] What is not seen or talked about becomes more fearful, not less.

Why should the tradition of public dying and expressive mourning wither and die in the same place between one end of a century and the other? One key to that may come from my own family history. My father, who was so terrified of death (though he died bravely in the end), was one of three sons of Lottie Gee, née Brown. Lottie herself was one of five children, three girls and two boys. But both Lottie's brothers were killed as private soldiers in the First World War, the first one, Jack, in the very same year that my father was born, 1914. She took it very hard. How it must have affected my father's early years I can only imagine. I remember Grandma telling me the story of her travelling after the war to France with her sister Kit, not speaking a word of French, and trying desperately to find their brothers' graves among so many. Neither of Grandma's sisters had children, so Lottie Gee's three boys were the only surviving members of that family. You can imagine her terror when the Second World War came and her three boys were of the age to fight. My father married and started a family while briefly on leave during the last years of that war in which so many millions of people died. Perhaps later on he simply grew allergic to death and mourning; perhaps he resented the hold it seemed to have upon his life. Perhaps the entire British nation had unconsciously resolved to banish death forever, in the aftermath of those two bloody wars in which altogether over seventy million people died. Perhaps it's an underlying explanation for 'Swinging London' and the cult of youth as well, with its reverberations all over the world. Instead of sending the very young off to die, we celebrated them, and tried to forget death in a gigantic street party.

In any case, what has been compulsively forgotten will be compulsively remembered. In my first novel, death leaps from every cranny of life. It begins with the apparent suicide of a young woman, Moira, but a reversal takes place in which every other person in her world dies, or has their death foreseen, while Moira chronicles their deaths and is alone alive at the end of the book, still typing.[7] My other six novels have been in very different styles and about very different subjects, yet there is often a dying fall in their pages, and they have been characterized by critics as elegiac. I don't think this is at all surprising; it would be surprising, really, if any of our activities weren't affected at some level by the Second World War, to which we are still so close in time, and which caused one of the greatest losses of life in 150,000 years of human history.

I have half an explanation, then, for our British silencing of death. But I offer no defence for our silence about emotion, the 'stiff upper lip' for which we are so famous.

The question of the British and the emotions is a complex one, for of course we are not all the same. I shall take a detour to talk about class here, another item from my list of taboos. A foreigner might be surprised to hear that the British find it hard to talk about class, since so many of our novels and plays seem to be about nothing else. But it's just a case of writers speaking the unspeakable again. Class still has such a powerful grip upon our lives, yet it is taboo as a direct topic of everyday conversation. It is impossible to ask a stranger what class they belong to, unthinkable to allude to your own. The British deduce these matters for themselves in silence, working from the little clues that voice, accent, habits, clothes supply. British writers write about class because it's their job to make explicit the implicit forces that shape our lives. To return to the British taboo on expressing emotion, I think it is the middle classes who have the stiffest upper lip, the middle classes who as Clare McIntyre says in her play are unable to say anything, the middle classes – at least those who are not in therapy – who make lack of emotion, especially negative emotion, a primary virtue in life. Theodore Zeldin quotes the nineteenth-century British Prime Minister and novelist Benjamin Disraeli's analysis of middle-class English as an 'expressive language': 'It consists, as far as I can observe, of four words; nice, jolly, charming, and bore, and, some grammarians add, fond'. Perhaps it was fortunate for my life as a writer that my family came from the working classes, and almost too freely expressed many, though not all, emotions.

Perhaps all this goes back to Empire and the military virtues; endure and say nothing; be stoical in the face of the sheer un-Englishness of the rest of the world. 'Mad dogs and Englishmen go out in the midday sun', Noel Coward wrote. Ignore physical discomfort and negative emotions because they make you vulnerable. In David Hare's 1978 play and film *Plenty*, the volatile, tragic, flamboyantly talkative heroine Susan demonstrates what happens if the emotions are allowed to run riot in a basically unemotional country; she destroys her husband, a decent civil servant, and then herself. Going back in time we see in

Virginia Woolf's work eccentric, badly-behaved or mad figures like Septimus Warren, Mrs Manresa and Miss La Trobe whose function is to be the necessary bull in the china shop, to express the suppressed, to upset the apple cart where those shiny, silent English apples are so neatly arranged. I do the same thing in my own work with truculent, selfish, passionate, difficult women like Lottie Lucas in *Light Years* or Paula Timms in *Grace*. And my dominant narrative voice is, I think, shaped to express the emotion my culture represses, through the use of rhythms like bodily rhythms, through repetition and half-rhymes, through my preference for verb forms with running participles, through rising and falling inflections.

The poet Philip Larkin, himself a master of emotional repression but a great poet all the same, satirized English emotional constipation in his poem 'Sympathy in White Major'. The 'I' of the poem imagines what people might say of him after he is dead:

> A decent chap, a real good sort
> Straight as a die, one of the best.
> A brick, a trump, a proper sport,
> Head and shoulders above the rest;
> How many lives would have been duller
> Had he not been here below?
> Here's to the whitest man I know –
> Though white is not my favourite colour.'

The poem refers to the now, I hope, obsolete phrase 'You're a white man', implying that the Anglo-Saxon abroad is uncoloured by dangerous and embarrassing emotions or any of the fearsomely unreliable behaviour we used to impute to foreigners, particularly black ones...

Which brings me to race, another topic on my 'forbidden' list. Here we suffer from a nervousness that's common to all nations with an imperial past and a history of slavery. It's called a bad conscience. The results of our history are still with us in the form of a racially mixed population with black people typically in poorer paid employment or unemployed, with lower life expectancy and a disproportionate number of arrests (though not necessarily convictions) from the police. Moreover, the level of racial attacks on black people in British cities is high today.[8] Guilt isn't a comfortable emotion. It's very easily stifled by the pretence that there's nothing wrong, nothing to worry about – which is something that comes very easily to the English.

One problem about racism in Britain is that it has been pushed underground but not crushed. It apparently no longer exists in polite discourse, because educated people are frightened of sounding racist. And yet the racial attacks continue, and it's difficult for black people to get high visibility jobs or be accepted in white English homes, to appear in advertisements or be cast in plays.[9] Moreover, if you listen to the familiar speech of less educated, less self-conscious white people, typically self-employed tradesmen or low-paid workers who feel their livelihood is threatened, the racial prejudices are virulent and apparently unmodified by the careful silence that has fallen upon the so-called 'chattering classes'.

The question of 'correct' language is often a distraction when we are thinking about race. It's easy enough to remember to say 'black' instead of 'coloured', or 'Native American' instead of 'Red Indian', or 'Caribbean' instead of 'West Indian' (though many older black people say 'West Indian'). To use what we imagine to be correct language is not necessarily to change our attitudes, and certainly doesn't change the underlying unfairness of the life of black people in Britain. I think the great anxiety that attends language about race, the tremendous sense that we are walking where we have been forbidden to walk, is a telling symptom of the fundamental divide between white and black people in Britain today.

In 1986 we moved to South Brent, which has one of the highest concentrations of black people in the country. This raised questions for me. Could I as a white writer write about black people, or through black characters? Are there some taboos that it is wrong to break? I wrote a novel about a racial murder that showed white racism at length, and had several black characters. It is the only novel I have written, since my first, which has proved difficult to publish. Which is a salutary reminder that the forbidding of language may mean something much stronger and more effective than mere disapproval. Perhaps I was too rash in thinking that every experience can be imagined, every taboo broken with impunity. No one, though, can un-write that novel, and it will probably be published one day. [*It was*].¹⁰ To speak of it here at any rate gives me the pleasurable experience of violating the English taboo on talking about failure and success.

I do think writers must be rash or nothing. In my own work I can see a consistent desire to go against the grain of British repression, to reach out for the ruby glowing in the darkness of denial, to find the forbidden truth, to transgress. It's what writers have always done. Chaucer wrote of the sexual and financial misbehaviour of the clergy; Shakespeare wrote of the folly of kings and princes; Cervantes satirized the pretences of knights. Jane Austen talked about the greed for money and social snobbery that lay under the surface of an apparently polite and genteel society. Thackeray wrote about the exploitation of innocence at the heart of the most aristocratic society of his day. Dickens wrote about the cruelty and stupidity of the institutions on which the Victorians most prided themselves, such as education and the law courts. E. M. Forster wrote about homosexual love, though he could not publish *Maurice* while he was alive. Virginia Woolf told unacceptable truths about the behaviour of Victorian patriarchal fathers and husbands, and the rebellious aspirations of their daughters and wives. James Joyce wrote about sexual and bodily functions including excretion, one of the last taboos on my list for this lecture – thus severely shocking Virginia Woolf, who said 'one hopes he'll grow out of it, but as Joyce is 40 this scarcely seems likely'. Which shows that even writers have their areas of forbidden language. More recently it's hard to find a taboo that writers haven't broken. Many have involved sex or violence or sexual violence. Writers like Martin Amis in *London Fields*, or Helen Zahavi in *Dirty Weekend*, express in a grotesquely exaggerated form the real anger and suspicion that exists between the genders today. They show how literature can be a field for pitched battle between the genders, rather than the playground for gender I have described.

The historian Theodore Zeldin reminds us in his brilliant book *An Intimate History of Humanity* (1994) that free speech is still something of relatively recent importance to human beings. He places his hopes for the future in the perpetually increasing possibilities for conversation, between people from different cultures and religions, between men and women, parents and children. In this country at the end of the twentieth century, children are no longer seen and not heard or required to speak only when spoken to. More and more parents answer their children's questions honestly, even if they are about sex or death, money, class, or emotion.

I do see the loosening of our tongues, and of the grip of taboos, as good. And yet, as a novelist I can't wholly welcome the dissolving of the fine web of taboos that helps define our culture. Throughout this lecture I have traced a connection between what is repressed and what the novelist is impelled most urgently to say. I do not think children who can always speak their deepest fears and desires will grow up to be novelists, though they may be artists in less mediated, more communal, instinctual and immediately pleasurable ways. They may be happier *not* performing linguistic marathons of self-definition and self-assertion.

Perhaps there are more connections than I would like to think between the lonely feats of endurance involved in writing theses and in writing novels. I have made writing sound very romantic. I have spoken of its bliss and release, but not of the passages of terrible drudgery, nor the necessary disciplines of writing and rewriting at such length. Yes, novelists rebel against their parents; but don't they also, in a convoluted way, try to impress and appease them? Writing a novel is not just the individual, anarchic act of finding one's own voice.

We can deduce other things about the novel from its early history in Spain, in Britain and elsewhere. The novel only flourishes in developed societies with a strong but problematic sense of the individual, where there is potential conflict between the inner and outer life, and where the structures of social repression are inflexible enough to force huge amounts of energy to run silently underground. As I speak in my own voice, I must also be aware of all those other forces speaking through me. It is that buried energy, that complex interaction between the culture saying *No* and the individual voice saying *Yes*, which bursts out, from time to time, in novels.

Acknowledgement

This essay was originally delivered as the 1996 William Matthews lecture at Birkbeck College, University of London. It has been updated by the author for this publication, including the addition of the following notes.

Notes

1 Oxford 1971, 'The influence of Surrealism on English writing of the thirties and forties', supervised by the poet John Fuller. Subsequently converted to an M Litt.

2 Wolverhampton 1980, 'A study of portraits of the artist in contemporary fiction: critical self-consciousness as a characterizing feature of twentieth-century writing', supervised by Vivienne Wylie and the novelist David Lodge.

3 *Where You Find It* (1996)

4 Yes. But alas, I did not see how that free-er kind of reviewing would at times deteriorate into narcissism and a desperate attempt to entertain on the part of the reviewer, as the literary pages lost confidence. I did try to muster a protest, when I was on the Management Committee of the Society of Authors, against the reversal of size and status between the names of author and reviewer that started in the 1990s and is now institutionalized, but no-one else thought it was worth protesting about. Yet so hard to write a book, so easy to write a review!

5 My most extended attempt at writing the truth about my body is in my memoir, *My Animal Life* (2010). My 2014 novel *Virginia Woolf in Manhattan* is a direct attempt (via the tragicomic indirections of fiction) to take on Woolf's challenge in the essay 'Professions for Women' – with Woolf as the protagonist in a tender sexual episode. Among many other things I wanted to say 'We can do this, now.'

6 This essay was of course written before the outpourings of public grief and mourning over the death and funeral of Princess Diana in 2004.

7 This is also a protest against the fetishizing of the self-destructive female artist which is central, once again, in *Virginia Woolf in Manhattan* – as teenage Gerda says of Sylvia Plath, 'What sense does it make to kill yourself? If she'd stayed alive, she'd have written more poems. So even if I'd wanted to kill myself, I won't, because I am going to Have a Life' (*VW*, 153).

8 Still true today. According to the latest statistics available from the Institute of Race Relations, 'Racial violence is largely underreported to the police. According to the Crime Survey for England and Wales (formerly the British Crime Survey), there were about 130,000 racially motivated "hate crimes" per year in the years 2009/10 and 2010/11'.

9 But I think in the issue of visibility, there has been real progress over the 18 years since I wrote this essay.

10 *The White Family*, published in 2002, seven years after I wrote it, by Lebanese editor and artist Mai Ghoussoub at the independent publisher, Saqi Books, was subsequently shortlisted for the Orange Prize for Fiction and the 100,000-euro International Impac Dublin Literary Award. Yet the novel had been rejected in 1995 by HarperCollins, to whom it was contracted, and then turned down by every mainstream publisher in London. The upside: to while away the time until someone liked *The White Family*, I wrote and published *The Ice People* (1998).

Notes on Contributors

Alexander Beaumont is Lecturer in English Literature at York St John University. His essays have appeared in the journal *Contemporary Literature* and the collection *Thatcher and After* (Palgrave Macmillan, 2010). He is author of *Contemporary British Fiction and the Cultural Politics of Disenfranchisement* (Palgrave Macmillan, 2015), which includes new appraisals of Jeanette Winterson, Hanif Kureishi, J. G. Ballard, Zadie Smith, Monica Ali, Ian McEwan, Kazuo Ishiguro and China Miéville.

Sarah Dillon is University Lecturer in Literature and Film in the Faculty of English at the University of Cambridge. She is author of *The Palimpsest: Literature, Criticism, Theory* (Continuum, 2007) and editor of *David Mitchell: Critical Essays* (Gylphi, 2011). She is General Editor of the Gylphi Contemporary Writers: Critical Essays series, and serves on the editorial board of *C21: Journal of Twenty-First Century Writing*. She has published widely on twentieth- and twenty-first-century literature, film and philosophy. Sarah is also actively involved in radio broadcasting and public engagement, and was a 2013 BBC New Generation Thinker.

Caroline Edwards is Lecturer in Modern and Contemporary Literature at Birkbeck, University of London. She is completing a monograph on time in contemporary fiction titled *Fictions of the Not Yet* and is co-editing *China Miéville: Critical Essays* (Gylphi, 2015). Caroline has published on twenty-first-century British fiction, utopian theory and literature, Marxist philosophies of time, and post-apocalyptic narratives in a number of journals, including *Modern Fiction Studies, Contemporary*

Literature, Radical Philosophy, Telos, and *Textual Practice.* She is Founding and Commissioning Editor of the open access journal of twenty-first-century literary criticism, *Alluvium,* and is a Founder and Director of the Open Library of Humanities.

Sarah Falcus is a Senior Lecturer in English Literature at the University of Huddersfield. Her research interests lie predominantly in contemporary women's writing and she has published critical work on authors such as Michèle Roberts, Pat Barker and Margaret Drabble. Her current research is in the area of literary gerontology, stemming from an interest in the intersection of gender and ageing. She is currently working on a study of narratives of dementia.

Irene Pérez-Fernández is a Lecturer at the University of the Oviedo, Spain. She researches on the notions of gender, space and identity in contemporary British literature and literatures in English. She has translated into Spanish Maggie Gee's short story 'The Artist' (*Maggie Gee: 'The Artist/Artista'* [Oviedo: KRK ediciones, 2011]) and published articles on the works of contemporary Black British Women Writers such as Andrea Levy, Zadie Smith, Monica Ali and Diana Evans.

Susan Alice Fischer is Professor of English at Medgar Evers College of The City University of New York, where she coordinates the Cross-Cultural Literature concentration and teaches British literature and literary theory. She is the Editor of the online peer-reviewed *Literary London Journal,* the publication of the Literary London Society. She is also Co-Editor of *Changing English: Studies in Culture and Education,* a Routledge/Taylor & Francis journal. She has published extensively on contemporary British novelists, including Andrea Levy, Zadie Smith and Sarah Waters. She is the editor of *Hanif Kureishi: Contemporary Critical Perspectives* (Bloomsbury, 2015), and she is completing a study on contemporary women's fiction.

Chris Maughan is currently reading for a PhD in English from The University of Warwick after obtaining full funding from the 'Warwick Postgraduate Research Scholarship'. His focus is the intersection between environmental activism and contemporary literature, particularly with regard to the politics which flow from and inform representations of environmental interventions.

Notes on Contributors

Monika Szuba completed her PhD on the subject of strategies of contestation in the novels of contemporary Scottish women authors at Gdańsk University, Poland. She has published a number of articles on contemporary fiction and poetry. She is co-organizer of International Literary Festival BACK 2 and BETWEEN in Sopot, Poland. She is also co-editor of the between.pomiędzy series published by the University of Gdańsk Press and one of the founding members of the Textual Studies Research Group as well as the Scottish Studies Research Group at the University of Gdańsk. Her research interests include contemporary British poetry and prose.

Adam Welstead is a 600th Anniversary Doctoral Fellow at the School of English, University of St Andrews. He is currently completing a PhD thesis entitled 'Imagining Intersubjectivities in Contemporary British Dystopian Fiction', and has research interests in modern and contemporary literature, critical theory and continental philosophy. Adam is currently the Co-Director of *Theoria: University of St Andrews Critical Theory Group*.

E. H. Wright is a playwright and Senior Lecturer in English and European Literature at Bath Spa University. Her most recent play *Vanessa and Virginia* (Play Dead, 2013) was nominated for five Off West End Awards. Her academic publications include a biography of Virginia Woolf (Hesperus, 2011) and various articles covering the Bloomsbury Group, Joseph Conrad and Henrik Ibsen. She is currently researching a monograph on Virginia Woolf and drama and writing a play entitled *Suicide's Symposium* sponsored by The Welcome Trust.

Index

Abrams, M. H. 72
Ackroyd, Peter 230
  Chatterton 253n.1
Adorno, Theodor 134
Africa 219, 220, 222, 225
ageing 14, 17, 79–99, 272
ageist
  discourses 88
  structures 93
Albion 195, 198
alcoholism 55
Aldiss, Brian
  Greybeard 109
Ali, Monica
  Brick Lane 182, 202n.2, 254
Amis, Martin
  London Fields 277
Amos, William
  Originals: An A-Z of Fiction's Real Life Characters, The 253n.2
antinatalism 75n.1
apocalypse 51, 52, 54–64, 64, 72, 74, 113, 124, 153, 163–165, 170, 173, 177
  dialectic of 75
  Judeo-Christian apocalyptic tradition 175
  literature and 28n.14, 48n.5, 48n.6, 76n.3
  nuclear 16, 40, 45, 70
  personal 15
apocalyptic natality 67–75
Arendt, Hannah 20, 106

Eichmann in Jerusalem 56
Human Condition, The 75n.2, 75, 162, 168–169, 172
natality 16, 53
On Violence 53, 56
Origins of Totalitarianism, The 53, 56
Promise of Politics 57
Armistead, Claire 26n.3
Armstrong, Isobel 264
Arthurian England 195–196
asexuality
  97n.4
atemporality 80
Atwood, Margaret 176
  Handmaid's Tale, The 18, 110
  Oryx and Crake 98n.5
  Republic of Gilead 111
  'ustopia' 179n.4
Austen, Jane 277
author fiction 22, 23, 230–237, 248–251 *see also* biofiction

Barker, Pat 266
  Ghost Road, The 267
  Toby's Room 254n.5
Barron, Stephanie
  White Garden: A Novel of Virginia Woolf, The 236
Barthes, Roland 251
  'Death of the Author' xv, 2, 229–231, 246
  'the hermeneutic code' 32

Beckett, Samuel 1, 22, 33, 230, 240
Beer, Gillian 264
Benjamin, Walter 47
Berger, John
   And Our Faces, My Heart, Brief as Photos 36
   G. 48n.2
biofiction 22, 231–233, 237, 245, 252, 253n.4, 255n.11 *see also* author fiction
biografiction 231
biographie romancée 231
Blair, Tony 7, 68
Bloom, Harold 240
   Anxiety of Influence, The 233, 254n.9, 256n.21
Bradbury, Ray
   Fahrenheit 451 49n.7
British Empire 59, 195, 204n.11
Buddhism
   compassion 212
   kōan 31–32, 35, 38, 47
Burdekin, Katharine
   Swastika Night 109
Bush, George 7, 68
Byatt, A. S. 230
   'The Conjugial Angel' 253n.1

cancer 63, 64
   breast 93
Canetti, Elias
   Crowds and Power 171
Case Against 8, The (film) 101
Certeau, Michel de
   'Concept-city' 189
Cervantes, Miguel de 277
Chapman, Robin 230
   Christoferus or Tom Kyd's Revenge 253n.1
Chaucer, Geoffrey xv, xvi, 277

   Troilus and Criseyde xiv
Chernobyl disaster 210
Chevalier, Tracy
   Girl with a Pearl Earring 235
Christian fundamentalism 111
Christianity 106–107, 110, 123, 123n.4, 209, 211, 212
Churchill, Winston 199
circularity
   of history 36
   of narratives 47, 243
   of stories 36
   of structure 16
class 84, 109, 139, 190, 195, 217–221, 232, 247–250, 262, 274, 278 *see herein* middle-class, working class
class-consciousness 248
class struggle 138
Cleave, Chris 183
climate change 7, 19, 70, 123n.7, 134, 133–157, 138
Cold War 72
Coleridge, Samuel Taylor 266
colonial history 56, 191, 195
colonialism 135, 182, 216, 218
Connor, Steven 28n.14, 242, 255n.12, 255n.16
consumer culture 86, 87, 91, 96
consumerism 17, 80, 87, 250
Coward, Noel 274
Craig, Amanda 183
Cunningham, Michael
   Hours, The 236, 241, 247, 254n.5

Dabydeen, David 182
D'Aguiar, Fred 182
Dante
   Inferno 253n.2
   Paradiso 216

Index

Darwin, Charles 136
Davies, Andrew 266
death 44, 47, 59, 61, 64, 67, 72, 79, 80, 81, 83, 87, 93, 96, 109, 119, 120, 153, 183, 200, 223, 244, 247, 255, 262, 270–274, 278
  denial of 14
  dying 14
  in battle 76n.5, 128n.24, 255n.12, 267
death drive 104, 114, 128n.27
Debord, Guy 20, 166, 168
Deleuze, Gilles
  and Félix Guattari
    What Is Philosophy? 173, 178
de Man, Paul 114
  anacoluthia 126n.17
demodystopia 18, 102, 109–112, 124 *see herein* demodystopian fiction, demodystopian literature 123n.7, 124n.8
demografiction *see* demodystopia
Derrida, Jacques 43, 62, 66, 125n.13, 126n.17, 129n.28
  'No Apocalypse, Not Now (Full Speed Ahead, Seven Missiles, Seven Missives)' 48n.6
Dickens, Charles 33, 277
  A Christmas Carol 27n.9, 27n.11, 123n.5
diegesis 42
diptych 22, 216–217, 223–225
Diski, Jenny 266
Disraeli, Benjamin 274
domestic violence 55, 209
dramatic irony 18, 102, 117–120

dualism 13, 27n.11, 28n.15
dystopia 16, 18–20, 94, 123n.5, 155n.4, 159–180
dystopian metropolis 159

ecocriticism 19, 136–138, 139, 155n.1
'ecopoetics' 33
Edelman, Lee
  No Future: Queer Theory and the Death Drive 102
  reproductive futurism 75n.1, 101–132
Edwin, Walter
  Peck's Shelley: His Life And Work 237
Eliot, George 27n.11, 33
  Silas Marner 123n.5
Eliot, T. S. 263
  'The Function of Criticism' 263
  'Tradition and the Individual Talent' 254n.6, 263
  Waste Land, The 170
embodiment 14, 55, 154, 196, 198, 200
Emecheta 182
environmental literary criticism *see* ecocriticism
Evans, Diana
  26a 182

Fairbairns, Zoe
  Benefits 18, 110–111
female sexuality *see* sexuality
First World War 191, 202n.3, 267, 273
Forster, E. M.
  Maurice 277
Foucault, Michel 185, 197
  heretopia 20, 175

Frank, Anne 55, 73
Freeman, Gillian 22
But Nobody Lives in Bloomsbury 236
Freud, Sigmund 26n.2, 161
Civilization and its Discontents 178n.1
Fuller, John 279n.1

Gadamer, Hans-Georg 143, 146
Gaia theory 22, 213–215, 223–224
Galloway, Janice 264
Gee, Maggie
  edited
    Anthology of Writing Against War: For Life on Earth 48n.3
  interviews
    with Elaine Showalter 26n.6
    with Margaret McKay 26n.4
    with Mine Özyurt Kiliç 27
  lectures
    'How May I Speak in My Own Voice?: Language and the Forbidden', William Matthews Lecture at Birkbeck College 12, 14, 27n.8, 215
    'Why Writers Can't Be Told They Have Responsibilities', 2004 Dawson-Scott Memorial Lecture at English PEN's International Writers' Day 6
  memoir
    My Animal Life 3, 13–14, 25, 27, 33–34, 76n.3, 209, 212, 216, 279n.5
  novels
    Burning Book, The xvi, 1, 4, 7, 28n.14, 31–50, 51, 54–61, 62, 66, 68, 70–73, 73, 74, 76n.4, 76n.6, 84, 204n.16, 215, 242–244, 255n.16, 269
    Dying, in Other Words 1, 11, 14, 25n.1, 55, 72, 76n.6, 243, 271
    Flood, The 4, 7, 27n.7, 28n.14, 47n.1, 48n.6, 51, 62, 67–75, 133–157, 159, 159–180, 204n.16, 243
    Grace xvi, 3, 7, 34, 94, 135, 269, 275
    Ice People, The 7, 51, 61–67, 94, 97n.3, 101–132, 135, 162, 280n.10
    Light Years 80, 94, 212, 215, 216, 275
    My Cleaner 28, 94, 183, 213, 216–223
    My Driver 11, 28, 94, 183, 213, 216–219
    Virginia Woolf in Manhattan xiii, xvi, 5, 9, 14, 229–260, 279n.5, 280n.7
    Where Are the Snows 51, 61–67, 72, 76n.7, 79–99, 266
    White Family, The 7, 34, 51, 61–67, 94, 141, 174, 176, 181–208, 215, 216, 243, 280n.10
  Oxford BLitt thesis on English Surrealism 262
  short stories
    Blue, The 8, 9, 10, 12–13, 203n.7
Genette, Gérard 38, 42
Gilman, Charlotte Perkins
  Herland 109

Index

Gilroy, Beryl 182
Glass, Rodge 134
Golding, William 213
  Lord of the Flies 161
grand narratives 36
Granta 183, 202n.2
Gray, Alasdair 266
Gunew, Sneja
  Displacements: Migrant Storytellers 203n.4

Hardy, Barbara 264
Hawkes, Ellen
  and Peter Manso
    Shadow of the Moth: A Novel of Espionage with Virginia Woolf, The 236
Heidegger, Martin
  Being and Time 75n.2
Heise, Ursula K.
  Chronoschisms: Time, Narrative and Postmodernism 36
heterodiegetic narrator 42
heteronormativity 18, 122n.3
hibakusha (or 'explosion-affected people') 16, 38–39, 57, 59
Hill, Susan 265
Hiroshima 16, 33, 39, 57, 60
historiography 137–138
Holocaust 55
Hopper, Edward 26n.5
Husserl, Edmund
  Einfühlen 234
Hutcheon, Linda
  'narcissistic narrative' 38
Huxley, Aldous
  Brave New World 20, 159–160, 165

illness 13, 15, 164, 247, 262, 271–272

immigration 21, 55, 182, 183, 186, 192
  laws 196, 202n.3, 203n.7
individualism 80, 84, 85, 87, 93, 160
Islamophobia 184

Jameson, Fredric 164, 176
  Political Unconscious, The 19, 138–141, 143–144, 146–149, 152–153, 154
  'The Politics of Utopia' 160, 178
James, P. D. 18
  Children of Men, The 106–110, 125n.11
Johnson, Amryl 182
Johnson, Linton Kwesi 182
Johnson, Lyndon B.
  'Daisy Girl' advertisement 76n.5
jouissance 67, 104, 105, 128n.27, 129n.28

Kapleau, Philip
  Three Pillars of Zen 31–32
Kew Gardens 59, 74, 163, 173–177, 244, 255n.16
Kiliç, Mine Özyurt
  Maggie Gee: Writing the Condition-of-England Novel xv, 5, 25n.1, 27n.11, 80, 81, 94, 96, 162, 164, 173, 176
Kipling, Rudyard
  'The Glory of the Garden' 191, 196
Kureishi, Hanif
  Buddha of Suburbia, The 202n.2
  My Beautiful Launderette 182

Lacan, Jacques 103, 104, 121, 128n.21
  sinthome 102, 120, 128n.25,

128n.27
Lamming, George
   Emigrants, The 182
Larkin, Philip 275
late capitalism 160, 164–165, 178
Lawrence, D. H.
   Lady Chatterley's Lover
     obscenity case 265
Lawrence, Stephen 7, 21, 27n.11, 34, 64–65, 183, 186, 216
Lee, Hermione 236
Lee, Sidney
   Principles of Biography 252
Lefebvre, Henri 155n.3, 185, 189, 193–194, 204n.8
Let the Right One In (film) 128n.23
Levy, Andrea
   Long Song, The 202n.2
   Small Island 182, 202n.2, 202n.3
Lippincott, Robin
   Mr Dalloway 247
Lodge, David 264, 279n.2
Lovelock, James 213
Lurie, Alison 90
Lyotard, Jean-François 43
   Postmodern Condition: A Report on Knowledge, The 35–36

Malalouf, Amin
   First Century After Beatrice, The 110
Malthus, Thomas 75n.1
Marxism 19, 94, 134, 136–152 see herein Marxist Theory
Marx, Karl
   Capital Vol. I 136–137
   'concrete history' 138
McEwan, Ian
   Atonement 254n.5
   Saturday 254n.5

McIntyre, Clare 274
   Thickness of Skin, The 262
McKibben, Bill 150, 155n.5
   'the end of nature' 137
McLeod, John 182–183, 193
mental illness 142
migration 21, 182, 183, 191
   inward 95
   post-Second World War immigrants 182
Miller, J. Hillis 126n.17
miscarriage 14
misogyny 21, 59, 118
Mitchell, David
   Bone Clocks, The 2
   Cloud Atlas 26n.3, 48n.5
Morgan, Clare 22
   Book for All and None, A 236
Moscovici, Serge
   Age of the Crowd, The 172
Moylan, Tom
   Scraps of the Untainted Sky: Science Fiction, Utopia, Dystopia 179n.3
multiculturalism 182–183

Nabokov, Vladimir 1, 22, 25, 27n.11, 230, 240
Nagasaki 16, 33, 39, 57, 60
natalist ideology 52
natality 54–61
National Service 197
Nazism 56
Nazi totalitarianism 56
necronarrator 9, 12
New York 92
Nicolson, Harold
   Some People 252
Nixon, Rob
   Slow Violence and the

Index

Environmentalism of the Poor 133–135
nuclear apocalypse 55
nuclear disaster 209
nuclear war 56, 57
  threat of 55
Nunez, Sigrid
  Mitz: The Marmoset of Bloomsbury 236, 241, 249
Nye, Robert 230
  Late Mr Shakespeare, The 253n.1

Orwell, George
  Nineteen Eighty Four 159, 160

Parekh Report
  Future of Multi-ethnic Britain, The 181
petits récits 36
Phillips, Caryl 202n.2
  Strange Fruit (play) 182
photography 239
physicality 14
Plato 42
post-apocalyptic 176
postcolonial relations 216, 225
posthuman 91, 93
postmodernism 230
Powell, Enoch
  'Rivers of Blood' (speech) 196, 204n.14
Praed, W. M. 263
pre-apocalyptic 176
Princess Diana
  death 280n.6
propaganda 192
Proust, Marcel 126n.17
psychoanalysis 105
psychoanalytic perspective 26n.2
psycho-sexual drive 215

public sphere 52, 66, 75
publishing 68

queer theory 122n.2

race 250, 275–276
racial discrimination 203n.6
racism 34, 55, 209, 276
  'polite' 218
Rancière, Jacques 106
realist novel 55
reproduction 51, 117–118
  biological and social 54
reproductive futurism *see* Edelman, Lee
Richards, I. A. 263
Richardson, Dorothy 267
Ricœur, Paul 41, 47
Riley, Joan 182
Rogers, Jane
  Testament of Jessie Lamb, The 110
Roth, Philip 90
Rousseau, Jean-Jacques
  Social Contract, The 161
Rupert Thomson 160
Rushdie, Salman 182, 202n.2

Sackville-West, Vita 252
same-sex marriage 101
scapegoat
  anthropological theory of 121n.1
Schopenhauer, Arthur 75n.1
Schwob, Marcel 231
Second World War 55, 193, 198, 244, 273
Selby, Hubert, Jr
  Last Exit to Brooklyn 265
Sellers, Susan
  Vanessa and Virginia 236, 241, 253n.4, 255n.11

Selvon, Sam
  Lonely Londoners, The 182
sex 14, 270, 278
sexual experience 267
sexuality 90–91, 166, 250, 272
  representation of female sexuality 97n.4
sexual violation 14
Shakespeare, William 277
Shelley, Percy Bysshe 263
Showalter, Elaine 5
slavery
  history of 275
Smith, Ali
  Hotel World 254n.5
Smith, Zadie 202n.2
  White Teeth 182, 204n.12
social repression 278
speculative and science fiction 109
spirituality 211
spiritual politics 209–227
Stephanie Barron 22
Stephen, Leslie
  Dictionary of National Biography 252
Sterne, Laurence
  Tristram Shandy 37
storytelling 36
  power of 47
Strachey, Lytton
  Books and Characters 252
  Elizabeth and Essex: A Tragic History 252
  Eminent Victorians 252
  Queen Victoria 252
suspension of disbelief 37
Suvin, Darko 166, 177
  'cognitive estrangement' 41
  'Theses on Dystopia 2001' 160, 179
Swift, Graham
  Waterland 36

taboos 276, 278
Taylor, Sam
  Republic of Trees, The 161
technology 250
temporality 38, 83, 86, 93
  disrupted 38
  fractured 16, 36
  futural 104
    129n.27
  linear 84, 103, 129n.28
  narrative 117
Tew, Philip 95
Thackeray, William Makepeace xiv, 27n.11, 33, 277
Thatcherism 80–81, 97n.1, 210
Thomson, Rupert
  Divided Kingdom 161
Tremain, Rose 183

Uganda 214, 216–218, 222
utopia 19, 20, 104, 109, 144, 155n.4, 159–180, 176
utopianism 176, 177

Vermeer, Johannes 235
Vonnegut, Kurt
  Player Piano 177

Weldon, Fay 90
  Rhode Island Blues 97n.4
Wells, H. G.
  Sleeper Awakes, The 20, 159, 165
  War of the Worlds 70
Winnicott, D. W. 126n.18
Winterson, Jeanette 254n.5
Woolf, Virginia 103, 230, 266, 268, 277

Index

"Am I a Snob?" 241
Between the Acts 244, 268–269
Common Readers, The 246
Flush: A Biography 241, 243, 252
Jacob's Room 252, 254
Mrs Dalloway 26n.2, 27n.11, 243, 254n.5, 255n.15
Orlando: A Biography 243, 246, 252, 254n.5
'Professions for Women' 265
Room of One's Own, A 241, 250, 264, 270
To the Lighthouse 174, 211, 242, 254n.5
Waves, The 241, 242, 244, 254n.5
Wylie, Vivienne 279n.2

Zahavi, Helen
 Dirty Weekend 277
Zeldin, Theodore 274
 An Intimate History of Humanity 278
Žižek, Slavoj 173
 Living in the End Times 163–165